CW01456593

POSSESSED

Cinema and Modernity A Series Edited by Tom Gunning

POSSESSED

Hypnotic Crimes, Corporate Fiction,
and the Invention of Cinema

STEFAN ANDRIOPOULOS

Translated by Peter Jansen and Stefan Andriopoulos

University of Chicago Press Chicago and London

Stefan Andriopoulos is associate professor of German
literature at Columbia University. He is the author of
*Unfall und Verbrechen: Konfigurationen zwischen juri-
stischem und literarischem Diskurs um 1900.*

The University of Chicago Press, Chicago 60637
The University of Chicago Press, Ltd., London
© 2008 by The University of Chicago

All rights reserved. Published 2008
Printed in the United States of America

17 16 15 14 13 12 11 10 09 08   1 2 3 4 5

ISBN-13: 978-0-226-02054-9 (cloth)
ISBN-10: 0-226-02054-1 (cloth)

Originally published as *Besessene Körper: Hypnose,
Körperschaften und die Erfindung des Kinos.* © 2000
Wilhelm Fink Verlag, München

Library of Congress Cataloging-in-Publication Data

Andriopoulos, Stefan.
    [Besessene Körper. English]
    Possessed: hypnotic crimes, corporate fiction,
and the invention of cinema / Stefan Andriopoulos;
translated by Peter Jansen and Stefan Andriopoulos.
        p.   cm.—(Cinema and modernity)
    Includes bibliographical references and index.
    ISBN-13: 978-0-226-02054-9 (cloth: alk. paper)
    ISBN-10: 0-226-02054-1 (cloth: alk. paper) 1. Hypno-
tism in motion pictures. 2. Hypnotism in literature.
3. Hypnotism and crime. 4. Corporations—Corrupt
practices. I. Title.
    PN1995.9.H95A5413   2008
    791.43'6556—dc22
                                2007039146

♾ The paper used in this publication meets the min-
imum requirements of the American National Standard for Information Sciences—Permanence of Paper
for Printed Library Materials, ANSI Z39.48-1992.

CONTENTS

ACKNOWLEDGMENTS

I would like to thank an anonymous reader for the University of Chicago Press for valuable suggestions on how to revise the German edition for an American readership. Susan Bielstein read the English manuscript in an early version and her comments and ideas were extremely helpful in revising the text. Yvonne Zipter has been a diligent and patient copy editor. I would also like to thank Anthony Burton for his professional support in producing this book. Annie Falk advised me on questions of linguistic usage. Timothy Frawley and Patrick Gallagher helped me with locating English translations of German and French sources. Tyler Whitney created the index and supported me in verifying bibliographical references.

I am grateful to Rachel Moore for her enthusiastic response to the German edition; and I would like to thank Tom Gunning for taking an interest in this book and for his generous support and friendship in publishing an English translation. Kelly Barry, Devin Fore, Brian Larkin, and Dorothea von Mücke read drafts of the new introduction, and their comments and feedback were extremely valuable. Translating this text from German into English coincided with my first years in New York, and I would like to thank my colleagues and coworkers in Columbia's Department of Germanic Languages for making the transition such a smooth and pleasant one. Publishing the text in English also gives me the opportunity to thank everybody who commented on, and thereby improved, the German edition. I am especially indebted to Jörg Schönert, Sebastian Scheerer, Anton Kaes, and Bernhard Dotzler.

Shiaolan has been the best of all possible reasons for moving to a different continent. Like the first edition of this book, I offer the English version στους γονείς μου.

New York, Fall 2007

INTRODUCTION

In the spring of 1887 Jean Mollinier participated as a subject in a number of public hypnotic exhibitions. The shoemaker, who practiced his trade on rue Chapon in the Third Arrondissement of Paris, was deeply affected by the experiments. Mollinier had a history of mental instability and now he came to regard the hypnotic phenomena as caused by supernatural agency. He believed himself under the influence of an invisible spirit that demanded his death. On the afternoon of May 21 he could no longer escape the power of these hallucinations. The craftsman donned his best apparel and went to a house on rue Lacépède. There, the neighbors noticed him engaged in an animated discussion, though nobody else seemed to be present. Finally Mollinier pulled out a revolver and shot himself—as if surrendering to the irresistible command of the invisible spirit.

Warning his readers against "The Dangers of Hypnotism," the journalist Hughes le Roux reported this story on June 1, 1887, in the newspaper *Le Temps*.[1] But a surprisingly similar plot was also at the center of a famous literary text, which had come out just a few days earlier. In Guy de Maupassant's *Le Horla* (1887), the nameless narrator witnesses a hypnotic exhibition that profoundly unsettles him, since it appears to confirm his obsessive fear of an "invisible being."[2] Like Mollinier, the unfortunate narrator gradually submits to the control of this invisible being and is eventually driven to suicide.

1. See Hughes le Roux, "La vie à Paris: Les dangers de l'hypnotisme" (1887). Unless otherwise noted all translations are mine.

2. Maupassant [1887] 1979/1990, 921/284. I am referring to the second version of *Le Horla* from 1887, which differs considerably from the shorter, first version that had appeared in October of 1886. Throughout this book, page references that are divided by a slash (/) indicate first the page number in the original version of the quoted text (921) and then the corresponding number in the published English translation (284). An asterisk * after the second number marks that the translation has been modified.

Since Maupassant's tale was published on May 25, 1887—only four days after Mollinier's violent death—the story of the shoemaker cannot have been a previously overlooked source for *Le Horla*.[3] Instead, the case history and the narrative emerged from a context that encompassed both Maupassant's literary production and Mollinier's hallucinations. A historically specific resonance thus gave currency to this cultural plot of hypnosis and possession. For in 1887 one could find in Paris alone "four to five hundred cabinets displaying somnambulists" and exhibiting the spectacular effects that hypnosis was capable of producing.[4] At the same time, an astonishing number of medical, juridical, and literary texts invoked the enormous power of hypnotic suggestion.

Maupassant's narrative cites the medical theories of the "Nancy school," which was known for raising the "terrifying specter of hypnotic crime."[5] Hippolyte Bernheim, the leading figure of this school, described the "rapport" between hypnotist and hypnotized subject as a relationship of unlimited power on the hypnotist's part. As Bernheim and many other physicians asserted, the hypnotized subject functioned as a sort of medium who could even be compelled to commit crimes against his or her own will. One particular fear concerned the possibility of implanting in a hypnotized person the idea to perform a criminal action, long after waking from the hypnotic trance. According to late-nineteenth-century medicine, the especially "insidious ruse" of such a "posthypnotic suggestion" consisted in the medium's assumption to be acting spontaneously, of his or her own free will, while in reality following an irresistible hypnotic order.[6] The belief in perfectly camouflaged suggestions thus pro-

3. Mollinier's suicide, which occurred on May 21, 1887, was first reported by the column "Les faits du jour" in the daily newspaper *Gil Blas* on May 23, 1887. The date of release of *Le Horla*, which appeared with the publisher Ollendorff in Paris, is given by the *Bibliographie de la France* (87:349) as May 25, 1887. On that day *Gil Blas* also contained an advertisement for the book. Maupassant's editor, Forestier, assumes that the narrative was written in January 1887.

4. The quote is from Gilles de la Tourette, *L'hypnotisme et les états analogues au point de vue médico-légale* [Hypnotism and analogous states from a medico-legal perspective] (1887), 392.

5. Schrenck-Notzing, "Die gerichtlich-medizinische Bedeutung der Suggestion" [The forensic significance of suggestion] (1900), 12.

6. Forel, "Der Hypnotismus und seine strafrechtliche Bedeutung" [Hypnotism and its forensic significance] (1889a), 184.

duced a powerful anxiety about numerous hypnotic crimes that could not be recognized as such.

At the same time juridical theories of invisible corporate bodies drew on similar figures of possession and control. Concurrent to the intense legal and medical discussion about the possibility of "criminal suggestion," a lively debate within the fields of civil and criminal law represented corporations as invisible but real "organisms" endowed with the ominous ability to commit crimes.[7] Otto von Gierke, Achille Mestre, Franz von Liszt, and others rejected the traditional notion of the "legal person" as a fictional entity and conceived of the corporation as an imperceptible being with a will and agency of its own. According to these legal theorists, the "plurality" of different corporate members merged into a cohesive "unity" with a distinct "aggregate will of its own."[8] The aggregate corporate organism therefore constituted an autonomous being that acted through its "possessed" members or "organs."[9] In a criminal suggestion, the hypnotist was alleged to exert his "indirect agency" through the possessed body of his medium.[10] Similarly in a corporate crime, the intangible corporation was perceived to be the "actual culprit," while the person executing the crime functioned merely as the "organ of a *foreign will*."[11]

Tracing the anxiety of being governed by a foreign power within literary, legal, and medical texts, this book explores the reciprocal exchange among representations of hypnotic and corporate agency in cultural production around the turn of the twentieth century and well into the years following World War I. Franz Kafka's novels *The Trial* (1914–15) and *The Castle* (1922) describe a merging of human and corporate bodies. Yet possession and hypnosis also became a prevalent theme in the newly emerging medium of film. On April 18, 1921, Victor Klemperer, a literary historian and avid moviegoer who had recently moved to Dresden, noted in his diary: "In the meantime I have been to the cinema twice

---

7. Gierke, *Das Wesen menschlicher Verbände* [The nature of human aggregates] ([1902] 1954), 12.

8. Gierke, *Genossenschaftstheorie* [Theory of associations] (1887), 25.

9. Ibid., 624–25.

10. Neumeister, *Mittelbare Thäterschaft und Hypnotismus* [Indirect agency and hypnotism] (1900).

11. Liszt, *Lehrbuch des deutschen Strafrechts* [Introduction to German criminal law] (1888), 166. Unless otherwise noted, all italicized passages are my emphasis.

already. On Thu. with Eva at the elegant *Princesstheater*. . . . The plot of the film itself—most popular subject: crime and suggestion. The eye of the criminal in close-up, enlarged, his one eye, since the film was called 'The One-Eyed Man.' "[12]

These short remarks about a now-forgotten film hint at the decisive role of the close-up for filmic representations of hypnosis. Simultaneously, Klemperer's description of "crime and suggestion" as cinema's "most popular subject" highlights the surprising number of movies that enacted the ostensibly unlimited power of the hypnotist on the cinematic screen. In representing hypnotic fascination, films like George Méliès's *Le Magnétiseur* (1897), Maurice Tourneur's *Trilby* (1915), Louis Feuillade's *Les yeux qui fascinent* (1916), Robert Wiene's *The Cabinet of Dr. Caligari* (1919), Fritz Lang's *Dr. Mabuse, the Gambler* (1922), Arthur Robison's *Shadows: A Nocturnal Hallucination* (1922), and Rex Ingram's *The Magician* (1926) testify to a structural affinity of cinema to hypnotism. At the same time, numerous physicians employed suggestion in order to produce visual film-like hallucinations in their hypnotized patients, while early theories of film described the new medium itself as exerting an irresistible hypnotic influence over its spellbound audience.

By analyzing representations of hypnotic crimes and corporate bodies in European cinema, literature, and science from the 1880s to the 1930s, the following chapters thus investigate a set of cultural fantasies surprisingly similar to our own. Today, modern media are perceived as surreptitiously influencing and manipulating their audiences. Simultaneously, globalization and the rise of multinational corporations create a fear of opaque corporate structures, which seemingly absorb human persons. At the turn of the last century, comparable anxieties about being controlled by a hidden force pervaded the domains of science, fiction, and film. Focusing on a previously neglected dimension of European cultural history, this study therefore inserts the ostensibly remote notion of "possession" into the analysis of Western modernity as it emerged around 1900.

In centering on corporate agency and hypnotism, the films and texts analyzed in this book seem to anticipate arguments central to recent poststructuralist theory. Franz Kafka's novel *The Trial* gives a detailed account of Joseph K.'s seemingly voluntary and gradual surrender to the

---

12. Klemperer, *Tagebücher* [Diaries] ([1918–24] 1996), 432; emphasis in the original.

living "judicial organism," thereby replacing simplistic notions of external coercion with a complex model that highlights the mutual interdependence of human and corporate bodies.[13] By focusing on K.'s response to the court's call, Kafka's literary text prefigures the famous
concept of "interpellation," developed by Louis Althusser in his essay
"Ideology and Ideological State Apparatuses" (1970) and further adapted
in Michel Foucault's studies on sujétion.[14] Similar to Kafka and the late-
nineteenth-century legal theorist Otto von Gierke, who considered the
corporate member "possessed" by an "invisible aggregate person," Foucault described the somatic effects of power as "passing through the
interior of the body."[15] Foucault's conceptualization of the relationship
between subject and power thus conceives of the human body as controlled by an intangible but real ubiquitous power—a notion already to
be found in legal and literary texts written around 1900.

Judith Butler's book The Psychic Life of Power (1997) also comes surprisingly close to juridical representations of "living," invisible, corporate organisms that seize and possess their members from within. Reminiscent
of not just Althusser and Foucault but also of Gierke and Kafka, Butler
defines subjection as a process in which individuals are simultaneously
produced and subjugated by an invisible power. Simultaneously, she
replicates late-nineteenth-century medical warnings against posthypnotic suggestion. According to the Swiss physician Auguste Forel, the
particularly "insidious ruse" of implanting a posthypnotic suggestion in
a hypnotized subject consists in the medium's belief to be acting on his
or her own free accord, while in reality following an external hypnotic
command.[16] In nearly identical terms, Butler indicts the hidden effects
of power that create an "insidious" semblance of freedom. Consequently
for Butler, "final responsibility" rests with the surreptitious workings of
power rather than with the ostensibly docile subject whose subordination only seems to be voluntary.[17]

---

13. The quoted phrase is from Kafka, The Trial ([1914–15] 1990/1998), 126/119.

14. See Foucault, Surveiller et punir 1975).

15. Gierke, Genossenschaftstheorie (1887), 624–25; Foucault, "Les rapports de pouvoir
passent à l'intérieur des corps" ([1977] 1994), esp. 231: "Le pouvoir atteint le corps"; see
also Foucault "Pouvoir et corps" ([1975b] 1994), 754: "L'investissement du corps par le
pouvoir"; also 756.

16. Forel, "Der Hypnotismus und seine strafrechtliche Bedeutung" (1889a), 184.

17. Butler, The Psychic Life of Power (1997), 6.

Yet instead of generalizing the figures and concepts analyzed in this study by formulating a comprehensive theory of the interaction or interdependence of human and corporate bodies, it may suffice to point out that comparable conceptualizations of modernity emerged already around 1900. When Durkheim's sociological study *Elementary Forms of Religious Life* (1912) described "mana" as a "diffuse and anonymous force"—simultaneously ubiquitous and intangible—Durkheim's text concurrently formulated a theory of the social that pertained not only to "primitive" societies but also to modern corporate aggregates and their effects on natural persons.[18] Durkheim emphasized that the forces of social cohesion work through complex "psychic mechanisms" that are not external to the subject but seize it from within. After participating in several hypnotic experiments, the unfortunate shoemaker Mollinier believed himself under the irresistible influence of an invisible foreign being. At the same time, the legal theorist von Gierke described the "psychic life" of the corporate member as *"determined* by the comprehensive force of an organized spiritual aggregate that works *inside* the individual."[19] As Durkheim stated in figures akin to Mollinier's hallucinations and Gierke's conceptualization of the "possessed" corporate member: "Because social pressure makes itself felt through mental channels, it was bound to give man the idea that outside him there are one or several powers, moral yet mighty, to which he is *subject.* Since they speak to him in a tone of commandment and sometimes even tell him to violate his most natural inclinations, man was bound to image them as being external to him."[20]

Anthropological theories from around 1900 thus describe social cohesion as a form of possession. In Durkheim's words: "The force of the collectivity is not wholly external; it does not move us entirely from outside. Indeed because society can only exist in and by means of individual minds, it must *enter into us* and become organized *within us.*"[21] That the social aggregate functions as a hypnotic force was emphasized even more strongly by Durkheim's contemporary Gabriele Tarde. In his

18. The phrase "diffuse and anonymous force" is from Durkheim, *Elementary Forms of Religious Life* ([1912] 1995), 197.

19. Gierke, *Genossenschaftstheorie* (1887), 774.

20. Durkheim, *Elementary Forms* ([1912] 1995), 211.

21. Ibid. Similarly, Henri Hubert and Marcel Mauss's *General Theory of Magic* describes magic as relying on the social, while society in turn becomes a magical category: "It is because society becomes activated that magic works, and it is because of magical beliefs that society becomes activated" ([1904] 1972, 133).

Laws of Imitation (1890), the French sociologist conceived of "social man" as a "veritable somnambulist."[22] Citing the medical theories of the Nancy school, Tarde affirmed the fact that "the social, like the hypnotic state, is only a form of a dream." Tarde described the members of primitive and of modern societies as "possessed" by a foreign power while simultaneously clinging to the "illusion that their ideas, all of which have been suggested to them, are spontaneous."[23] "Society is imitation and imitation is a kind of somnambulism" constituted Tarde's explanatory formula for the rise and cohesion of social unities.[24]

Tarde's and Durkheim s theories emphasized seemingly primitive phenomena such as somnambulism or hypnosis, states that late-nineteenth-century anthropological discourse considered the European equivalent to non-Western forms of trance and possession.[25] The heated debate about the irresistible power of hypnotic suggestion, the rising importance of invisible corporate bodies, and the newly emerging projection of moving images thus speak to a modernity that seems quite different from the "disenchantment of the world" described by Max Weber.[26] Yet instead of simply subscribing to the theories and conceptions inherent in medical, legal, and literary texts from around 1900, this book engages in a semiotic and historicist analysis of these discourses, simultaneously linking the textual representations of hypnotic and corporate agency to the concurrent emergence of cinema.

In exploring the historically specific currency and resonance of figures of possession and control as they circulated within literature, science, and visual culture around the turn of the last century, the subsequent chapters will accordingly combine literary and visual analysis with a cultural history of media and the "sciences"—a term that I employ here as including medical and legal theory and practice. Cutting across the fields of media studies, cultural history, comparative literature, and the history of science, this book interpolates literary fiction, theater, and film with other representational practices such as law and medicine. Before addressing the intricate question of how to conceptualize the com-

22. Tarde, *The Laws of Imitation* ([1890] 1903), 76–77.

23. Ibid., 77.

24. Ibid., 87.

25. See, esp., Stoll, *Suggestion und Hypnotismus in der Völkerpsychologie* [Suggestion and hypnotism in ethnopsychology] (1894).

26. Weber, *Wissenschaft als Beruf* [Science as a vocation] ([1917–19] 1992), 87.

plex interaction of technological media and cultural discourses, I will therefore first outline how to conceive of the interdiscursive exchange among literary, legal, and medical texts.

One of the lasting merits of poststructuralism and the "poetics of culture" built on its premises has been the insight that rhetorical figures and narrative forms are constitutive of literary as well as theoretical, medical, and legal texts.[27] Yet whereas Paul de Man once postulated an unbridgeable "disjunction" allegedly separating the figurative, rhetorical dimension of literary or philosophical texts from any historiographical approach, my analysis aims at historicizing precisely the gaps and lacunae that mark late-nineteenth-century juridical discourse in its conceptualization of legal persons and corporate organisms.[28] The German legal theorist Rudolph von Jhering accounted for the juridical reliance on fictional modes of representation by emphasizing a "theoretical deficiency" or "emergency" that justified the recourse to the "technical lie" of fiction.[29] Another legal scholar from the period, von Gierke, turned against Jhering's definition of the corporation as a fictional person. But in describing the "life" of invisible corporate organisms, Gierke himself borrowed from the contemporary literature of the fantastic, thereby compensating for what he called the "linguistic deficiency" of juridical discourse.[30]

In contrast to traditional studies of the relationships among literature, law, and medicine, this book is therefore not concerned with investigating how law as an ostensibly prediscursive reality is "reflected" or "depicted" in literature.[31] Nor are the legal and medical sciences con-

---

27. The "poetics of culture" is Greenblatt's phrase (*Shakespearean Negotiations* [1988], 5).

28. Disjunction is de Man's term. "Sign and Symbol in Hegel's *Aesthetics*" ([1982] 1996, 104).

29. "Theoretischer Nothstand"; "technische Nothlüge": Jhering, *Geist des römischen Rechts* [Spirit of Roman law] (1865), 288.

30. "Sprachlicher Notstand": Gierke, *Das Wesen der menschlichen Verbände* ([1902] 1954), 19.

31. Such an approach marks, for instance, Klaus Petersen's book *Literatur und Justiz in der Weimarer Republik* [Literature and the law in the Weimar Republic] (1988), which sets out to reconstruct the "reality" of "the law" in order to ascertain "the relationship in which the [literary] image of reality stands to that reality itself" (12). Petersen thus seems oblivious to the fact that legal discourse itself consists of linguistic representations.

sidered a mere arsenal of motifs from which literary texts borrow their metaphors. Instead, the following chapters set out to explore a reciprocal exchange of discursive elements among literary, juridical, and medical representations.[32] Legal and medical texts are analyzed as if they were literary, without neglecting the specific cultural function of each discursive practice.[33] Late-nineteenth-century theories of hypnotism and corporate agency testify to a surprising convergence of law, literature, and medicine on the textual level. Nevertheless each of these discursive realms does remain embedded in a particular institutional context. A literary, medical, or legal text may therefore engender markedly different consequences even when employing the very same figures and tropes.[34]

While acknowledging the institutional boundaries that separate science from fiction, the following study still assigns an epistemic function to literature that goes beyond the mere preservation and storage of outdated scientific models and theories.[35] Close reading shows that medical and legal texts rely on narrative forms and rhetorical figures, which function as necessary but not sufficient conditions for the formulation of new theories. Accordingly, literary fiction can play a constitutive role for the emergence of new juridical and medical knowledge. As Michel Fou-

32. In his *Learning to Curse* (1990), Stephen Greenblatt formulates this point in the following manner: "The idea is not to find outside the work of art some rock onto which literary interpretation can be securely chained but rather to situate the work in relation to other *representational* practices operative in the culture at a given moment" (170). Or, to put it in terms borrowed from Foucault's *Archaeology of Knowledge* (1969), literary as well as medical and juridical texts are read as "monuments" and not as "documents" (see 1972, 7–8 and 138–39).

33. In transferring techniques of literary analysis to the reading of legal texts, this book thus partakes in the "law as literature" movement as it has emerged over the last two decades. Peter Brooks's essay "Narrativity of the Law" (2002) gives a good overview of the field.

34. On this crucial difference, see also Brooks (2002), 8: "'It is so ordered': this rhetorical topos inevitably fascinates the literary analyst, who normally deals with texts that cannot call on such authority."

35. Already in 1978, Wolf Lepenies assigned such a function to literature in his essay on "Der Wissenschaftler als Autor" [The scientist as author] (1978), esp. 141–45. Instead of providing an exhaustive bibliography of the vast scholarship on literature and the sciences, I would like to limit myself to indicating two journals that assemble essays devoted to the field: *Configurations*, which is published by the Society for Literature, Science, and the Arts, and *Scientia Poetica*, a yearbook for the history of literature and the sciences, published in German since 1997.

cault once stated: "Knowledge is to be found not only in demonstrations, it can also be found in fiction, reflexion, narrative accounts, institutional regulations, and political decisions."[36] The late-nineteenth-century forensic debate about (fictional) hypnotic crimes, for instance, was based on literary stories and theatrical simulations. At the same time, the juridical and sociological representations of invisible corporate organisms drew on the literature of the fantastic in conceptualizing the autopoetic agency of large supra-individual organizations.

On the other side of the transfer, literary texts like Guy de Maupassant's *Le Horla* or Franz Kafka's *The Trial* borrow from scientific disciplines such as medicine and law. While scientific texts can be read, up to a point, as literature, literary texts lend themselves to a corresponding reading "as science." Narrative fiction, however, adapts legal and medical concepts not only in the mode of a simple, identical repetition. Instead, different forms of appropriating scientific theories can be distinguished within literature, testifying to various degrees of internal complexity or "literariness."

Novels like Gregor Samarow's *Under a Foreign Will* (1888) or Wilhelm Walloth's *Under the Spell of Hypnosis* (1897) perform a simple reiteration of scientific notions, taking up and highlighting figures that had previously been moved from literature into scientific discourse. These tropes remain virtually unchanged when reappropriated within narrative fiction. Hermann Broch's modernist trilogy *The Sleepwalkers* (1928–32), in contrast, draws on the scientific discourses of law and medicine in a more intricate manner. In its increasingly depersonalized mode of narration, Broch's three-part novel develops a literary equivalent to economic theories that describe human individuals as disempowered by abstract opaque organizations. A close reading of Broch's text consequently shows that discursive figures and concepts may undergo an alteration when transferred from one cultural sphere to another, thereby allowing for a literary transformation of scientific notions. Franz Kafka's *The Trial* even comments on contemporary legal discourse, not by merely repeating medical and juridical figures but by taking the figurative dimension of juridical tropes literally, simultaneously linking these legal concepts to medical notions. In this manner, the novel engages in a transformation and critical revaluation of scientific figures and concepts.

The disciplinary identity of literary history is therefore neither un-

---

36. Foucault, *Archaeology of Knowledge* ([1969] 1972), 183–84.

dermined nor threatened by redeploying the established critical tools and concepts of rhetoric and narratology to a formal analysis of nonliterary scientific texts. Nor are literary texts in such a project reduced to mere "illustrations" of other cultural practices. Instead, the transdisciplinary approach of this book is based on a clearly defined disciplinarity that adheres to the techniques and methods of literary history. The critical exploration of how discursive material is transferred from one cultural realm to another presupposes the demarcation of these different spheres, for examining the various literary appropriations of scientific figures and concepts consistently emphasizes affinities as well as differences between literature and other cultural realms. Or to put it in different terms: the insight into the permeability of the boundaries that separate law, literature, and medicine does not deny the differentiation among these discourses, which also—but not exclusively—follow their own internal logic.

Comparable studies of narrative structures in juridical discourse have reconstructed, above all, exchanges among representations of crime in literature, penal law, and criminology.[37] More recently, statistics and accident insurance have been established as crucial for Kafka's literary writings.[38] But the juridical representation of corporate bodies and legal persons, first analyzed in its relevance for literary history by Walter Benn Michaels, still deserves more attention.[39] Ahistorical studies of organic and bodily metaphors within social and legal theory have postulated a constancy of the same figures "over thousands of years."[40] This book, in contrast, historicizes the juridical representation and construction of corporate bodies around 1900, interpolating these legal theories to contemporary representations of hypnotism. This juxtaposition allows

37. See especially the volume *Erzählte Kriminalität* [Narrations of criminality] (Schönert 1991).

38. On the relationship between Kafka's office and literary writings, see, above all, Benno Wagner's studies (2002, 2004, 2006); see also Wolf (2006). On interrelations between representations of accident and crime around 1900, see Andriopoulos (1996a, 1996b).

39. In his innovative essay "Corporate Fiction" (1987), Michaels links the juridical debate about corporations to Frank Norris's *Octopus* ([1901] 1986) and Josiah Royce's *The Feud at Oakfield Creek* (1886) and succeeds in establishing the crucial role of legal theory for American literary naturalism.

40. Hörisch, "Die Armee, die Kirche und die Alma mater" [Army, church, and alma mater] (1990), 547.

us to introduce a new perspective into the history of the human body; for while medical and literary representations of hypnotism center on the psychic and the somatic effects of suggestion, juridical and literary texts describe corporate organisms as exerting a corporal impact on natural persons that seem to be absorbed by these intangible organizational structures.[41]

Before tracing figures of hypnotic and corporate possession within the realm of theater and film, this book will first explore interrelations of narrative literature, law, and medicine. An analysis of competing late-nineteenth-century medical theories of "suggestion" will establish the constitutive role of literary fiction for the lively scientific debate about hypnotic crimes (chapter 1). Whereas Jean-Martin Charcot and his disciples denied the possibility of so-called criminal suggestions, the physicians of the Nancy school substituted literary stories for actual cases within their treatises about hypnotism and crime. At the same time, narratives and novels such as Maupassant's *Le Horla* or Gregor Samarow's *Under a Foreign Will* (1888) cited the forensic debate about the irresistible power of suggestion, thereby imbuing the literary description of possessed bodies with scientific legitimacy. The enormously popular tales of hypnotic crime accordingly emerged from a mutual exchange of rhetorical tropes, scientific concepts, and narrative patterns among law, literature, and medicine. Juridical, literary, and medical representations of criminal suggestion mutually presupposed and engendered each other.

An interaction between literature and legal theory was also constitutive of the late-nineteenth-century juridical debate about the demonic power of invisible corporate bodies, analyzed in chapter 2. The strain of continental legal theory based on a modernization of Roman law expressly relied on fictional modes of representation, thereby compensating for the "theoretical deficiency" of juridical discourse in conceptual-

41. A structurally similar interaction from the same period is explored in Mark Seltzer's *Bodies and Machines* (1992), which traces a "coupling" of bodies and machines around 1900 (191n32). Among the numerous volumes on body history I mention here, only some texts are on hysteria, such as Georges Didi-Huberman's *Invention of Hysteria* ([1982] 2003); Jan Goldstein, "The Uses of Male Hysteria" (1991); Elaine Showalter, *Hystories* (1997); Felicia McCarren, *Dance Pathologies* (1998); Ruth Rae Brown, "From Charcot to Charlot" (2001). Ingrid Kollak's book *Literatur und Hypnose* [Literature and hypnosis] (1997) concentrates on animal magnetism and mesmerism in the early nineteenth century and does not go beyond the insights of Maria Tatar's early and commendable study *Spellbound* (1978).

izing legal persons.[42] But a merely "fictional person" was not considered capable of committing crimes. In diametrical contrast, other legal theorists such as von Gierke and Franz von Liszt regarded the corporation as an invisible yet real organism that could compel its possessed members to commit criminal acts.[43] The executing "organ" was described as the tool of a foreign will and hence as not responsible for its own actions—just like a hypnotized medium. This connection between theories of corporate agency and hypnotism was not, however, one of monocausal determination. Instead, the legal representations of intangible corporate organisms participated in a discursive network of the fantastic that also included contemporary literary texts such as Guy de Maupassant's *Le Horla* and Joseph Conrad's *Heart of Darkness* (1902). Juridical invocations of invisible corporate bodies and their seemingly preternatural demonic power thus testified to a precarious proximity of legal theory and horror fiction.

In addition to narrative patterns and rhetorical figures, theatrical and iconographic forms also circulated among the scientific, dramatic, and cinematic representations and enactments of corporate and hypnotic crimes. Jean-Martin Charcot and Paul Richer's study *Les démoniaques dans l'art* (1887) shows how the iconography of demonic possession pervaded the clinical nosography or medical description of "grand hysteria." In his famous Tuesday Lectures, which took place in the amphitheater of the Salpêtrière Hospital, Charcot presented a "demonic variant" of the neurosis, inducing artificial hysterical attacks before an audience that consisted of students, physicians, artists, and authors. But it was not only the spectacle of the *grande attaque hystérique* that unfolded as an elaborately choreographed performance. As we will see in chapter 3, a fundamental theatricality also marked late-nineteenth-century medical research into the forensic significance of hypnosis. Striving to establish the possibility of real criminal suggestions, medical researchers staged the "strange spectacle" of artificial hypnotic crimes.[44] The physicians presented these simulations—enacted with wooden daggers and blank cartridges—as evidence for the unlimited power of suggestion. Skeptical

---

42. "Theoretischer Nothstand": Jhering, *Geist des römischen Rechts* (1865), 288.

43. "Unsichtbare Verbandsperson": Gierke, *Das Wesen menschlicher Verbände* ([1902] 1954), 30. See also Liszt, *Lehrbuch des deutschen Strafrechts* (1888), 166.

44. Salten, "Über Schnitzler's hypnotische Versuche" [On Schnitzler's hypnotic experiments] ([1932–33] 1984), 55.

opponents, however, criticized these "fake crimes," denouncing them as scientifically worthless "performance" and "comedy."[45]

The young Arthur Schnitzler, who conducted similar experiments in the Vienna Polyclinic, consequently reappropriated the "comedy of hypnosis" on the stage of the Vienna Burgtheater. In *Electra* (1903), Hugo von Hofmannsthal similarly comments on the theatricality of medical research into hysteria and hypnosis, concluding the tragedy with a hysterical attack that replaces the murder of Clytemnestra at the hands of the somnambulist Electra. Instead of simply equating theatricality with the cultural institution of theater, this study therefore conceives of it more broadly—as a mode of cultural performance whose semiotic structures pervade plays by Schnitzler and Hofmannsthal as well as Charcot's Tuesday Lectures and medical experiments with "criminal suggestion."[46] It is an intermedial interaction among texts, performances, and the pictorial iconography of painting, photography, and film that gave rise to late-nineteenth-century visual and textual figures of possession.[47] In order to undertake a methodologically consistent analysis of literature, science, and visual culture around 1900, it is thus necessary to conceptualize the emergence and cultural appropriation of cinema.

In theorizing the reciprocal interaction of media and culture, this book grasps technological media like print, photography, and film as material, necessary, but not sufficient conditions for the (re)production of texts and images. The work of Friedrich Kittler has provided us with important insights into how new media give rise to cultural change, highlighting the previously ignored importance of such media as the typewriter, the gramophone, and film for literature and scientific dis-

45. "Scheinverbrechen": Freud, "Rezension von A. Forel *Der Hypnotismus*" [Review of A. Forel, *Hypnotism*] ([1889] 1987), 138/1:101–2*; "performance": Hugo Münsterberg, "Hypnotism and Crime" (1908), 223; "comedy": Fuchs, "Die Komödie der Hypnose" ([1890] 1895), 7.

46. In a similar vein, Felicia McCarren's *Dance Pathologies* (1998) investigates the "overlapping arenas of print, performance, and medical practice" (28) in relation to hysteria and dance.

47. The dialogic interaction of performance, iconography, and discourses is also emphasized in Gabriele Brandstetter's *Tanz-Lektüren: Körperbilder und Raumfiguren der Avantgarde* [Readings of dance: body images and figures of space in the avant-garde] (1995), esp. 22–23 and 29. Similarly to this study, Brandstetter introduces the notion of the "cultural sign" as bridging the divide between textual and visual media (22).

courses around 1900.[48] Yet while opening up a new perspective on technological modernity, Kittler ultimately considers "hardware" to be more fundamental than the discourses and imaginations that allow for its emergence and shape its contingent realization and appropriation.[49] While striving to emulate the archival richness that marks the archaeology of media as practiced by Kittler and others, this study therefore assumes a mutual interaction between the emergence of a new technology and its surrounding cultural discourses.[50]

Interpolating the "invention" of a new medium to its contingent cultural contexts thus allows us to avoid a simple determinism that threatens to reduce culture to a mere epiphenomenon. Elsewhere I have tried to show how the gradual emergence of television in the late nineteenth and the early twentieth centuries was dependent not only on factors immanent to technology but also on spiritualist research into the clairvoyance of somnambulist mediums.[51] Important components of early television sets—such as the cathode ray tube—were designed by scientists also engaged in psychical research. At the same time, occultist descriptions of "psychic organs" invoked technological innovations such as wireless telegraphy as proof for thought transference and telepathy. Ostensibly obscure theories of "psychic television in time and space" thus played a crucial role for the concurrent emergence of the technological medium, while newly emerging communication media engendered a surprising wave of psychical research.

48. For English translations of Friedrich Kittler's work, see esp. *Discourse Networks 1800/1900* ([1985] 1990); *Gramophone, Film, Typewriter* ([1986] 1999); and the anthology *Literature, Media, Information Systems* (1997).

49. Accordingly, Kittler considers a Foucauldian discourse analysis as unable to grasp medial and cultural constellations after 1850. See, for instance, Friedrich Kittler, *Discourse Networks 1800/1900* ([1985] 1990), 369; and *Gramophone, Film, Typewriter* ([1986] 1999), 5.

50. In the last two decades the history and theory of media has been an extremely productive field in Germany. While the work of younger scholars such as Bernhard Dotzler, Christoph Hoffmann, Wolfgang Schäffner, Stefan Rieger, and Niels Werber still remains untranslated, there are, in addition to the texts by Friedrich Kittler mentioned in n. 48 above, English editions of the anthology *Materialities of Communication*, ed. Hans Ulrich Gumbrecht and Karl-Ludwig Pfeiffer ([1988] 1994) and of Bernhard Siegert's *Relays: Literature as an Epoch of the Postal System* ([1993] 1999).

51. See Andriopoulos, "Psychic Television" (2005).

In a similar vein, this book sets out to explore the contingent but none-theless mutually constitutive interrelation that links hypnotism and cin-ema's emergence and cultural appropriation around 1900. At that time, the staging of hypnotic crimes was not limited to the venues of medi-cine and theater; as already noted, "crime and suggestion" was also the "most popular topic" of cinema.[52] Chapter 4 will accordingly analyze how films such as Robert Wiene's *The Cabinet of Dr. Caligari* (1919–20) and Fritz Lang's *Dr. Mabuse, the Gambler* (1922) appropriated a lively scientific debate about the unlimited power of suggestion. Furthermore, contemporary medical and psychological representations of the new medium spoke to a structural affinity of cinema and hypnotism: physicians employed verbal suggestion in order to produce visual film-like hallucinations in their hypnotized patients; and cinema itself was described as exerting a suggestive irresistible influence on its spellbound audience. It was even feared that films depicting violent actions would induce similar crimes, since the posthypnotic influence of the moving images would control susceptible spectators after leaving the movie theater. The numerous cin-ematic representations of hypnosis thus not only adapted a medico-legal discussion about the possibility of "criminal suggestion." By employing specifically filmic devices such as the close-up and the point-of-view shot, these films also enacted the alleged hypnotic power of cinema.

In tracing an intermedial exchange among medical representations of suggestion, cinematic enactments of hypnosis, and medical concep-tualizations of film, this study analyzes sequences from Wiene's *Caligari* and Lang's *Mabuse* while simultaneously interpolating these films with contemporary discourses. Tom Gunning and Anton Kaes have contex-tualized the cinema of attractions and Weimar cinema within a wider culture of modernity.[53] Similarly, I will combine cultural history with formal film analysis in exploring the interaction of cinema and hyp-notism. Without reducing the technological modernity of 1900 to the

52. Klemperer, *Tagebücher* ([1918–24] 1996), 432.

53. See Kaes, "The Cold Gaze" (1993), "German Cultural History and the Study of Film" (1995), and *Shell Shock* (forthcoming). See also Gunning, *The Films of Fritz Lang* (2000) and his numerous essays. Jonathan Crary's *Suspensions of Perception* (1999) simi-larly links visual media from the late nineteenth and the early twentieth centuries to contemporary discursive constellations. Karin Bruns's study *Kinomythen* [Cinema myths] (1995), in contrast, embeds Thea von Harbou's "film drafts" [*Filmentwürfe*] in an interdiscursive web of legal theory, medicine, and occultism, without taking an interest in the filmic visualization of these "drafts."

"hardware" of the apparatus, this book therefore examines textual and visual modes of representation, embedding the visuality of cinematic images in a discursive network that responded to, and shaped, the emergence and cultural appropriation of cinema.

Following a historical trajectory that shifts its focus from Paris, over Vienna, to Berlin as exemplary sites of European modernity between 1885 and 1930, the subsequent study is thus structured, above all, according to the different genres and media of narrative literature, theatrical performance, and film. Yet after analyzing the intermedial crossings among medical, dramatic, and filmic enactments of possession and hypnotic control, the final chapter of the book turns back to narrative fiction. Tracing modernist literary representations of human and corporate bodies, I will engage in a close reading of Hermann Broch's novel *The Sleepwalkers* (1928–32). The text appropriates medical notions of somnambulism while employing an increasingly depersonalized mode of narration that functions as a literary equivalent to legal and economic representations of corporate agency. Franz Kafka's novels *The Castle* (1922) and *The Trial* (1914–15), in turn, emphasize the somatic pressures exerted on K. through his dealings with an intangible "living" organization. By linking contemporary medical theories of neurasthenia to the description of bureaucratic "organisms," Kafka's novels center on a merging of human and corporate bodies. Finally, the epilogue outlines how medical theories of "depersonalization" and "psychic automatism" became crucial for the modernist avant-garde and the surrealist *écriture automatique*.

I TALES OF HYPNOTIC CRIME

Medical practice has no real autonomy; it lives on borrowings and applications.
Jean-Martin Charcot, *Lectures on the Diseases of the Nervous System* (1886)

It is here that the actual hypnotic novel begins. Albert von Schrenck-Notzing,
*The Czynski Trial: Expert Opinion on the Impairment of Free Will as a Consequence
of Hypnotic-Suggestive Influence* (1895)

In Guy de Maupassant's *Le Horla*, it remains uncertain whether the possession by an alien being, so minutely recorded in the unnamed narrator's diary, does in fact occur at the level of concrete action and plot.[1] Even the narrator himself considers the possibility that he has become the "plaything of his fevered imagination"—unless he is somehow a "somnambulist or the victim of one of those precisely documented but nevertheless inexplicable influences called *suggestions*."[2] As this reference to precise documentation indicates, the literary narrative appropriates a vast medical debate about hypnosis and suggestion. *Le Horla* not only refers to late-nineteenth-century theories of brain localization that ascribed specific mental functions to certain areas of the brain: "Men who have survived accidents lose their capacity for remembering names or verbs or numbers or just dates. The locations of all parts of thought have now been definitely established." At a dinner given by his cousin, the narrator also encounters a physician who reports extensively on the astounding experiments performed in contemporary medical research on

1. This structural ambiguity is also emphasized in Tzetvan Todorov's *The Fantastic* (1975), 86.
2. Maupassant, *Le Horla* ([1887] 1979 1990), 921/283.

hypnotism: "I found myself seated next to two young women, one of whom was the wife of a physician, Doctor Parent, who has a considerable interest in nervous disorders and the unusual phenomena which are currently being generated by experiments in hypnosis and suggestion. He told us at some length about the startling results obtained by English researchers and the doctors of the Nancy School."[3]

The leading figure of this *école de Nancy* was the physician Hippolyte Bernheim, who cooperated closely with Ambroise Liébeault, Henri Beaunis, and Jules Liègeois. After the publication of Bernheim's *De la suggestion dans l'état hypnotique* (On suggestion in the hypnotic condition [1884]), this group of medical researchers became the most important opponent of the "Paris school" centered around the famous neurologist Jean-Martin Charcot, who practiced at the Salpêtrière Hospital. In Germany and Switzerland, the physicians Albert Moll and Auguste Forel aligned themselves with Bernheim's theories, whereas the young Sigmund Freud studied at both places—in Paris at the Salpêtrière and in the southern town of Nancy—translating books by Charcot and by Bernheim from French into German.[4] The heated debate between these two medical camps revolved around the status of hypnosis: Was it a physiological epiphenomenon of hysteria or a general psychological process? This disagreement about how to conceive of suggestion was further linked to an intense discussion about the possibility of crimes committed under hypnosis. Whereas Charcot and his disciples strictly refuted these so-called hypnotic crimes, the adherents of the Nancy school took recourse to literary narratives, invoking stories instead of actual cases in their medical and juridical treatises on the unlimited power of suggestion.

Bernheim versus Charcot: The Nancy School and the Salpêtrière

Charcot's scientific reputation legitimized hypnosis as a subject of serious medical study. In 1882, five years before the publication of Maupas-

3. Ibid., 928/291, 922/284–85. The English researchers referred to are probably Hack Tuke and his disciples—see, for instance, Tuke, *Influence of the Mind upon the Body in Health and Disease* ([1872] 1884), and Tuke, *Sleep-Walking and Hypnotism* (1884).

4. See Charcot 1886, [1887] 1892; Bernheim [1886b] 1888, [1891] 1892. In contrast to the unreliable English editions of Bernheim's and Charcot's texts, Freud's translations are remarkably faithful and elegant. On the evolution of Freud's increasingly critical attitude toward Charcot's theories, see also below, 70 n. 17.

sant's tale, Charcot had been awarded a new chair at the Salpêtrière, specifically established for research into diseases of the nervous system. Subsequently, Charcot's medical studies evolved from his *Lectures on Localization in Diseases of the Brain* (1878)—also mentioned in *Le Horla*—to a dynamic theory that no longer traced nervous diseases exclusively to organic lesions. According to Charcot's *Lectures on the Diseases of the Nervous System* (1886), the neurosis of hysteria did not result from injuries or dysfunctions with a demonstrable anatomical substrate but from "traumatic agents" such as the "nervous shock" brought about by an "accident."[5]

Charcot's insight into the "pseudo-organic" or psychological character of hysteria resulted from the observation that the phenomena of anesthesia and paralysis afflicting both female and male hysterical patients at the Salpêtrière could be traced to a "mechanism analogous to the [artificial] induction of paralysis through hypnotic suggestion."[6] Charcot demonstrated this discovery in his nosography of hysterical "monoplegia," which he described as the paralysis of a single limb caused by ideas that were fixed through autosuggestion. "By means of suggestion," Charcot succeeded in producing a "perfect imitation of monoplegia" that resulted, like the neurosis itself, not from anatomical changes but from ideas.[7]

Yet despite this shift in interest from purely somatic to psychosomatic ailments, Charcot remained committed to his method of a physiologically anchored nosography. Focusing on "somatic phenomena," he aimed

5. Charcot, *Leçons sur les maladies du système nerveux* ([1886] 1890/1889), 352/302*, 355/305. See also Charcot [1888] 1895. For a more detailed account of how the meaning of the word "trauma" in late-nineteenth-century neurology gradually shifted from denoting material or physical shocks to referring to psychological shocks, see Esther Fischer-Homberger, *Die traumatische Neurose: Vom somatischen zum sozialen Leiden* [The traumatic neurosis: from somatic to social affliction] (1975). See now also Ruth Leys, *Trauma: A Genealogy* (2000).

6. Charcot [1886] 1890/1889, 359/308*. On Charcot's representation of male hysteria, see Goldstein (1991), Micale (1990), and Ouerd (1984). As Michèle Ouerd has shown, the old, seemingly abandoned theory of the migrating uterus reinscribed itself in Charcot's representation of male hysteria, since Charcot's late case histories emphasize the low social status of male hysterics, ascribing to them a "pathological urge to migrate." Charcot [1888] 1895, 278. See Ouerd 1984, 26–27.

7. Charcot [1886] 1890/1889, 351/302*. See also 349/302: "The *imitation* that we have achieved is truly perfect."

for a "truly scientific, exact description" of hysteria and hypnosis and claimed to base the medical classification of various pathological conditions "only on well-proven experiences," thereby "excluding any simulation" by his patients.[8] Charcot thus developed a detailed description and iconography of *grande hystérie* and characterized the "grand hysterical seizure" as unfolding in four highly distinct phases: the "epileptoid period" (*période épileptoide*), mimicking the individual phases of an epileptic seizure, the "period of contortions and grand movements" (*période des contorsions et des grands movements*), the period of "passionate attitudes" (*attitude passionnelles*), and the "terminal period" (*période terminale*).[9]

Similarly, Charcot defined three distinct phases of "grand hypnotism": catalepsy, lethargy, and somnambulism, phases that could be distinguished from each other by specific physiological characteristics, especially on the level of "neuro-muscular phenomena."[10] In catalepsy the hypnotized subjects remained rigid, with their eyes wide open, preserving any position that was given to them. By contrast, in lethargy the patients' eyes were "completely or at least halfway closed," while their unresisting, flaccid bodies presented "the appearance of a corpse before the onset of rigor mortis." Furthermore, any consciousness or sensitivity to pain was "completely suspended" in this state. In the final phase of grand hypnotism, a "heightened capacity . . . of the individual senses" was alleged to set in, enabling the hypnotist to enter into a "rapport" with the somnambulist who would execute simple commands.[11] In all three phases, which according to Charcot were marked by distinct physiological symptoms, the hypnotized mediums could be returned to a waking state by blowing on their eyes.

Charcot established such a close link between hysteria and hypnosis that he believed only hysterics could be hypnotized. Georges Gilles de la Tourette, Paul Richer, Charles Richet, and Pierre Janet also held this

8. Charcot 1889, iii, iii, iv. On the "nosographic method" that, based on the "description" of "pathological conditions," isolates differential-diagnostic symptoms or "defining characteristics" of diseases before developing their etiology, see also Charcot [1886] 1890/1889, 10 ff./8 ff.

9. The "drama" (Charcot and Richer 1887, 95) of the "grand hysterical attack" is analyzed in more detail in chapter 3, "Staging the Hypnotic Crime."

10. Gilles de La Tourette, *L'hypnotisme* (1887), 81. For a more detailed discussion of lethargy, catalepsy, and somnambulism, see ibid., 81–112.

11. Ibid., 91, 91, 95, 93.

assumption.[12] Tourette put it succinctly when he asserted: "As natural somnambulism is a precursor of hysteria, so hypnotic somnambulism is only a further manifestation of hysteria."[13] For Charcot and his disciples, hypnosis represented nothing short of an artificially induced hysterical neurosis; consequently they thought its therapeutic potential to be limited to the treatment of hysterical symptoms, which could be not only imitated but also eliminated by suggestion.

In stark contrast to Charcot's theories, the *école de Nancy* conceived of hypnosis not as a pathological disease of the nervous system but as a state akin to sleep. This conception was first formulated in Ambroise Liébeault's study *Du sommeil et des états analogues* (Of sleep and states analogous to it [1866]) and then adapted in Bernheim's works, which found enormous resonance in the 1880s.[14] In the preface to his *On Suggestion and Its Therapeutic Applications* (1886), Bernheim opposed Charcot directly, insisting that the hypnotic state was "not a neurosis analogous to hysteria."[15] As Bernheim asserted, the "induced sleep" did not differ from a "natural" one. The affinity of hypnosis to natural sleep also explained why "the overwhelming majority of persons" were "suggestible," even though they did not suffer from hysterical symptoms. But to account for the role of suggestion, Bernheim expanded Liébeault's notion of hypnosis. In a circular equation of hypnosis and suggestion, Bernheim affirmed: "To define hypnosis as an induced sleep, is to give a too narrow meaning to this word. . . . I define hypnotism as inducing a specific psy-

12. See Janet, *État mental des hystériques* [The mental state of hysterics] (1893); Gilles de la Tourette, *Traité clinique et thérapeutique de l'hystérie d'après l'enseignement de la Salpêtrière* [Clinical and therapeutic treatise on hysteria according to the teachings of the Salpêtrière] (1894); Babinski, *Hypnotisme et hystérie* [Hypnotism and hysteria] (1891), 17. Because Gilles de La Tourette, after whom Charcot named the "Tourette syndrome," is more commonly known simply by the name Tourette, all future in-text references will use that shortened form of his name while notes and the bibliography, for documentary purposes, will retain his full surname.

13. Gilles de La Tourette, *L'hypnotisme* (1887), 174.

14. According to Maria Tatar, just five copies of Liébeault's book were sold between 1866 and 1871. However, it was reissued in two volumes in 1889 and 1891, before being translated in 1892 into German as well (see Liébeault 1866, 1889, 1891, [1866] 1892; also Tatar 1978, 33, and Gauld 1992, 320).

15. Bernheim, *De la suggestion et ses applications à la thérapeutique* ([1886a] 1888/1964), iii/418.

chic condition of *increased suggestibility*. . . . It is suggestion that generates hypnosis."[16]

Comparable to Charcot's description of male hysteria, Bernheim's medical experiments subverted a binary notion of gender that regarded only women as suggestible: "It must not be assumed that only . . . women can be hypnotized; on the contrary, most of my observations refer to men whom I have chosen on purpose to refute this belief."[17] But in denying a link between hysteria and hypnosis, Bernheim questioned the physiological characteristics that, according to Charcot, marked the various phases of "grand hypnotism." Whereas Charcot and his disciples characterized hypnosis as a physical condition of "heightened neuro-muscular excitability," Bernheim conceived of hypnosis as a mental or "psychic condition," marked by an "increased suggestibility."[18] Since the mental factors of suggestion and autosuggestion were fundamental to all somatic effects of hypnosis, Bernheim regarded the "allegedly physical phenomena" of catalepsy, lethargy, and somnambulism as "psychic . . . effects of suggestion."[19] His medical conception of "psychotherapy" thus emphasized the healing "effect exerted by the spiritual upon the physical."[20]

The hypnotic power of the mind over the body, however, went so far as to render the control of the hypnotist over his medium boundless. In his description of the somnambulist phase of "grand hypnotism," even Charcot asserted: "Our power does not encounter any limits in this domain; for we can extend our influence almost toward the infinite."[21]

16. Ibid., ii/417, iii/418, 22/15*.

17. Ibid., 6/5*. See also Moll 1924, 58: "Gender does not exert a significant influence. It is an error to assume that the female is better suited for hypnosis than the male."

18. "L'hyperexcitibalité neuro-musculaire": Gilles de la Tourette, *L'hypnotisme* (1887), 82. Bernheim ([1886a] 1888/1964), 22/15*. The opposition between physiology (Salpêtrière) and psychology (Nancy) can also be understood as a repetition of diverging explanations of the phenomena of "animal magnetism" that around 1800 were traced to either an invisible fluid or the somatic effects of the imagination (see Tatar 1978, 32).

19. Bernheim [1886a] 1888/1964, iii/418*.

20. "These facts should suffice to recall the effect exerted by the spiritual upon the physical, by the mind [*esprit*] upon the body, by the psychic functions of the brain upon the organic ones. . . . The task of suggestion and the goal of psychotherapy is letting the mind [*esprit*] intervene in order to heal the body" (Bernheim, *Hypnotisme, suggestion, psychothérapie: études nouvelles* [1891]/[1891] 1980, 48/36*).

21. Charcot, *Leçons sur les maladies du système nerveux* ([1886] 1890), 340/293*.

Bernheim in turn represented the hypnotized subject as an "automaton controlled by a *foreign* will."[22] The German physician Albert Moll accordingly described the hypnotized subject as "completely devoid of a will of his own" and asserted that certain people could even be hypnotized "against their own will."[23] In the act of hypnosis the personality of the hypnotized medium was alleged to disappear, while his or her body dissolved into individual members that defied the subject's control. To quote from Albert Moll's textbook *Hypnotism*: "I have shown above by the example of the second subject how easy it is for me to render that person's arm immobile, merely by instilling the *idea* that the arm was inert. In precisely the same fashion, the muscles of the legs, of the torso, of the larynx, etc. can be made to defy the volition of the subject. 'You cannot raise your arm, cannot stick out your tongue': that suffices to make the prohibited movement impossible."[24]

In contrast to mesmerist theories of the early nineteenth century, these phenomena were not explained by an invisible magnetic fluid but by suggestion and autosuggestion. Bernheim affirmed that without the subject's autosuggestion, hypnosis would be impossible: "There is no magnetizer and no magnetic fluid. . . . The induction of sleep does not depend on the hypnotist but on the hypnotized subject; it is his *own belief* that puts him to sleep."[25] But despite this insight into the fundamental role of autosuggestion, the relationship between the hypnotist and the

22. "Automate dirigé par une volonté étrangère": Bernheim ([1886a] 1888/1964), 84/60*. In the sexual pathology of the period—especially in Ulrichs's texts—male homosexuality is similarly represented as the presence of a female will in a male body. See also Vestenhof's novel *Der Mann mit den drei Augen* [The man with the three eyes] (1913), where the head of the male protagonist simultaneously contains the brain of a jointly developed female twin who repeatedly seizes control over his body, forcing him to commit crimes and acts of "sexual inversion." On the treatment of "sexual inversion" by means of hypnosis, see Schrenck-Notzing's *Die Suggestions-Therapie bei krankhaften Erscheinungen des Geschlechtssinnes: Mit besonderer Berücksichtigung der conträren Sexualempfindung* [Suggestion therapy in the treatment of pathological sexual phenomena: with special consideration of contrary sexual orientation] (1892).

23. Moll, *Der Hypnotismus* (1889), 14; also 26.

24. Ibid., 37. The dissolution of the body into different members also comes to the fore in the medical practice of "semi-lateral hypnosis" (ibid., 54).

25. Bernheim ([1886a] 1888/1964), 259/190*. A good analysis of the tension between Bernheim's emphasis on the constitutive role of autosuggestion and his representation of the hypnotist's unlimited power is to be found in Borch-Jacobsen's "The Bernheim Effect" (2006).

somnambulist medium was usually described as one of unilateral dependence, thereby raising the all-important question of whether somnambulists could be forced to commit criminal acts against their own will.

Medical and Legal Debates about Hypnotic Crime

After 1885, an astonishing wave of legal and medical books and articles
warned of the "terrifying specter of hypnotic crime."[26] Only two cases
of alleged criminal abuse of hypnosis were tried in Europe during these
years, those of Gabrielle Bompard in Paris in 1890 and Ceslav Lubic Czynski in Munich in 1894.[27] Nonetheless, the theoretical speculation was
endless as to whether it was possible to force a hypnotized medium to
carry out so-called criminal suggestions. Liégeois, Liébeault, Schrenck-
Notzing, and Forel, in particular, affirmed "that in deep somnambulism
the individual, devoid of its own will, is at the mercy of the hypnotist

26. "Schreckgespenst des hypnotischen Verbrechens": Schrenck-Notzing (1900), 12;
see, for instance, Liégeois, *De la suggestion hypnotique dans ses rapports avec le droit civil
et le droit criminel* (1884); Obersteiner, *Der Hypnotismus mit Berücksichtigung seiner klinischen und forensischen Bedeutung* (1887); Forel, "Der Hypnotismus und seine strafrechtliche Bedeutung" [Hypnotism and its forensic significance] (1889a); Liégeois, *De la
suggestion et du somnambulisme dans leur rapports avec la jurisprudence et la médecine légale*
(1889); Prel, *Das hypnotische Verbrechen und seine Entdeckung* (1889); Delboeuf, "Die verbrecherischen Suggestionen" [Criminal suggestions] (1893–94); Schapira, *Der Hypnotismus in seiner psychologischen und forensischen Bedeutung* [Hypnotism in its psychological
and forensic significance] (1893); Crocq, *L'hypnotisme et le crime* [Hypnotism and crime]
(1894); Liébeault, "Criminelle hypnotische Suggestionen: Gründe und Thatsachen,
welche für dieselben sprechen" [Criminal hypnotic suggestions: reasons and facts
that corroborate them] (1894–95); Schrenck-Notzing, "Die gerichtlich-medizinische
Bedeutung der Suggestion" (1900); etc. Apart from these monographs and essays,
whose enumeration is by no means complete (compare also Campili 1886, Garnier
1888, Ladame 1888, Rieger 1888, Bell 1889, Höfelt 1889, Drucker 1893, Loos 1894, Kuh
1898, etc.), the textbooks by Auguste Forel, Albert Moll, and Leopold Loewenfeld all
devote individual chapters to discussing the criminal applicability of hypnosis. Forel's
book even grew out of a long essay titled "Hypnotism and Its Forensic Significance"
and went through twelve increasingly voluminous editions (see bibliography).

27. Gabrielle Bompard testified in court that her lover Michel Eyraud had forced
her by means of posthypnotic suggestion to participate in the murder of the bailiff
Alexandre Gouffé; for an excellent analysis of the controversy surrounding the case,
see Harris, "Murder under Hypnosis in the Case of Gabrielle Bompard" (1985). See also
Harris (1989), 155–207; and Laurence and Perry (1988), 248–59.

and becomes defenseless in both a moral and physical sense."[28] "Like the cane in the hand of a wanderer," so, they asserted, a somnambulist could be used for carrying out a criminal suggestion as "a docile, unresisting instrument, . . . executing *any* command."[29]

Since there were no unequivocally verified cases of crimes committed under hypnosis, many medical researchers staged simulated hypnotic crimes in order to prove their possibility. Auguste Forel, who taught in Switzerland, described one such experiment in the following manner: "To an older man of good suggestibility, whom I had just hypnotized, I gave a revolver that Mr. Höfelt himself had previously loaded with blanks only. Pointing to H., I explained to the hypnotized that the latter was a thoroughly evil person and that he should shoot him dead. With utter determination he took the revolver and fired a shot directly at Mr. H. Mr. H., *simulating an injured person*, fell to the floor. Then I explained to the hypnotized man that the fellow was not quite dead yet and that he should shoot him again, which he did without hesitation."[30] In addition to Forel, the physicians Bernheim, Bérillon, Beaunis, Crocq, Schrenck-Notzing, and the young Arthur Schnitzler staged similar "performances"—for the purpose of proving to their largely judicial audiences that hypnotic crimes were indeed feasible.[31]

Bernheim furthermore explored "suggesting to a somnambulist actions . . . which were to be carried out not during hypnosis but after awakening."[32] Bernheim conceived of such a suggestion as "sleeping unconsciously in the brain into which it had been implanted under hypnosis."[33] When the time arrived for its execution—which could be months later—the embedded suggestion took control of the body and was

28. Loewenfeld, *Der Hypnotismus* (1901), 434.

29. "Cane": Beaunis (1886), 181; "instrument docile et sans volonté . . . accomplir tous les actes": Bernheim [1886a] 1888/1964, 226/160*.

30. Forel, *Der Hypnotismus* (1895), 198–99.

31. "Vorstellungen": Schnitzler ([1920] 1981), 313. The staging of simulated hypnotic crimes by numerous physicians is also mentioned by Gauld, *A History of Hypnotism* (1992), 500. On the largely juridical audience of these performances, see Franz von Liszt's letter to Auguste Forel from April 19, 1891 (Forel 1864–1927, 257). I will analyze the theatricality of these medical performances and the appropriation of these medical simulations in contemporary drama in more detail in chapter 3, "Staging the Hypnotic Crime."

32. Bernheim, *De la suggestion* ([1886a] 1888), 45/31*.

33. Ibid., 54/38*.

promptly carried out. In retrospect, Freud described these posthypnotic suggestions as demonstrating before psychoanalysis the existence and agency of the unconscious.[34]

Auguste Forel came to see a particular danger in the employment of posthypnotic suggestions in which, in addition to a crime and the time set for its execution, the idea of "free volition" was implanted in the hypnotized subject, causing the medium committing the crime to believe in his or her own free will. As Forel put it: "One of the most insidious ruses of suggestion, however, lies in the use of timing along with implanting amnesia and the idea of free volition in order to prompt a person . . . to perform a criminal act. That person then finds himself in a situation that is bound to create in him every illusion of spontaneity while in reality he is only following the command of someone else."[35] The belief in perfectly camouflaged suggestions thus produced the powerful paranoia that there might be an unlimited number of unknown hypnotic crimes that could not be recognized as such—a terrifying medicolegal scenario that finds a compelling narrative adaptation in Maupassant's *Le Horla*.[36]

In Maupassant's tale, the figure of Dr. Parent gives an extensive report

34. See Freud, "Das Unbewußte" [The unconscious] ([1915] 1946/1953–74), 267/14:168–69*: "Incidentally, even before the time of psychoanalysis, hypnotic experiments, and especially posthypnotic suggestion, had tangibly demonstrated the existence and agency of the mental unconscious."

35. Forel, "Der Hypnotismus und seine strafrechtliche Bedeutung" (1889a), 184. Schrenck-Notzing wrote in nearly identical terms: "One of the most insidious ruses of posthypnosis is the suggestion of free volition in committing the deed" (1900, 9); see also Moll (1889), 119; (1924), 523. In the fifth edition of his textbook from 1907, Forel changed his warning against posthypnotic suggestions from an assertive declaration to the indication of a mere possibility; but he refrained from completely deleting it: "One of the most insidious ruses of suggestion, however, *would be* the *not impossible* use of timing along with implanting amnesia and the idea of free volition in order to prompt a person . . . to commit a criminal act" (1907, 258).

36. On this paranoia, see, for instance, Ivers (1927), 68: "Cases of this nature have . . . certainly come to trial in the past. But the court is unable to recognize the real cause of the criminal act . . . when free volition or amnesia have been suggested"; and "We shall be confronted with a psychological enigma and find the acting person guilty" (23). See also Adolphe Belot's novel *Alphonsine* (1887), in which the innocent medium is convicted because the court does not realize that Berthe Mauclair acted under a foreign will when following the irresistible hypnotic command to murder.

about the "startling results . . . of the Nancy School." He tries in vain to refute the objections of his skeptical listeners. Finally, he hypnotizes the narrator's cousin and orders her to obtain, under false pretenses, five thousand francs on the next day, after being awakened from hypnosis: "She [Sablé] sat in an armchair and he [Parent] began staring hypnotically into her eyes. . . . I saw Mrs. Sablé's eyes grow heavy, her mouth tense up, and her chest begin to heave. Ten minutes later, she was asleep. . . . The doctor commanded, 'You will get up tomorrow at eight o'clock. Then you will pay a visit to your cousin in his hotel and implore him to give you five thousand francs that your husband wants from you and that he needs before his next trip' Then he woke her up."[37]

Sablé promptly carries out the order received under hypnosis and persists in the belief that she is acting on behalf of her husband, even after the narrator tells her that she is only executing Parent's post-hypnotic command:

> I went on: "Do you have any recollection of what happened yesterday at your house?"
>
> "Of course."
>
> "Do you remember Doctor Parent hypnotizing you?"
>
> "Yes."
>
> "Well, he ordered you to come here this morning and borrow five thousand francs from me, and you are now merely obeying that suggestion."
>
> She thought for a few moments and then answered: "But you must understand it is my husband who is demanding the money."
>
> For a whole hour I tried persuading her, but I failed utterly.[38]

Sablé, who believes she is acting of her own volition, is in reality "dominated by the *irresistible* order she has received."[39] She cannot therefore be held accountable for the actions that she carries out under the compelling hypnotic influence of another person.

The numerous juridical treatises about hypnotic crimes, such as Karl

37. Maupassant, *Le Horla* ([1887] 1979/1990), 922/285, 923/286.
38. Ibid., 925/288.
39. Ibid.

von Lilienthal's *Hypnotism and Criminal Law* (1887), Max Heberle's *Hypnosis and Suggestion in German Criminal Law* (1893), and Georg Neumeister's *Indirect Agency and Hypnotism* (1900), accordingly regarded "the person dominated by such a suggestion as legally not responsible for his actions."[40] Even though there existed no proof of actual hypnotic crimes, these legal texts considered the "victim of a suggestion" as caught in an "exceptional state of body and mind that rendered the afflicted person physically or mentally defenseless against the influence" of the hypnotist. Hence neither "free volition" nor "normal determination by motives" applied to the possessed somnambulist.[41] Instead, the responsibility for the hypnotic crime was ascribed to the hypnotist, who acted through his medium: "The responsibility of the hypnotist cannot in the least be doubted. He must be . . . treated as the *indirect agent [mittelbarer Thäter].*"[42]

Tales of Hypnotic Crime

The appropriation of medical and juridical figures and concepts that can be observed in *Le Horla* did not constitute the unilateral citation and popularization of a purely scientific debate by a fictional literary text, as

40. *Unzurechnungsfähig*: Lilienthal, *Der Hypnotismus und das Strafrecht* (1887b), 106; Heberle, *Hypnose und Suggestion im deutschen Strafrecht* (1893), Neumeister, *Mittelbare Thäterschaft und Hypnotismus* (1900). Lilienthal's treatise first appeared as an extensive essay in the prestigious legal periodical *Zeitschrift für die gesamte Strafrechtswissenschaft* [Journal for complete criminal jurisprudence], which in 1889 also published a lengthy essay by Auguste Forel. On hypnotism in relation to civil law, see Bentivegni (1890).

41. Lilienthal (1887b), 106. For a more detailed analysis of how responsibility (*Zurechnungsfähigkeit*) in late-nineteenth-century German criminal law is no longer defined as "free volition" by modern legal theorists but as "normal determination by motives" (*normale Bestimmbarkeit durch Motive*), see Andriopoulos (1996b), 78 ff. A more extensive account of juridical texts describing the irresponsibility (*Unzurechungsfähigkeit*) of somnambulist mediums is to be found in Andriopoulos (1998).

42. Lilienthal 1887b, 110. The same theory of "indirect agency" is proposed by Mößmer, *Die mittelbare Thäterschaft in gleichzeitiger Berücksichtigung des Hypnotismus im Strafrecht* [Indirect agency, with concomitant consideration of hypnotism in criminal law] (1892); Heberle (1893); Liszt, *Lehrbuch des deutschen Strafrechts* (1898), 164, 220–21; Neumeister (1900); Mezger, "Die Suggestion in kriminalpsychologisch-juristischer Beziehung" [Suggestion in the context of forensic psychology and jurisprudence] (1912); Ivers, *Die Hypnose im deutschen Strafrecht* [Hypnosis in German criminal law] (1927), esp. 71 ff. Compare also Borchert 1888, Hirsch 1896, and Höpfner 1902.

one might expect. Instead, the medical discussion invoked in Maupassant's narrative relied on the very same rhetorical figures and narrative patterns as are found in literary discourse. While being adapted in narrative fiction, forensic representations of criminal suggestion conversely drew on literary tales. Given the lack of firmly established actual cases, the "peculiar spectacle" of staged hypnotic crimes remained the only ostensibly empirical evidence for the possibility of criminal suggestions.[43] Yet these medical experiments enacted mere artificial simulations, entertaining their audiences in the same manner as Donato's or Hansen's popular public exhibitions of somnambulism. An equally thrilling "dread" (Grauen) was also produced by the numerous literary texts that centered on hypnotic crimes.[44] Commenting on the popularity of these sensationalist narrative accounts of hypnotism, the German psychiatrist Binswanger remarked in 1892: "Today, the horror novels [Schauerromane] of former times celebrate their resurrection in the depiction of criminal suggestions."[45]

Literary texts such as Jules Claretie's Jean Mornas (1885), Adolphe Belot's Alphonsine (1887), Charles Epheyre s Possession (1887), Gregor Samarow's Under a Foreign Will (1888), Daniel Dormer's The Mesmerist's Secret (1888), Carl du Prel's The Cross on Ferner (1890), Willard Coxey's A Hypnotic Crime (1896), and Wilhelm Walloth's Under the Spell of Hypnosis (1897) were not only extraordinarily successful, they were also closely tied to the scientific discourses from which they borrowed.[46] In the preface to Jean Mornas (1885), Jules Claretie called his text both a "narrative" and a "forensic study" on "guilt and responsibility."[47] In the tale itself, his protagonist, Doctor Pomeroy, proves that the power of hypnosis has turned the virtuous Lucie Lorin into a murderess, who acts as the "unconscious instrument of an unknown criminal."[48] In addition, Pomeroy also declares that

43. "Peculiar spectacle": Salten, "Über Schnitzler's hypnotische Versuche" [On Schnitzler's hypnotic experiments] (1932), 55.

44. Grauen: Schnitzler, "Die Weissagung" [The prophecy] ([1902] 1989), 136.

45. Binswanger 1892, 7.

46. The original titles of the German texts are Samarow, Unter fremdem Willen (1888); du Prel, Das Kreuz am Ferner ([1890] 1928); Walloth, Im Banne der Hypnose (1897). Charles Epheyre is a pseudonym of the famous neurologist Charles Richet, and Gregor Samarow is a pseudonym of Oskar Meding.

47. Récit; étude médico-légale: Claretie 1885, v, vi; Claretie [1885] 1889, 4.

48. L'instrument inconscient d'un criminel inconnu: Claretie 1885, 134.

he reads the medical writings of Liégeois, Liébeault, and Charcot as he would read a novel—"Je lis ça comme je lirais un *roman*"—thereby highlighting the convergence of science and fiction.[49]

A comparable confluence of literature and medicine can be observed in Adolphe Belot's novel *Alphonsine* (1887), which describes two murders committed under hypnosis. *Alphonsine* explicitly refers to Claretie's *Jean Mornas* and summarizes, over a stretch of thirty pages, medical treatises by Liébeault, Liégeois, Delboeuf, and Charcot.[50] In this manner the novel serves to introduce the reader to the forensic aspects of hypnotism, emphasizing—like numerous juridical texts—the spectacular effects that can be produced by criminal suggestions.[51]

Carl du Prel's novel *The Cross on Ferner* (1890) similarly aspires "not only to entertain but also to instruct the reader." A scientific appendix therefore supplements the actual narrative. While the literary story details how Theodor, the "compliant tool" of Doctor Somirof, poisons the Countess Leonore von Karlstein "under the power of a foreign will," the medicolegal supplement invokes Carl du Prel's own treatise *Das hypnotische Verbrechen und seine Entdeckung* (The hypnotic crime and its discovery [1889]) as well as studies by Auguste Forel and Jules Liégeois.[52]

The astonishing popularity of these novels was capped off by the success of Jules Claretie's *Jean Mornas*, which went through thirty-six editions in the first year of its publication and was translated into German in 1889 and into English in 1892.[53] Literary accounts of criminal suggestion thus gained wide circulation and shaped the perception of hypnotism for lay audiences. The psychiatrist Albert Eulenburg even complained about a female patient who, "after reading Samarow's horror novel *Under a For-*

49. Ibid., 131; on Claretie's novel *Les amours d'un interne* (1881), a love story set in the Salpêtrière, see Beizer (1994), 15 ff.

50. See Adolphe Belot, *Alphonsine* (1887), 228–59. For the reference to Claretie, see Belot, *Alphonsine* (1887), 278.

51. For equivalent texts in the United States, see, for instance, Willard Coxey, *A Hypnotic Crime, and Other Like True Tales: Being a Free Adaptation from the Minutes of the Society for Psychical Research* (1896). Already in its subtitle, the book presents itself as an appropriation of scientific studies undertaken by the Society for Psychical Research, which counted William James among its members. Compare, in addition, Ford 1891, Coryell 1892, and Collins 1892.

52. Du Prel ([1890] 1928), v, 465, 457, 547n31.

53. Compare Claretie, *Jean Mornas* ([1885] 1889), and Claretie, *Hypnotism* ([1885] 1892).

eign Will, which she had just happened to come across, was stricken with such a fear of hypnotism that in blind terror she eschewed all treatment and took to her heels as fast as she could."[54]

Yet in addition to frightening their lay readers, these works and their representations of hypnotic crimes also had an impact on legal scholarship and medical research. In 1893, the *Zeitschrift für Hypnotismus* (Journal of hypnotism), founded one year earlier by Auguste Forel, featured a review of Paul Lindau's play *Der Andere* (The other [1893]).[55] Treating the literary text as if it were a medical one, the physician Albert Moll judged the drama—about a district attorney who during somnambulism commits crimes that he would abhor while awake—as "by all means corresponding to the experiences of scientific observation."[56] In the same way, Claretie's literary tale *Jean Mornas* (1885), in which reference is made to the medical debate about criminal suggestions, was cited by Schrenck-Notzing as seemingly empirical proof for the possibility of hypnotic crimes: "With great factual knowledge Jules Claretie in his novella 'Jean Mornas' describes such a hypnotic crime."[57] The reliance of forensic science on literary modes of representation even extended to a trial that took place in 1895 in Munich. The court found the defendant Ceslav Lubic Czynski guilty of having used hypnosis to force the Countess Hedwig von Zedlitz to become his wife and transfer all of her property to him. Czynski's suggestive powers were considered so dangerous that he had to leave the courtroom before the countess was called to the witness stand; for it

54. Eulenburg, "Gutachten über Hypnose und Suggestion" [Expert opinion on hypnosis and suggestion] (1892), 24.

55. Lindau, *Der Andere: Schauspiel in vier Aufzügen* [The other: drama in four acts] (1893).

56. Moll, "Die Bewusstseinsspaltung" [The dissociation of consciousness] (1893), 310. On Lindau's explicit reference to medical experiments with hypnosis, see Lindau (1893), 24: "Now [science] no longer laughs, since it has determined by unbiased observation that certain facts in the field of hypnotism and suggestion are simply undeniable."

57. Schrenck-Notzing 1900, 9. In his discussion of criminal suggestions, Bernheim also referred to literature—see Bernheim (1891), 160–61/118*: "A distinguished writer, M. Henri de Parville, to whom no scientific question is foreign, understood this subject with his usual wisdom." At the same time, Charcot's disciple Charles Richet not only wrote the novel *Possession* (1887), which came out under the pseudonym Charles Epheyre with the same publishing house as Maupassant's *Le Horla*; he also characterized literary representations of hysteria as "exact descriptions" (*déscriptions exactes*) that could "complete" (*completer*) the medical nosography of the disease (Richet 1880, 346).

was feared that he might otherwise hypnotize his victim one more time, compelling her to exculpate him by false testimony. Without doubting the veracity of the prosecution's claims, the physician Schrenck-Notzing referred to the "facts in the case" as "a boldly plotted *novel*."[58]

The constitutive role of narrative fiction for the scientific debate about hypnotic crimes was already recognized, however, by late-nineteenth-century medical researchers who rejected the possibility of criminal suggestions. In his essay "Hypnotism and Crime" (1890), Charcot criticized exaggerated notions of the danger posed by the criminal abuse of hypnosis, emphasizing that the hypnotized subject might at any moment suffer a hysterical seizure instead of executing the crime.[59] His disciple Georges Gilles de la Tourette subjected the belief in criminal posthypnotic suggestions to a more extensive critique and expressed his regret "that literary fiction has taken hold of the subject, finding an inexhaustible trove of stories that are as dramatically effective as they are mysterious."[60] Like Charcot, Tourette emphasized that the hypnotized medium would likely suffer a hysterical attack while attempting to carry out the suggested crime. At the same time, he denounced the circulating case histories and narratives that were meant to prove the possibility of criminal suggestions as "obscure and unscientific tales," equating them to "novel[s]."[61]

58. Schrenck-Notzing, *Der Prozess Czynski: Thatbestand desselben und Gutachten über Willensbeschränkung durch hypnotisch-suggestiven Einfluss, abgegeben vor dem oberbayerischen Schwurgericht zu München von Prof. Dr. Grashey in München, Prof. Dr. Hirt in Breslau, Dr. Freiherr von Schrenck-Notzing in München, Prof. Dr. Preyer in Wiesbaden* [The Czynski trial: facts in the case and expert opinion on the impairment of free will as a consequence of hypnotic-suggestive influence, rendered before the trial court of Upper Bavaria in Munich by Prof. Dr. Grashey in Munich, Prof. Dr. Hirt in Breslau, Dr. Baron von Schrenck-Notzing in Munich, Prof. Dr. Preyer in Wiesbaden] (1895), 1; see also 4. On the Czynski trial, see also Fuchs, "Gutachten in dem Prozesse Czynski" [Expert opinion in the Czynski trial] (1895); and Preyer, *Ein merkwürdiger Fall von Fascination* [A strange case of fascination] (1895). For literary texts with similar plots, see Adolphe Belot, *Alphonsine* (1887), W. Somerset Maugham, *The Magician* (1908), Hans Hyan, *Die Somnambule* (1929), etc.

59. See Charcot, "Hypnotism and Crime" (1890), esp. 164.

60. See Gilles de la Tourette, *L'hypnotisme et les états analogues au point de vue médico-légal* (1887), which contains the most extensive discussion of the forensic aspects of hypnotism from the perspective of the Salpêtrière. A German translation with a new preface by Charcot was published in 1889. The quote is from Gilles de la Tourette (1887), 490; see also 374.

61. "Tales": ibid., 376; "novel": ibid., 380.

Yet, despite his skeptical turn against the "tales" of hypnotic crime, Tourette himself took recourse to literary case histories if they confirmed his own theories. To be sure, Tourette rejected the possibility of criminal suggestions, but he asserted that criminal acts might be committed in the state of natural or spontaneous somnambulism.[62] He therefore ascribed authenticity to the following story about an abbot who only by chance escaped the murderous attack of a sleepwalking monk. Tourette quotes in detail from the narrative account, underscoring its claim to veracity by preserving the first-person voice of the abbot:

> One day I had not lain down at the accustomed hour but was working . . . at my desk, when suddenly I heard the door to my room open, and a moment later the lay brother entered, in a state of deep somnambulism. His eyes were wide open, but fixed, . . . he had a long knife in his hand, walked directly over to my bed, . . . and it appeared that he was making sure by running his hands over the bed that I was there. Then he struck three blows with such force that the blade penetrated the covers and . . . cut deep into the mattress. . . . When he had struck his blow and turned around, I could observe . . . that his face . . . bore an expression of gratification.[63]

Tourette borrowed this "observation," whose status as scientific evidence he considered beyond any doubt, from François Fodéré's *Treatise on Forensic Medicine and Public Hygiene* (1813).[64] However, it is rather unlikely that the incident in question was truly related to Fodéré "by an eye witness," since the same story was reported as early as 1756 in the appendix to Johann Gottlob Krüger's *Experimental-Seelenlehre* (Experimental psychology).[65] The

62. This view is also held by modern sleep research—see, for instance, Brody, "When Can Killers Claim Sleepwalking as a Legal Defense?" (1996).

63. Gilles de la Tourette (1887), 183.

64. Fodéré, *Traité de médecine légale et d'hygiène publique* (1813).

65. On the assertion of an eyewitness as the source of the story, see Gilles de la Tourette (1887), 183. On Krüger's use of this story, see Schmidt-Hannisa, "Das eiserne Szepter des Schlafes: Über die Unzurechnungsfähigkeit von Schlaftrunkenen, Nachtwandlern und Träumern im 18. Jahrhundert" [The iron scepter of sleep: on the legal irresponsibility of sleepers, somnambulists, and dreamers in the eighteenth century] (1998), 66–67. For a literary tale from the same period that represents a murder committed in somnambulism, see Brown, "Somnambulism" ([1805] 1987).

"fantastical story," which Tourette invoked as an authentic example of a crime committed in natural somnambulism, was even reappropriated within the literature of the fantastic when Hanns Heinz Ewers included it—with slight changes—in his novel *The Sorcerer's Apprentice; or, The Devil Hunters* (1910).[66]

> His [Pietro's] eyes were wide open and stared fixedly into space. . . . At last he found the cabinet of utensils and pulled out a long, pointed butcher knife. . . . Pietro stepped straight toward the bed, which stood close to the window, he took the knife in his mouth and cautiously felt with both hands for the head of the bed. . . . Finally he seemed sure of his purpose; he seized the pillow with his left hand, grabbed the knife and struck a blow of insane intensity. Once more he pulled up the knife and struck again, then he ran his hand over his eyes as if the blood had spattered his face. And again and again he stabbed the knife up to the hilt into the pillows. A blissful smile full of innermost gratification played on his lips.[67]

As the migration of this allegedly authentic case history clearly shows, the literary texts about hypnotic crimes emerged by no means from a

66. "Histoire fantastique": Gilles de la Tourette (1887), 183. In addition to such case histories, Tourette cites the representation of natural somnambulism in *Macbeth* (1887, 178). Tourette's teacher, Charcot, also characterized Shakespeare as "a remarkable observer of physiology [and] medicine" (Charcot [1887] 1987, 41). An extensive psychoanalytic interpretation of *Macbeth*, which—in analogy to Freud's *Interpretation of Dreams*—conceives of somnambulism as the fulfillment of sexual wishes, can be found in Sadger's *Nachtwandeln und Mondsucht: Eine medizinisch-literarische Studie* [Sleepwalking and somnambulism: a medical-literary study] (1914), 143–69. Sadger invokes literary texts as seemingly empirical confirmation for his medical theories: "I intend . . . to resort to literature in order to solve the immensely difficult and dark problems of somnambulism. For, despite psychiatry and psychology, it is our poets who possess the deepest knowledge of the human soul. They intuitively found a solution to the riddles of the soul, centuries before science learned to illuminate them" (1914, 58).

67. Ewers, *Der Zauberlehrling oder Die Teufelsjäger* (1910), 208–9. Ewers also adapts Charcot's nosography of "grand hypnotism" with its three phases of catalepsy, lethargy, and somnambulism—see ibid., 108 ff.; cf. also Ewers's *Alraune* [Mandrake] (1911a), 218 ff., and his *Der Geisterseher* [The ghost seer] (1922), 435–36, on the magnetic influence of Dr. Teufelsdrökh on the prince.

unilateral adaptation of purely scientific debates within narrative fiction. Instead, one can observe a reciprocal exchange between medicine and literature. Tropes that had earlier migrated from literature into medicine were reappropriated in literary texts and vice versa. Rhetorical figures and scientific concepts, narrative patterns and case histories thus circulated among literary, legal, and medical representations of criminal suggestion. The intensity of the scientific debate emerging from this interaction of narrative fiction and forensic research is even more astounding when one considers the absence of verified cases; for apart from the paranoid invocation of unknown posthypnotic crimes that could not be recognized as such, evidence for the terrifying specter of criminal suggestion was restricted to theatrical simulations and literary tales.[68]

But the physicians and writers who denied the possibility of hypnotic crimes also formed an alliance. Authors and medical researchers like Paul Lindau, Albert Moll, Albert von Schrenck-Notzing, and Jules Claretie pointed to the respectively opposite discourse of literature or medicine that would seem to legitimize their own position.[69] At the same time, the writer Karl Emil Franzos edited the anthology *Suggestion and Literary Fiction* (1892), assembling expert opinions by Otto Binswanger, Friedrich Fuchs, Richard von Krafft-Ebing, and others for the purpose of prevent-

68. A comparable recourse to literary texts is constitutive for late-nineteenth-century criminological and legal theories of the "born criminal." The crisis of criminal law in representing the cases of "diminished responsibility," which simultaneously posed an "increased danger" to society, is then adapted in Robert Musil's novel *Man without Qualities*, which thereby appropriates and transforms concepts from a juridical debate that in itself relies on borrowings from narrative fiction—for a detailed analysis of this interaction of law and literature, see Andriopoulos, *Unfall und Verbrechen. Konfigurationen zwischen juristischem und literarischem Diskurs um 1900* [Accident and crime: configurations between literary and legal discourse around 1900] (1996b).

69. The strategy of legitimizing the literary representation of hypnotic crimes by explicitly citing scientific research is still to be found in Richard Condon's cold war novel *The Manchurian Candidate* (1959), which quotes books such as Paul Reiter's *Antisocial or Criminal Acts and Hypnosis* (1958)—see Condon ([1959] 2003), 40–45. Like Condon's novel, Frankenheimer's film adaptation from 1962 ostensibly introduces the representation of criminal suggestion for the purpose of characterizing the "totalitarian" Eastern bloc. But at the same time the film speaks to a profound unease about the manipulative power of television and advertising. On the context of the *Manchurian Candidate*, see also Genter (2006). See, too, Walter Herman Wager's *Telefon* (1975) for another novel with a similar plot, adapted into a movie as well.

ing literary "naturalism" from "abusing the theory of suggestion in the same manner as the theory of heredity."[70] In his introduction, Franzos turned against the notion that "any one of us" could "unwittingly" become "the *machine* of another" and thereby be "*forced* to unconsciously carry out all commands, be they ever so pernicious."[71] Deeply unsettled by this scenario, Franzos claimed that the consulted medical experts all had responded with an "unequivocal 'no'" to his question whether such criminal suggestions were indeed conceivable.[72] Yet this allegedly "unequivocal" negative response "from every side" speaks more to Franzos's wishful allegiance to the program of German poetic realism than to the actual content of the volume; for in it, Auguste Forel stuck to his assertion that hypnotic crimes were indeed possible: "Nevertheless, in contrast to Delboeuf and Gilles de la Tourette, I must insist that crimes can be suggested." In addition, Richard von Krafft-Ebing and Albert Eulenburg did not exclude the possibility of hypnotic crimes.[73]

By publishing this anthology, Franzos was engaging in a somewhat desperate attempt to suppress literary representations of hypnotism, and thereby narrative naturalism in general, in the hope of preserving German literary realism, which presupposed a "measure of self-determination, however limited."[74] His anthology is thus an extraordinarily apt example of the tension between the realist "poetics of transfiguration," as it had been formulated around 1850, and the cultural impact of medical theories from the second half of the century.[75] The lasting significance of "poetic realism" (*poetischer Realismus*) for German narrative fiction from the late nineteenth century was, however, power-

70. Franzos, preface (1892), xxvii; Franzos's book initially appeared in 1890 as vol. 9, no. 7, of the journal *Deutsche Dichtung* [German literature]. In 1892 it then came out as a separate monograph under the title *Die Suggestion und die Dichtung*.

71. Franzos, preface (1892), xxii.

72. Ibid., xxvii.

73. Forel, "Gutachten" [Expert opinion] (1892), 51. See also Krafft-Ebing (1892), 95; and Eulenburg (1892), 16.

74. Franzos, preface (1892), vii.

75. This tension has been analyzed extensively in regard to other texts by Horst Thomé—see Thomé, *Autonomes Ich und 'Inneres Ausland': Studien über Realismus, Tiefenpsychologie und Psychiatrie in deutschen Erzähltexten (1848–1914)* [Autonomous ego and "inner foreign lands": studies on realism, depth-psychology, and psychiatry in German narrative fiction (1848–1914)] (1993); "poetics of transfiguration" (*Verklärungspoetik*), 282.

ful enough to allow for only a surreptitious appropriation of the medical discussion about hypnosis and suggestion within canonical literary texts such as Gottfried Keller's novel *Martin Salander* (1886).[76] Similarly, in Thomas Mann's early narrative *Gefallen* (Fallen [1894]), hypnosis is invoked only on the figurative level of narrative discourse.[77] In German literature, an explicit enactment of suggestion on the level of the story was hence limited to marginal naturalist or fantastic tales like Gregor Samarow's *Under a Foreign Will* (1888), Carl du Prel's *The Cross on Ferner* (1890), Wilhelm Walloth's *Under the Spell of Hypnosis* (1897), Moritz von Ebner-Eschenbach's *Hypnosis Perennis* (Eternal hypnosis [1897]), Alfred Kubin's *Die andere Seite* (The other side [1909]), or Hanns Heinz Ewers's *The Sorcerer's Apprentice; or, The Devil Hunters* (1910).[78]

Franzos and Eulenburg accordingly regarded Guy de Maupassant's *Le Horla* as the most notorious literary text about the uncanny power of hypnotic suggestion. As Franzos put it: "Today, novellas and novels in which one person forces an unwitting victim under his spell by means of suggestion . . . are common in France and England. In Germany, too, such texts are no longer unheard-of exceptions, . . . though, fortunately . . . , not one can be found among them that is written in as riveting a style as Maupassant's 'Le Horla.'"[79]

A close reading of Maupassant's tale shows, however, that *Le Horla* not

---

76. For a more detailed analysis of Keller's novel, see below, 64–65.

77. See Mann (1894), 17: "And while till now he had been as though under a weight, under a heavy necessity, *as if under hypnosis*, he was now acting with a free, straightforward, jubilant will."

78. Many of these literary texts link hypnosis to spiritualism—a connection that was not embraced by all physicians working on hypnotism and is also criticized in Bölsche's novel *Die Mittagsgöttin* [The noonday goddess] (1891). (On this point, see also Thomé [1993], 247.) The boundary between neurology and occultism is, however, not as impermeable as Thomé suggests (cf. Thomé 1993, 256); for established neurologists like Charles Richet, who received the Nobel Prize for medicine in 1913, simultaneously engaged in psychical research. On Richet's experiments with clairvoyance, see Andriopoulos, "Psychic Television" (2005).

79. Franzos, preface (1892), x; see also Eulenburg (1892), 23: "It could be predicted that hypnotism would yield rich material for our sensationalist narrative fiction; and indeed the latter has taken hold of it and adapted it with greater or lesser talent and in more or less frightening fashion (worst, most likely, in Guy de Maupassant's *Le Horla*)." For British and French literary texts that represent hypnotism, see also Doyle (1884, 1895); Cushing (1887); Dormer (1888); Bierce ([1891] 1966, [1897] 1966, [1903] 1966); Cuninghame (1891); Valdès (1891) Daudet ([1894] 1984); Du Maurier (1895).

only stands in the literary tradition of the Gothic novel, which, according to Otto Binswanger, "celebrated its resurrection" in the representation of criminal suggestions.[80] The narrative also undertakes a complex formal appropriation of the medical debate about imaginary hypnotic crimes. The downright clinical journal of the narrator, who repeatedly questions his own sanity and minutely records the smallest details, seems to adopt Charcot's medical nosography, which was based on precise documentation and drew "only . . . [on] well-proven experiences," thereby excluding "any simulation."[81] In a parallel manner, Maupassant's unnamed narrator conducts "experiments" that are meant to preclude any deception and prove the existence of the Horla beyond any doubt.[82] *Le Horla* thereby transforms Charcot's medical nosography into a literary mode of writing. At the same time, Maupassant's tale points to a link between the scientific discussion about criminal suggestions and another, seemingly remote discursive sphere that invoked the same figures and concepts.

In *Le Horla* it is impossible to determine if the possession by an invisible being actually happens within the diegetic world of the narrative or whether it is just a pathological hallucination of the narrator. This uncertainty may be read as a literary metacommentary on the scientific debate from which the story emerged—the undecidable question of whether hypnotic crimes are in fact possible or whether they merely constitute a paranoid fantasy or "tale." Yet while appropriating the medical representations of hypnosis and suggestion, Maupassant's literary text also refers to a lively discussion about intangible corporate organisms. That late-nineteenth-century juridical debate conceived of corporations as "living beings"—invisible but real organisms with the ominous ability to commit crimes through their possessed members or "organs."[83]

The episode of the narrator's cousin who punctually executes Doctor Parent's posthypnotic suggestion functions in *Le Horla* to lend credibility to the narrator's minute description of being gradually possessed by an "invisible being."[84] After the narrator becomes convinced that he is indeed acting under the inescapable influence of a foreign being, he notes in his journal: *"In exactly the same way* my cousin was possessed

80. Binswanger, "Gutachten" [Expert opinion] (1892), 7.
81. Charcot, preface (1889), iv.
82. Maupassant, *Le Horla* ([1887] 1979/1990), 920/283.
83. Gierke, *Genossenschaftstheorie* [The theory of associations] (1887), 121.
84. Maupassant, *Le Horla* ([1887] 1979/1990), 921/284.

and dominated on that day when she tried to borrow the five thousand francs. She was obeying a foreign will that that had entered into her . . . like a *parasitic*, dominating soul. But the one who dominates me, who is he, that unrecognizable being?"[85] The narrator's description of his cousin obeying Dr. Parent's "parasitic," posthypnotic command echoes Charcot's remark that a hypnotically implanted idea lodges "like a *parasite* in the mind of the hypnotized person."[86] The gradual possession of the narrator by this "unrecognizable being" thus corresponds to the irresistible power of hypnotic suggestion. The nameless narrator does, in fact, try to save his freedom and agency, making a desperate attempt to leave his country house. But he can no longer escape the dominating influence of the Horla, since he lacks the ability to execute this "simple act" of his "free volition": "I am lost! Someone is seizing possession of my soul and dominating it! Someone is controlling every movement of mine, every action, every thought. . . . I decide to go out. But I cannot. *He* does not want me to, and I stay, helpless and trembling, where he holds me transfixed. I want to get up, just to be able to believe that I am my own master. I cannot! I remain nailed to my prison."[87]

Just as in the case history of the shoemaker Mollinier, an invisible being seizes control of the narrator and drives him to suicide. But whereas Mollinier believed himself under the influence of an invisible spirit, Maupassant's narrator ascribes an "imperceptible body" to the foreign being that has taken control of his thoughts and actions.[88] In the next chapter, we will see that this invocation of an invisible body is not confined to Maupassant's literary fiction. For *Le Horla* appropriates not only late-nineteenth-century medical and juridical representations of "criminal suggestion," which in turn can be shown to take recourse to literary works. In addition, the story also draws on juridical texts that ascribe the demonic power of possession to invisible corporate bodies.

85. Ibid., 930/293*.
86. Charcot, *Leçons sur les maladies du système nerveux* ([1886] 1890/1889), 335/289*.
87. Maupassant, *Le Horla* ([1887] 1979/1990), 929–30/293*.
88. "Corps imperceptible": ibid., 936/300*.

II INVISIBLE CORPORATE BODIES

Poesy will thus contain the law, as the law will include poesy. Jakob Grimm, *On Poesy in Law* (1816)

Concurrent to the popular medical, juridical, and literary tales of hypnotic crime, late-nineteenth-century legal theorists engaged in a lively debate about the status of corporations or "legal persons" within civil and criminal law.[1] Following Roman jurisprudence, German scholars such as Savigny, Jhering, and Binder proposed the "fiction theory," which defined a corporation as a fictional person, represented by physical or natural persons in legal transactions. In diametrical contrast, other legal thinkers such as Otto von Gierke and Franz von Liszt regarded a corporation as an invisible yet real aggregate person. While highlighting the rhetoricity and fictionality of law as a linguistic system of representations, the diverging conceptions of legal personality also had far-

1. Since Continental law lacks the device of the trust, the French notion of *personne morale* and the equivalent German concept of *juristische Person* refers to commercial corporations as well as to funds or endowments. In the following chapters, the German term *juristische Person* will be consistently rendered as "legal person," even though some English translations also employ the phrases "juridical" or even "juristic person." For a more detailed account of the specific legal characteristics of the joint-stock company or the company with limited liability (Gesellschaft mit beschränkter Haftung, or GmbH), which was introduced into German commercial law in 1892, see Pohl (1982).

reaching implications when it came to criminal law. In May 1888, the Third Penal Senate of the German Imperial Court concluded that a joint-stock company did not bear any "responsibility under criminal law." According to the court, the fact that a joint-stock company was "legally entitled and *bound* in consequence of legal transactions performed on its behalf by its representatives" had "no significance for criminal law," for a "fictional legal subject" that lacked "natural agency" could not be held responsible for crimes committed in its name.[2] In pronouncing this verdict, the Imperial Court replicated opinions advanced in Friedrich Savigny's *System of Modern Roman Law* (1840), which had sought to reestablish the Roman principle *societas delinquere non potest* (an association cannot commit crimes).

Legal Fictions of Personality

In his work, Savigny posited an original identity between the "concept of person or legal subject" and "the concept of man."[3] It was only for "legal purposes," Savigny stated, that the notion of personality was "extended to artificial subjects *feigned by a mere fiction*." Since no actual beings corresponded to these "fictions," the legal person—though capable of holding rights—lacked real volition and agency. "Like minors and demented individuals," the corporation had to be "represented" by a natural person in legal transactions.[4] Yet as a merely fictional being, a corporation could not be deemed culpable. Savigny therefore denied that a "legal person" might bear the legal responsibility for a criminal action:

> The criminal law has to do with natural man as a thinking, willing, and feeling being. The legal person, however, is nothing of this sort, but simply a being that owns property, and lies therefore completely outside the reach of the criminal law. Its real existence relies upon the representative will of specific individuals, which, *in consequence of a fiction*, is attributed to it as its own will. Such a representation, however, without the exercise of a personal will, can be acknowledged only in matters of private, and not of criminal law. . . . Any action which one regards as the crime of a legal

2. Third Penal Senate 1888, 123.
3. Savigny, *System des heutigen Römischen Rechts* (1840), 2:2.
4. Ibid., 235, 282, 283.

person, is always only the crime of its members . . . and, therefore, of individual men or of natural persons. In this regard, it is also completely immaterial whether the corporate relationship may have been the motive or purpose of the crime.[5]

Savigny's definition of the corporation as a "fictional person" and his refusal to hold a corporation legally responsible for crimes—even if they resulted from the "corporate relationship"—were modified numerous times. Nonetheless, the basic outlines of his conception came to dominate German adaptations of Roman law well into the early twentieth century, thereby shaping juridical definitions of *The Concept and Nature of So-Called Legal Persons*, as Ernst Zitelmann titled his prize-winning treatise from 1873.[6]

In his *Spirit of Roman Law* (1865), Rudolph von Jhering, for instance, set out to circumvent the "technical lie" of fiction, which he viewed as "bridging" a "theoretical deficiency" or even "emergency" of the law.[7] Instead of defining the corporation as a *persona ficta*, Jhering conceived of the corporate members as the truly existing legal subjects of the corporation. Yet Jhering's remark that the actual "plurality" of the corporate members figured in law as a "collective unity . . . for reasons of utility" did, in fact, reintroduce the ostensibly abandoned fictional mode of representation.[8] For the "residual fiction of equation" retained a constitutive function for this conception of the corporation's legal personality.[9]

A surreptitious replication of the traditional concept of *persona ficta*

5. Savigny [1840] 1884, 312–13/232*.

6. Zitelmann, *Begriff und Wesen der sogenannten Juristischen Personen* (1873). As Felix Schikorski has shown, some adaptations of Roman law from the second half of the nineteenth century rejected the responsibility of a legal person under criminal law but recognized its liability within civil law (1978, 92 ff.).

7. "Technische Nothlüge," "theoretischer Nothstand": Jhering, *Geist des römischen Rechts* (1865), 288.

8. Ibid., 210. Christian Meurer, too, in *Die juristischen Personen nach deutschem Reichsrecht* [Legal persons according to German imperial law] (1901), defined the corporation in nearly identical terms: "The legal subject of the corporation (*universitas personarum*) is the plurality of its members, which is treated by the law only *like* a unity and accordingly is regarded as such without being in reality an actual unity distinct from that plurality" (19).

9. "Fiktionsresiduum der Gleichsetzung": Demelius, "Ueber fingirte Persönlichkeit" [On fictional personality] (1861), 126.

can also be observed in Hugo Böhlau's *Legal Subject and Impersonated Role* (1871), which adapted previous definitions of the corporation as a "property" created for a specific "purpose" (*Zweckvermögen*). According to Böhlau, a "property without a physical subject," such as a joint-stock company, was not a physical person but a "role . . . *impersonated*" by that property "for the benefit of the physical persons designated by its purpose."[10] Böhlau's definition of the corporation as an "impersonated role" relied, however, on the same strategy of figuration that had replaced the explicit notion of a fictional person within Jhering's *Spirit of Roman Law*. The underlying comparison of the joint-stock company to an actor even introduced a double fiction, since the figurative analogy presupposed the simile of a person who was then alleged to impersonate the role of a second, equally fictional person.

The various definitions of the legal person that emerged from modernizing Roman law thus resorted to fictional modes of representation, while simultaneously rejecting the assumption that a corporation was capable of committing crimes; for a merely fictional being lacked the ability to act in a culpable manner.[11] But the juridical reliance on the notion of a *persona ficta* was also criticized for undermining the law in its status as a consistent closed conceptual system by introducing "the deceit of fiction" into legal theory.[12] In countering this charge, Felix Somló asserted that the legal fiction was "not a fiction in the conventional sense."[13] Similarly, Gustav Demelius, in his *The Legal Fiction in Its Historical and Dogmatic Significance* (1858), and Josef Esser, in his *The Value and Significance of Legal Fictions* (1940), claimed that legal fictions had to be considered not as descriptive statements, intended to grasp or represent reality, but as normative statutes.[14] Demelius rejected Josef Unger's

10. Böhlau, *Rechtssubjekt und Personenrolle* (1871), 16 and 17.

11. A more extensive overview of further conceptualizations of fictional persons within nineteenth-century legal theory is to be found in Schikorski (1978).

12. "The deceit of fiction": Regelsberger, *Pandekten* [Pandects] (1893), 292.

13. Somló, *Juristische Grundlehre* [Basics of jurisprudence] (1917), 524–25.

14. Demelius, *Die Rechtsfiktion in ihrer geschichtlichen und dogmatischen Bedeutung* (1858); see also Esser, *Wert und Bedeutung der Rechtsfiktionen* (1940), 17: "Since laws are commandments and not epistemic tools, they cannot contain fictions in an epistemological sense." See also Fuhrmann (1983), 415: "Fiction and imaginary entities: it would be easy to assume that Roman law had strayed far into the realm of poetry. That is not the case: the terminological correspondence does not reflect an actual convergence. The proper fiction (the fiction of literature) belongs to the realm of the

critique of the legal fiction as "bending the facts" by stating that "if that were the case, then, I concede, these fictions would indeed be, if not *poesy*, then certainly *legal fabrications akin to literature*."[15] But according to Demelius, juridical fictions did not simulate "facts" not given in reality. Instead, he considered the legal fiction a "mere form of expression" according to which reality had to be legislated.[16]

The distinction between prescriptive and descriptive modes of representation, however, not only failed to acknowledge the difference between the normative statutes of the law and the theoretical texts of jurisprudence. It furthermore could not obscure the fact that the slippages involved in representing reality through recourse to fiction also applied to legal verdicts about that reality—such as the decision of the Imperial Court from May 26, 1888, which regarded a joint-stock company as a fictional person that, although capable of engaging in economic transactions, could not commit crimes. At a time when the number and power of joint-stock companies and other commercial corporations were rapidly rising, German courts thus upheld a peculiar divide between the legal recognition of corporate agency in civil and criminal matters.

The Criminal Agency of Invisible Corporate Organisms

The opinion of the Imperial Court was opposed by Otto von Gierke, Franz von Liszt, Ernst Hafter, Josef Kohler, and others who vehemently argued that a corporation had the ability to commit crimes.[17] Instead of describ-

---

descriptive sentence, the statement; the legal fiction, in contrast, is part of a normative code, of commandments, of statutes—but commandments and statutes cannot contain a fiction in the conventional sense of the word. In Roman law, the fiction served as a means to cautiously expand the law."

15. "Wäre dem so, dann gestehe ich, wären die Fiktionen in der That, wenn nicht *Poesie*, [so] doch *Rechtsdichtung*": Demelius (1861), 115; see also Demelius (1858), 87. "Bending the facts": Unger, "Zur Lehre von den juristischen Personen" [On the concept of legal persons] (1859), 166.

16. Demelius 1861, 116.

17. See Bouvier, *De la responsabilité civile et pénale des personnes morales* [On the responsibility of legal persons in civil and criminal law] (1887); Gierke, *Die Genossenschaftstheorie und die deutsche Rechtsprechung* [The theory of associations and German legal practice] (1887), esp. 743–801; Liszt, *Die Grenzgebiete zwischen Privatrecht und Strafrecht* [Liminal areas between civil and criminal law] (1889), esp. 43 ff. ; Mestre, *Les personnes morales et leur responsabilité pénale* [Legal persons and their criminal responsibility]

ing corporations as fictional persons, these legal thinkers considered them as real entities. Ernst Freund, who in 1897 introduced the "organic theory" to an American readership, summarized its basic assumption succinctly: "The corporation as a person distinct from its members is not a fiction, but a reality."[18]

Ferdinand Regelsberger defined legal persons as "social organisms" that were "not visible to the physical eye [and] could not be grasped by hand." Nonetheless, as Regelsberger put it, "not only the corporal" was "real."[19] Otto von Gierke, the most influential proponent of this school, claimed to revive a lost tradition of medieval and early modern Germanic law. Yet despite its invocation of Germanic tradition, Gierke's theory was a thoroughly modern construction. In representing the "conglomerates of partially gigantic proportions" as the "actual protagonists of economic life," Gierke conceived these "commercial enterprises" not as fictional entities but as "social organisms" with a material substrate that was both corporate and corporal.[20] Whereas Regelsberger distinguished between "reality" and "corporality," Gierke consistently characterized the "imperceptible unities" of corporations as "social *bodies*."[21] In contrast to the human body, however, these "social bodies" could not be apprehended "as a whole," since the "unity of their life [remained] invisible."[22] For Gierke then, the invisible corporate body was real even while eluding immediate

(1899); Rhomberg, *Körperschaftliches Verschulden* [Corporate culpability] (1899); Krüger, *Die Haftung der juristischen Personen aus unerlaubten Handlungen* [The liability of legal persons for illegal actions] (1901), esp. 54 ff.; Hafter, *Die Delikts- und Straffähigkeit der Personenverbände* [The ability of associations to commit crimes and their legal responsibility] (1903); Esch, *Die kriminalistische Deliktsfähigkeit der Körperschaften* [The corporate ability to commit crimes] (1910); Kohler, "Die Straffähigkeit der juristischen Person" [The punishability of the legal person] (1917); Marcuse, "Die Verbrechensfähigkeit der juristischen Person" [The ability of the legal person to commit crimes] (1917). See, in addition, Bamberg 1896; Klingmüller 1900; Busch 1933.

18. Freund, *The Legal Nature of Corporations* (1897), 14. For further English texts on Germanic corporate theory, see Maitland, "Translator's Preface" (1900); and Machen, "Corporate Personality" (1911).

19. Regelsberger 1893, 291, 292.

20. Gierke 1889, 40; "sociale Lebewesen": Gierke 1887, 121. See also Schäffle [1875a] 1896, 144.

21. "Unsinnliche Einheiten": Gierke 1895, 471; "gesellschaftliche Körper": Gierke, *Das Wesen der menschlichen Verbände* [The nature of human aggregates] [1902] 1954, 20.

22. Gierke [1902] 1954, 20. See also Gierke 1895, 268: "Personality is a legal concept. . . . It is *neither tangible nor visible*. . . . The aggregate personality is equally impercep-

sensory perception—just as the "material nature" of the Horla remains "imperceptible for the human senses" in Maupassant's narrative.[23]

. Gierke rejected the "excesses" of "organicism," which conceptualized the corporate body as gendered—states were considered male, while churches were female.[24] But he did assume a fundamental similarity between the human and the corporate organism. Invoking the analogy of the human body's different parts and organs forming a unity, Gierke described how the "plurality" (*Vielheit*) of the different corporate members merged into the distinct "unity" (*Einheit*) of a cohesive autonomous "aggregate person" (*Verbandsperson*).[25] The "personality of the corporation" was "not an externally feigned illusion but an inner quality of its essence."[26] In this manner, Gierke not only postulated the reality of corporate unities; he also considered the corporation as endowed with a will and agency of its own: "The aggregate person is not a dead conceptual thing that would require representation by other persons, it is a *living organism that wills and acts as such*."[27]

Gierke, who drew heavily on the life science of late-nineteenth-century biology, thus formulated an early version of systems theory,

---

tible but also equally *real*"; see also Gierke 1883, 1139, on the "invisible corporate personality." Also Schäffle [1875a] 1896, 91; and Hafter 1903, 44.

23. "Nature materielle," "imperceptible pour nos sens": Maupassant, *Le Horla* ([1887] 1979/1990), 927/290*.

24. Gierke [1902] 1954, 16 and 17. The distinction of the female church and the state as the "embodiment of *male* totality" (Bluntschli 1853, 110), which was highly common in the Middle Ages, is ignored by Jochen Hörisch (1990), who considers the body of the corporation as principally female, since it allegedly corresponds to a male desire. Hörisch thus neglects not only the historical sources but also the possibility of a homosocial desire directed at male bodies (on the category of the "homosocial," see Sedgwick [1985], esp. 85 ff.).

25. Gierke 1887, 174. The merging of the corporate members into one body, as described by Gierke, thus corresponds to the merging of individuals into one organism in a magical rite, as described by Henri Hubert and Marcel Mauss's *General Theory of Magic* ([1904] 1974): "It is then that the corporate social group genuinely manifests itself, because each different cell, each individual is closely merged with that of the next, like the cells which make up an individual organism" (133).

26. Gierke 1887, 176. In Gierke's view, both the "individual person" and the "aggregate person" were "natural persons," which became "legal persons" through their "recognition"—rather than "creation"—by the law (see Gierke, *Deutsches Privatrecht* [German civil law] [1895], 471).

27. Gierke 1895, 472.

which, anticipating the later concept of "autopoiesis," described the corporate organism as a distinct entity with its own "life."[28] The representation of the corporation as a real "aggregate person," however, concurrently implied a depersonalization of the natural persons who as "individuals incorporated into the aggregate *disappeared* behind that unity."[29] While the plurality of members merged into the unity of the aggregate person, the identity of the human individual dissolved. Because Gierke considered the aggregate person to be endowed with an "aggregate will *of its own*"—distinct and "independent from the individual will of its members"—these members became mere organs of the corporation, dominated by a foreign will.[30] As Gierke put it, relying on a bodily analogy: "When the mouth speaks or the hand grasps, it is man who speaks . . . and grasps. In the same way, when *the controlled* organ properly functions in its assigned position, the living unity of the whole directly exerts its agency. The *invisible aggregate person* manifests itself through its organ as a perceiving, . . . willing, and acting unity. The legal person is . . . a subject that autopoetically [*selbsttätig*] intervenes into the external world."[31]

Gierke describes here a form of indirect agency, in which the "invisible aggregate person" employs its controlled and functioning organ as its medium. The legal responsibility for a corporate crime can therefore not be ascribed to the executing individual. Instead, it is the corpora-

28. Whereas Maturana simply substitutes the concept of "autopoiesis" for the older biological notion of "life," Niklas Luhmann seeks to distance himself from Maturana's conception of "social systems' as "living." *Social Systems* [1984] 1987/1995, 293n13/547n12.

29. "Eingegliederte Individuen, . . . [die] hinter dieser Einheit *verschwinden*" (Gierke 1889, 34). See also Gierke 1887, 24: "The individual wills *merge* [*verschmelzen*] into a new, unified will."

30. Gierke 1887, 25. The difference between the individual will of the members and the "aggregate will of the corporation" is also emphasized by Hafter in *Die Delikts- und Straffähigkeit der Personenverbände* (1903), 43 ff.

31. Gierke 1902, 30. Similarly, Ferdinand Regelsberger also criticized the assumption that a natural person would represent the fictional legal person as its deputy: "When a deputy acts, two legal subjects come into consideration, the representative and the represented, and, to the extent that the latter is able to act, two wills and two minds. In short, the representative stands outside of the personality represented by him. In contrast, the corporation itself acts through the corporate organ, as man acts through his mouth or his hand. The willed action of the organ, unlike the decisions of a deputy, is not just attributed in its consequences to the corporation; rather, it is the latter's will that manifests itself through the organ" (1893, 323).

tion itself that acts through its organ: "The corporation is held legally responsible . . . for its own illegal action, which is carried out by an organ functioning as such within its corporate position."[32] Gierke's theory of the corporate crime thus attributed agency not only to persons but also to organizations. But faced with the "linguistic deficiency" of legal discourse,[33] Gierke could not describe the "life" of complex organizations without personifying them by taking recourse to anthropomorphic figures.

As a concession to existing law, to which his theory of corporate crime was diametrically opposed, Gierke did admit "a residue of independent individual culpability." In his view, the "punishment imposed on the corporation as such" did not exclude a "punishment imposed on the holders . . . of organ positions who are guilty as individuals." Yet for Gierke, the actual author of the corporate crime was "that sphere of the aggregate spirit . . . in which the psychic life of the individual is *determined* by the comprehensive force of an organized spiritual aggregate that works inside the individual."[34] The controlled and properly functioning member did not act autonomously but was dominated by the foreign will of the corporate organism. The "organ" was possessed, as it were, by the corporation:

> [It] is the aggregate person itself that wills and acts through its organ. One cannot speak anymore of one person represented by another person, enlisted in its service from outside, . . . of one whole represented by a coherent, equivalent whole that would be distinct from it. Instead, the corporate organism *possesses* in each organ a part of itself; the aggregate personality that wills and acts thus coincides completely with the functioning organ; the whole is embodied by the part insofar as the homogenous life of the whole passes through that very part.[35]

32. Gierke 1895, 530. See also Gierke 1887, 758: "An aggregate person commits those culpable acts . . . that a functioning organ commits as such in its assigned role." Georg Simmel's *Soziologie* [Sociology] ([1908] 1992) likewise described the "unaccountability" (*Verantwortungslosigkeit*) of "individual persons" as resulting from "the heightened sociological *deindividualization*" that characterized "the mystery of group action" (453).

33. "Sprachlicher Notstand": Gierke [1902] 1954, 19.

34. Gierke 1887, 768, 774.

35. Ibid., 624–25; see also Marcuse 1917, 489.

Gierke thus described the corporation as an invisible organism that, like the Horla, demonically assumes control of its possessed organs.

At the same time, the juridical demonization of invisible corporate beings that seize possession of their "functioning" organs found a surprising equivalent in the realm of theological discourse. Within the contemporary debate over whether the devil ought to be regarded as a real being or as a fictional personification of evil, the Protestant theologian Daniel Schenkel compared Satan to a legal person for the purpose of illuminating the supra-individual power of the devil: "Evil is always personal; there is no evil outside of the self-manifestation of personal life. But Satanic evil is no longer subjectively but collectively personal. Satan is a person, juridically speaking: a so-called legal person, a collective person of evil; and this is the source of his, at least relatively, extraordinary supra-individual power."[36]

Late-nineteenth-century juridical discourse described corporations as demonic invisible beings, while theology appropriated legal notions in order to conceptualize the devil's personality and power.[37] But juridical representations of invisible corporate bodies did not only rely on theological concepts in order to compensate for the *inopia*, the "linguistic deficiency," of legal discourse in describing the autopoetic agency of corporations.[38] In representing the corporate crime, juridical theories drew above all on the lively debate about the possibility of criminal suggestions. The legal descriptions of corporate agency thus invoked the medical, legal, and literary tales of hypnotic crime, in which figures of demonic possession also occupied a central position.

Late-nineteenth-century criminal law conceived of a "criminal sug-

---

36. Schenkel, *Christliche Dogmatik* [Christian dogmatics] (1859), 294.

37. It might be a promising topic for a different study to analyze the interrelation of theological representations of demonic possession and juridical representations of serfdom (*Leibeigenschaft*) that constituted, in the Middle Ages and the early modern period, a peculiar counterpart to the conceptualizations of corporate and hypnotic crime around 1900. This parallel seems also suggested by Freud's essay "A Seventeenth-Century Demonological Neurosis" ([1923] 1940); for in the case history, which is retrospectively diagnosed by Freud as a case of hysteria, the actual term "serf" (*leibeigen*) is at the center of the contract between the devil and his possessed victim (327). For an anthropological analysis of the relationship between corporations and possession in modern Malaysia, see Aihwa Ong, "The Production of Possession: Spirits and the Multinational Corporation in Malaysia" (1988).

38. Gierke [1902] 1954, 19.

gestion" as an irresistible hypnotic command for which the person executing the crime could not be held responsible. Instead, the hypnotist was the "indirect agent" (*mittelbarer Thäter*) who controlled his hypnotized medium.[39] The corporate crime was described in nearly identical terms, since the invisible corporate organism was perceived as exerting its will and agency through the possessed functioning medium. As if referring to a hypnotic crime, the German legal theorist Franz von Liszt characterized the corporation as the "actual culprit," while the person physically carrying out the offense constituted merely the "organ of *a foreign will*."[40]

Simultaneously, Franz Mößmer, in his juridical study *Indirect Agency, with Concomitant Consideration of Hypnotism in Criminal Law* (1892), described a criminal suggestion in terms that seem borrowed from Gierke's conceptualization of the corporate crime. According to Mößmer, the hypnotized medium was a mere "body without a mind," controlled by the irresistible foreign will of the hypnotist.[41] The plurality of hypnotist and possessed medium therefore merged into a unity that, for Mößmer, "constitute[d], as it were, *one* criminal person." Shifting from a figurative comparison to an assertive declaration, Mößmer concluded: "Thus a crime perpetrated by way of indirect agency actually involves only *one criminal person* [*eine Verbrechensperson*], a person who rises from the *merging* of the person exerting a will and the one mechanically executing it."[42] Franz von Liszt and Otto von Gierke represented the invisible corporate organism as if describing a criminal hypnotist who exerted his indirect agency through his possessed medium. Mößmer, in turn, conceptualized the hypnotic crime as the deed of a supra-individual unity in which only one aggregate person acted.

The circulation of tropes and concepts between representations of hypnotic and corporate crime does not, however, infer an unambiguous, causal relationship between these two distinct cultural realms. The medical and juridical debate about criminal suggestion functioned as a

39. Lilienthal 1887b, 110.
40. "Der eigentlich Schuldige," "Organ fremden Willens": Liszt 1888, 116.
41. "Körper ohne Geist": Mößmer 1892, 59; see also 62: "body without a soul."
42. Ibid., 64, 70; see also: "It is evident . . . that both [the indirect and the physical actor] constitute, as it were, *one criminal person*" (ibid., 64); and: "Indeed it is only *one criminal person*; only one *spiritus sceleris* commits an infraction of the legal order" (63).

necessary but not sufficient condition for the contemporary discussion about corporate crimes and vice versa. Both debates also resonated with an anxiety about the "criminal crowd," which pervaded literary texts such as Émile Zola's novel *Germinal* (1885). Conversely, Gustave le Bon's popular study on the *Psychology of the Crowd* (1895) relied on the concept of hypnosis as it had been defined by the Nancy school in order to explain the phenomenon of "mental contagion."[43] Similarly, the French sociologist Gabriel Tarde described the "Crimes of the Crowd" (1893) as caused by the power of suggestion; and he regarded "social man" in general a "veritable somnambulist."[44] The mutual exchange between conceptions of corporate agency and notions of hypnotism thus eludes a monocausal explanation that would turn forensic debates about criminal suggestion or theories of corporate organisms into the effects of an underlying determining basis. Instead, the popular literary, medical, and legal tales of hypnotic crime participated in the same discursive network of the fantastic that also included juridical representations of invisible corporate bodies.

Legal Theory and Literature of the Fantastic

Gierke's personification of the corporation as a real "aggregate person" allowed him to hold the corporation legally responsible for a corporate crime while avoiding the explicit recourse to a fictional mode of representation. But the notion of a real aggregate personality nonetheless relied on the rhetorical strategy of prosopopoeia, which was characterized by Gierke himself in his treatise *Humor in German Law* (1871)—

43. Gustave le Bon's *Psychologie des foules* (1895) was translated into English as *The Crowd: A Study of the Popular Mind* (1895). See also Scipio Sighele's *La folla delinquente: Studio di psicologia collectiva* [The criminal crowd: a study in collective psychology] (1891), which was translated into French in 1892 and into German in 1897. An explicit juridical comparison between the corporate crime and the crime of the crowd is to be found in Hafter's *Die Delikts- und Straffähigkeit der Personenverbände* (1903), 55–56 and 99–103. In analogy to the corporation, Hafter assumed the existence of a "distinct will" (*Sonderwille*) (101) of the crowd. But the crowd's lack of "understanding" led Hafter to conclude that the "crowd as such cannot be held legally responsible under criminal law" (101). Hence, for Hafter, only its individual constituents could be prosecuted.

44. See Tarde, "Les crimes des foules" (1893) and *The Laws of Imitation* ([1890] 1903), 76. On Tarde's theory of society, see also above, 6–7.

quoting from Jakob Grimm's *On Poesy in Law* (1816)—as an "animation of the inanimate."[45] In ascribing life to invisible, ghostly beings that could exert their agency at multiple locations, late-nineteenth-century juridical discourse thus shared common ground with contemporary literary texts of the fantastic and the cultural practice of occultism.[46]

The extraordinary power of corporate bodies indeed appeared preternatural when compared to the power of "natural persons." Max Weber emphasized that organizations consisted not of persons, who could be replaced or exchanged, but of positions.[47] Gierke, who spoke in this context of "organ positions" and their "holders," accordingly asserted that corporate bodies do not die a natural death. As Gierke remarked in discussing the "termination of the aggregate person," the corporation lives on, even after holders of one or more organ positions have died: "The mere loss of organs does not destroy a social body as long as it retains the ability to regenerate the necessary organs."[48] Corporate organisms are not only able to act—"with a hundred arms"—at different places at the very same time.[49] Unlike the human body, which is always threatened by death, the corporate body is also far more durable.[50]

45. "Belebung des Leblosen": Gierke 1871, 11; see also ibid., 14. The connection between the legal person and "animation" was also emphasized in Jhering's *Scherz und Ernst in der Jurisprudenz* [Humor and seriousness in jurisprudence] ([1884] 1992): "It is especially with the concept of personality that modern legal theory . . . has contrived to . . . spiritualize lifeless matter and to animate it by legal means" [die leblose Materie zu durchgeistigen und juristisch zu beleben] (12; also 7). Jhering explicitly called attention to the constitutive power of literary modes of representation within legal scholarship by describing the "inundation of jurisprudence by semi-poetry [halbe Poesie]"; but he regarded the "excess of poetic fantasy . . . within the field of juridical literature" as essentially avoidable (275). On the constitutive role of prosopopoeia in the law, see also Schlossmann's *Persona und Prosopon im Recht und im christlichen Dogma* [Persona and prosopon in the law and in Christian dogma] (1906).

46. This effect of prosopopoeia has already been emphasized by Paul de Man: "When one speaks of the legs of the table or the face of the mountain, catachresis is already turning into prosopopoeia and one begins to perceive a world of potential ghosts and monsters" ([1978] 1996, 42).

47. See Max Weber's analysis of the "bureaucratic form of government" in his *Wirtschaft und Gesellschaft* [Economy and society] (1910–20).

48. Gierke 1887, 832, 834.

49. Regelsberger 1893, 328.

50. See also Georg Simmel's sociological representation of the "immortality of the group," which he explains by invoking the independence of the "corporation"

In Maupassant's narrative *Le Horla* (1887), the supernatural powers of the "invisible being" that seizes possession of the narrator are described in nearly identical terms: the "transparent, unknowable, spiritual body" of the Horla is not subject to "pain, injuries . . . , and premature death." The narrator is therefore unable to liberate himself from his pursuer by a physical attack: "Kill him? How? For I cannot reach [*atteindre*] him. Poison? He would see me mix it with the water. And our poisons, would they have an effect on his invisible body? No . . . definitely no."[51]

The imperceptible body of the Horla eludes a physical attack just as the intangible body of the corporation cannot be imprisoned or executed. In *Le Horla*, the narrator sees no escape from this dilemma but suicide. Gierke's juridical treatises, by contrast, recommended fines or liquidation as modes of punishment against criminal corporations.[52] Maupassant's narrative drew on juridical representations of invisible corporate bodies, while Gierke conversely borrowed from the literature of the fantastic in describing the extraordinary power of organizations. But the juridical reliance on tropes of supernatural agency positioned legal theory in precarious proximity to horror fiction.[53]

The structural affinity between late-nineteenth-century juridical representations of intangible corporate organisms and the invocation of invisible supernatural agents within the literature of the fantastic thus constitutes the demonic equivalent to the mutual exchange of rhetori-

---

from the "fate of [its] members": "In reference to the East India Company it has been stressed that it attained domination over India by no other means than the Grand Mogul in earlier times: its advantage in comparison with the other usurpers in India was the simple fact that it could not be assassinated" (Simmel [1908] 1992, 568–69)—see also his "Die Selbsterhaltung der sozialen Gruppe" [The self-preservation of the social group] ([1890] 1992), esp. 320 ff.

51. Maupassant [1887] 1979, 1990, 938/302*, 936/300*. On the occultist representation of indestructible "astral" or "ethereal bodies," see also Myers, *Human Personality and Its Survival of Bodily Death* ([1903] 1975).

52. See Gierke 1887, 773 ff.

53. The structural affinity between representations of corporate agency and horror fiction also becomes evident in recent sociological theories of organizations that transfer the notion of "actor" from human beings to supra-individual corporate agents—see, for instance, Coleman's *Power and the Structure of Society* (1974), 57: "It is like the recurrent science-fiction nightmare—the robot created by man coming to have a will of its own, and out from under the control of man. The fact that these robots are merely intangible organizational structures makes them no less real in their effects."

cal figures and narrative patterns between the Gothic novel and political economy around 1800—an interrelation that I will outline here only briefly.[54] In Horace Walpole's *The Castle of Otranto* (1764) and Clara Reeve's *The Old English Baron* (1778), it is the supernatural intervention of a benign "invisible hand" that restores the threatened "genealogical equilibrium." Similarly, in Adam Smith's narrative representation of the economic process, the closure of that process—the economic equilibrium—is attributed to the interposition of an "invisible hand."[55] In his early text *The History of Astronomy*, Smith assumed an ostensibly enlightened stance, explaining how in polytheism terrifying natural events like lightning or thunder are ascribed to the "invisible hand of Jupiter." Yet since the "obscurity" of the economic process rendered a purely conceptual representation of the market's self-regulation impossible, Smith himself took recourse to this figure in *The Wealth of Nations* (1776). Only by invoking the supernatural interposition of a benign "invisible hand" could Smith thus reject the mercantilist demand for state intervention in the economic process.[56]

Around 1900, this trope of an "invisible hand," which at first generated little attention, became a frequently cited figure for the market's marvelous self-regulation. Simultaneously, literary representations of demonic agency such as Maupassant's *Le Horla* (1887), H. G. Wells's *The Red Room* (1896), and Gustav Meyrink's *The White Dominican: From the Diary of an Invisible Being* (1921) invoked the very same trope, while contemporary juridical and economic representations of corporate agency warned against the threat posed to common welfare by intangible "gigantic" conglomerates.[57] The popular practice of spirit photography—described

---

54. For a more detailed analysis of this interrelation, see Andriopoulos, "The Invisible Hand: Supernatural Agency in Political Economy and the Gothic Novel" (1999).

55. "Invisible hand": Walpole [1764] 1993, 22; Reeve [1778] 1967, 14; "genealogical equilibrium": Mishra 1994, 61; "invisible hand": Smith [1776] 1976, 1:477.

56. Smith [1758] 1976, 49; [1776] 1976, 1:33.

57. Gierke 1889, 40. The extent to which representations of the economic process draw on tropes of the supernatural is also demonstrated in Ferdinand Kürnberger's reaction to the first German stock market crash of 1873: "Surveying the enormous throngs of those arcanists, alchemists, . . . necromancers, and Rosicrucians with which the eighteenth century is teeming, the question arises: where have they gone in the nineteenth? They have joined the devil, you say. . . . But what does the devil do with their substance, . . . seeing that there is no matter to annihilate but only to transform. . . . In the nineteenth century he turns them into entrepreneurs, syndicates,

in treatises like James Coates's *Photographing the Invisible* (1911) or Joseph
Peter's *Die Photographie des Unsichtbaren* (1921)—even produced a "photographic image of an invisible hand" that was included in Cesare Lombroso's *Studies in Hypnosis and Spiritualism* (1909).[58] The spiritual member
was alleged to have left its imprint—not through simple exposure but
by means of "a radioactive process"—on a photographic plate, which had
been wrapped in opaque material but was grasped and lifted by an invisible agent during a spiritualist séance (fig. 1).[59]

Paying attention to the late-nineteenth-century occultist debate
about "phenomena of materialization" and manifestation therefore allows us to glimpse the structural affinity between spiritualist theories
and Gierke's invocation of the "manifestation" or "apparition" of the
invisible aggregate person in the actions of its possessed organs.[60] The
reciprocal exchange among legal representations of imperceptible cor-

bankers, . . . speculators, in short, 'strange fantasts'" ([1873] 1967, 86). On the "invisible
hand" in late-nineteenth-century and early-twentieth-century literary texts, see Maupassant ([1887] 1979/1990), 927; Wells ([1896] 1989), 177; (1897), 66; Meyrink *Der weiße
Dominikaner: Aus dem Tagebuch eines Unsichtbaren* (1921), 37, 151, 291; cf. also Meyrink
([1916] 1998), 109 and 212.

58. For a seminal, brilliant analysis that combines cultural and media history in
examining the boom of spirit photography in the nineteenth and early twentieth
century, see Gunning, "Phantom Images and Modern Manifestations" (1995a). On
spirit photography, see also *Im Reich der Phantome* [In the realm of phantoms] (Loers,
Aigner, and Stahel 1997); *The Perfect Medium* (Chéroux 2005); and Albert von Schrenck-
Notzing, *Materialisationsphaenomene: Ein Beitrag zur Erforschung der mediumistischen Teleplastie* (1914). The latter was published in English as *Phenomena of Materialization: A
Contribution to the Investigation of Mediumistic Teleplastics* (1920).

59. Lombroso, *Ricerche sui fenomeni ipnotici e spiritici* (1909), 233–34. For an analysis
of the circulation of rhetorical tropes and narrative patterns between Lombroso's
anthropological criminology, which represented the "born criminal" as a blood-
sucking vampire, and late-nineteenth-century horror fiction such as Bram Stoker's
novel *Dracula* ([1897] 1979), in which Dracula is explicitly classified as a "criminal
type" (406) in Lombroso's sense of the term, see Stefan Andriopoulos, "Ungeheuer,
Vampire, Werwölfe: Fiktionale Strategien der Horrorliteratur in kriminologischen
Darstellungen von Serienmördern" [Monsters, vampires, werewolves: figures of horror fiction in criminological representations of serial killers] (2004).

60. "Erscheinung": Gierke 1883, 113; 1895, 472. Just as the observation of occult
spheres, according to Emil Feden's *Der Spiritismus* [Spiritualism] (1921), required su-
persensory "spiritual eyes" (65), Otto von Gierke's *Deutsches Privatrecht* [German civil
law] described the "intangible corporate persons" as perceptible "to the *spiritual eye*
that is schooled through inner experience" (1895, 471).

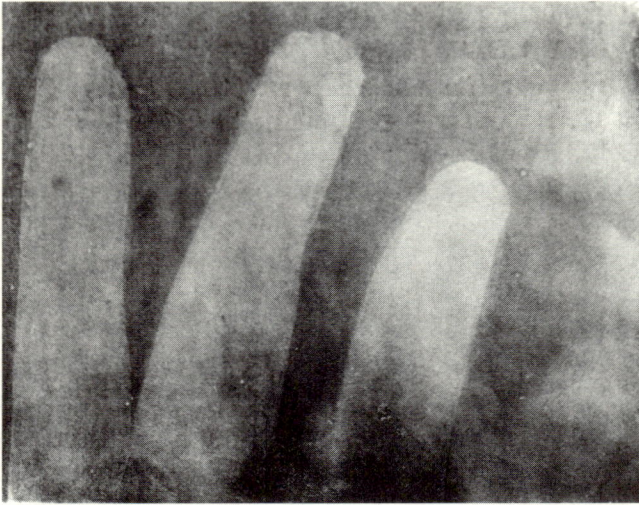

FIGURE 1. "Photograph of an Invisible Hand." From Cesare Lombroso, *Studies in Hypnosis and Spiritualism* (1909).

porate beings, the literature of the fantastic, and occultism was even noticed by contemporary legal scholars. For in his treatise *The Problem of Legal Personality* (1907), Julius Binder compared Gierke's conception of an invisible corporate body to the occultist belief in the materialization of invisible spirits: "The fact that this notion of invisible bodies has its appeal has been demonstrated by . . . corporate legal theory, which has allowed itself to be misled . . . into objectifying the purely spiritual, *disembodied* law, or, if we are allowed to employ an *occultist* term, into *materializing* it and then to engage in a quite *ghostly* dissemination of the concepts thus obtained."[61]

The juridical animation of invisible corporate bodies that can be simultaneously present at different locations comes surprisingly close to the spiritualist belief in the materialization of invisible spirits. Gierke criticized the juridical reliance on fictions for introducing the "*specter* of

61. Binder, *Das Problem der juristischen Persönlichkeit* (1907b), 48. On the critique of such an objectification of legal terms, see also Binder (1907a), 43–44: "When we give names to juridical concepts, a strange . . . process takes place. . . . Purely intellectual things . . . even though they lack any real existence, turn into things that exist outside of us, almost in a *bodily* sense."

the *persona ficta*" into scholarly, legal discourse.[62] Yet in turning against this "phantom," Gierke himself relied on modes of representation that were borrowed from spiritualism and the literature of the fantastic.[63] Gierke's unintended replication of the "fiction" that he strongly criticized was also pointed out by Christian Meurer, who wrote in 1901: "Gierke wants to escape the *fiction*, which he disdains, and fails to realize that he is entangled in an even worse *fiction*. He explains the legal treatment of the legal person as a unity by presupposing the reality of this unity—an organic entity with body and soul, endowed with a will and a consciousness. Thus it is a *phantom* that he puts at the center of the legislative injunctions, which latter then carry on their antics as reflections of a purely *fantastical light source*."[64]

Meurer, who in 1885 had attributed a real existence to the legal person, here compares Gierke's conception of an intangible but real corporate body to the belief in a phantom created with a magic lantern or the cinematograph, an invention that had been publicly presented for the first time in 1895.[65] In establishing this relation between Gierke's legal theory and the deceptive power of late-nineteenth-century visual media, Meurer simultaneously emphasizes the rhetoricity of law as a linguistic discourse.[66] According to Meurer, Gierke "confuses" the figurative meaning of juridical terms with their literal meaning. Even though "all personifications [represent] only an *image*," Gierke equates the legal fiction

62. Gierke 1887, 605.

63. Ibid., 5: "The core of the theory of associations is contained in the concept of the corporation as a real aggregate person, contrary to the *phantom* of the *persona ficta*." See also Gierke (1895), 267.

64. Meurer, *Die juristischer Personen nach deutschem Reichsrecht* [Legal persons according to German imperial law] (1901), 25.

65. On the attribution of existence to the legal person, see Meurer, *Der Begriff und Eigenthümer der heiligen Sachen Zugleich eine Revision der Lehre von den juristischen Personen* [The concept and proprietor of sacred objects, being at the same time a revision of the doctrine of legal persons] (1885), 73 ff. and 84 ff.

66. The cinematic animism subtext of Gierke's corporate theory seems particularly prominent in the following passage from his *Das Wesen menschlicher Verbände* [Nature of human aggregates] ([1902] 1954), where he asserts: "The aggregate persons persist. We would have to tolerate them, even if they were *deceptive images* [*Trugbilder*]. But does their tenacious resistance not imply that they are by no means *ghostly shadows* [*gespenstische Schatten*] but living beings [*lebendige Wesen*]?" (9).

with physical reality.[67] His juridical representation of an imperceptible corporate organism thus all but coincides with the representation of invisible supernatural agents in the literature of the fantastic.

The interrelation of Otto von Gierke's *Theory of Associations* (1887) and Guy de Maupassant's *Le Horla* (1887) cannot, however, be attributed to conscious adaptation or influence; it seems unlikely that these authors would have read each other's work. Instead their texts appear linked by "a set of interlocking tropes and similitudes that function not only as the objects but as the conditions of representation."[68] Even though late-nineteenth-century legal theory, the literature of the fantastic, and occultism were embedded in different pragmatic and institutional contexts, the discursive boundaries among these cultural realms were surprisingly permeable. It is true that legal theory strove for an enclosure that would have rendered the ostensibly "pure" conceptual language of jurisprudence independent of rhetorical figures. Yet the limits of an exclusively juridical terminology were supplemented by fictional strategies and narrative patterns, taken over from the literature of the fantastic. Late-nineteenth-century narrative fiction thus played a constitutive role for the emergence and formulation of new legal theories that represented the autopoetic agency of organizations. While the legal scholars who adapted and modernized Roman law introduced the notion of a fictional person into juridical discourse, the theories of a real aggregate personality compensated for the "deficiency" of legal discourse by resorting to figures of supernatural agency.[69] Conversely, within narrative fiction, the literary invocations of supernatural beings and clandestine "associations" took recourse to juridical concepts, so that the legal and literary representations of invisible demonic agency mutually presupposed and engendered each other.[70]

67. Meurer (1901), 45; see also 157.

68. I borrow this phrase from Greenblatt's *Shakespearean Negotiations* (1988), 86.

69. "Theoretischer Nothstand": Jhering 1865, 288; "sprachlicher Notstand": Gierke [1902] 1954, 19.

70. A literary adaptation of juridical texts that describe the depersonalization of "organs" in the unity of an "aggregate person" is also to be found in Meyrink's *Der weiße Dominikaner* [The white Dominican] (1921). There, a demonic "secret society" pursues the goal of "restoring the *unity* from the *plurality*," hoping to "redeem" humanity from the "burden of personality" (all quotations, 275).

Corporate Bodies in Literary Fiction

The corporation consequently became the functional equivalent to the devil within literary texts that refrained from introducing "marvelous," supernatural agents.[71] In Joseph Conrad's *Heart of Darkness* (1902), it is the "company" that determines the conduct of the novel's human personnel, despite remaining in the background. The "phantom" Kurtz, which is described as a "supernatural being" and "something altogether without a substance," can therefore be read as an embodiment of the corporation that becomes the actual protagonist of the novel. The company even controls the actions of the narrator Marlow, who at the beginning of the novel sells his soul by joining the corporate organization: "I found myself . . . in the waiting-room with the compassionate secretary, who . . . made me sign some document. . . . You know I am not used to such ceremonies, and there was *something ominous* in the atmosphere. It was just as though I had been let into *some kind of conspiracy*—I don't know—something not quite right."[72]

Marlow's entry into the company ostensibly takes the form of a "free contract"; but after signing the papers, Marlow finds himself "incorporated" into "a monarchically structured entity" that "by [its] compelling force" deprives him of his freedom and his ability to act autonomously.[73] He must now follow the principles of the company that are exclusively geared toward "efficiency" and "profit." Marlow is bound by his contract— "It was written I should be loyal to the nightmare of my choice." Accordingly, he can draw no profit from his pact with the demonic corporation. As Marlow notes: "No fool ever made a bargain for his soul with the devil."[74]

Another unexpected variation on the literary representation of criminal corporate agency can be found in Mark Twain's legal "farce" *Those Ex-*

71. Volker Hoffmann, who emphasizes the naturalization of the supernatural in nineteenth-century literary tales of a pact with the devil, neglects these literary representations of economic organizations ("Teufelspaktgeschichten des 19. Jahrhunderts" [Tales of pacts with the devil] 1991], esp. 123 and 125). On the genre of the "marvelous," see Todorov 1975, 41.

72. Conrad, *Heart of Darkness* (1902), 25; "phantom": 97 and 122; 24; 79.

73. Gierke, *Die soziale Aufgabe des Privatrechts* [The social task of civil law] (1889), 40.

74. "Efficiency": Conrad 1902, 20; "profit": 28 and 110; 104, 82.

traordinary Twins (1894).[75] In his study *The Anatomy and Life of the Social Body* (1896), the German sociologist Albert Schäffle emphasized the figurative dimension inherent in the sociological and juridical representations of supra-individual unities, which join the plurality of members into a real, distinct aggregate person. Warning against an overly literal reading of these organic figures, Schäffle emphasized: "The individual persons who *grow together into one social body* do not *corporally grow together.*"[76] Twain's novel, in contrast, literalizes the legal and sociological conceptions of supra-individual aggregates by describing the Siamese twins Luigi and Angelo as the literal merging of two individuals into a corporal unity. Like a corporation, this unity has the ability to commit crimes and simultaneously evades punishment under criminal law.

Since the "possession of power" over their body alternates weekly between Luigi and Angelo, control of their body is precarious. When one of the twins commits a crime, the corporation of the twins therefore eludes punishment. The "identity" of the perpetrator is "so merged in his brother's" that the jury is unable to decide which of the two is the culprit: "It appears to have been a mistake to bring the charge against them as a *corporation*; each should have been charged in his capacity as an individual."[77] Calling for a reform of American penal law, Henry D. Lloyd described this exemption of corporations from punishment in ominous terms: "Corporations possess the power to act as persons, as in the commission of crimes, with exemption from punishment as persons."[78] In Twain's novel, the figure of Judge Robinson likewise criticizes the jury's verdict: "You have set adrift, unadmonished, in this community, two men endowed with an awful and mysterious gift, a hidden and grisly power for evil—a power by which each in his turn may commit crime after crime of the most heinous character, and no man will be able to tell which is the guilty or which is the innocent party in any case of them all. Look to your homes—look to your property—look to your lives—for you have need."[79]

In contrast to Twain's or Conrad's comparatively direct representation

---

75. "Farce": Twain, *Those Extraordinary Twins* ([1894] 1984), 303.

76. "Die zum socialen Körper verwachsenden Einzelpersonen verwachsen nicht leiblich" (Schäffle, *Bau und Leben des socialen Körpers* [(1875a) 1896], 18).

77. Twain [1894] 1984, 278, 271; "possession of power": 259.

78. Lloyd, *Wealth against Commonwealth* (1894), 519.

79. Twain, *Those Extraordinary Twins* ([1894] 1984), 279.

of corporate agency, late-nineteenth-century German literary fiction was still dominated by a program of poetic realism that upheld a "measure of self-determination" and even, as in the case of Karl Emil Franzos's *Suggestions and Literature*, attempted to censor literary representations of possession and control (see above, 37–38).[80] Consequently, corporations or organizations could not occupy a central position in these literary texts. Already in Gustav Freytag's *Debit and Credit* (1856), the most influential literary representation of the economic process in nineteenth-century Germany, the "honorable" family business of Schröter that holds center stage is led by autonomous individuals.[81] Even the Jewish antagonists Itzig and Ehrenthal, whose "black hand" effects the economic ruin of the noble Rothsattel family, remain personalized.[82] The domination of economic life by impersonal corporations is therefore projected onto a distant America, from where Fink, in his letters to Anton, reports on the "constraints" imposed by corporate structures on his activities: "I praise a fellow who becomes a scoundrel *of his own free will*; at least he has the pleasure of making a smart *contract* with the devil. . . . My lot is less agreeable than that. I am being driven . . by the *compelling force* of the roguish tricks that others have contrived."[83]

Like Conrad's *Heart of Darkness*, Freytag's *Debit and Credit* evokes the pact with the devil to describe the relationship between the possessed individual and the controlling corporate organism. But the power of corporate structures in which the individual must obey "external constraints" remains limited to a distant America—"over there"—while the actual story of the novel concentrates on the opposition between the "honorable" family enterprise of Schröter and the Jewish speculators Itzig and Ehrenthal. Fink, in contrast to Conrad's protagonist Marlow, therefore succeeds in "liquidating the company," asserting one more time his status as an autonomous person.[84]

The same strategy of exoticizing intangible economic organizations

80. "Measure of self-determination": Franzos (1892), vii.

81. "Honorable": Freytag ([1856] 1896), 1:550.

82. "Black hand": ibid., 1:449. On the constitutive role of anti-Semitism for Freytag's novel, see Wagner, "Verklärte Normalität. Gustav Freytags *Soll und Haben*," [Transfigured normalcy: Gustav Freytag's debit and credit] (2005).

83. Freytag ([1856] 1896), 1:493–94.

84. Ibid., 1:550, 2:99. See also Anton's remark about Fink: "It is a strange twist of fate that he [Fink], . . . who is so little inclined to obey *external constraints* [*äußerm Zwang*], must in his present position always work with his hands tied. The mechanism

can be observed in Gottfried Keller's novel *Martin Salander* (1886), which appeared at about the same time as Gierke's *Theory of Associations* (1887) and Émile Zola's *L'argent* (1891). In Keller's novel, the protagonist, Martin Salander, faces financial ruin due to the criminal collapse of the "Atlantic Shoreline Bank of Rio de Janeiro," in which he had invested his entire fortune. The bank's directors and employees disappear without a trace so that nobody can be "threatened with arrest and prosecution."[85] The economic situation in Switzerland, however, is represented as exclusively controlled by individuals or natural persons. The firm "Damagemiller & Company," the Swiss business partner of the Atlantic Shoreline Bank, is accordingly the creation of Louis Wohlwend, who, as Salander's "evil idol," has already once before ruined him financially.[86]

Wohlwend, who serves as the personified embodiment of an anonymous corporate organization, exerts a controlling influence over Salander. His suggestive recitation of Schiller's poem "Die Bürgschaft" (The guaranty), which Salander remembers even after seven years as accurately as if it had taken place "the night before," functions—without explicitly being characterized that way—as a posthypnotic suggestion. Just like the narrator's cousin in Maupassant's *Horla*, Salander obeys the suggestion in a somnolent state by vouching for Wohlwend with his entire fortune: "In fifteen minutes I had become the first to put my name as a guarantor and co-signer on a document that lay prepared in Wohlwend's house, and immediately afterward I went to *sleep*."[87] As the plot of the novel further unfolds, Wohlwend succeeds one more time in putting Salander into a "dreamlike state," "lulling . . . his critical faculties."[88] Yet the realist "poetics of transfiguration" forces Keller's adaptation of the contemporary medical discussion about hypnosis and suggestion to remain half-hidden—just as the numerous economic crimes described

of those speculations is so firmly established in America that a single partner can do little to change it." Freytag [1856] 1896, 1:550.

85. Keller, *Martin Salander* ([1886] 1943), 57, 65.

86. "Damagemiller & Company" [Schadenmüller & Co.]: ibid., 57; "evil idol" [*Ölgötz*]: ibid., 23, 297.

87. Ibid., 18–21, 19.

88. Ibid., 272, 294. See, in particular, 294: "Meanwhile, Wohlwend was indeed preaching a sort of sermon, but one to which Salander in his distraction did not listen at all. The sound of words otherwise devoid of meaning only served to *lull his critical faculties* even more, and his thoughts, too, wandered off into the distance, as though a *foggy haze* were enveloping them."

in the novel are attributed exclusively to culpable individuals and not to the agency of intangible corporations.[89]

The exclusion of impersonal forms of association, which can be observed in Freytag's *Debit and Credit* and in Keller's *Martin Salander*, also marked the numerous German business novels from the late nineteenth century that "either ignored or explicitly vilified" corporate organizations.[90] The anonymity of the joint-stock company, the *societé anonyme*, as it was called in French, was alleged to dissolve the entrepreneur's responsibility for his undertakings. This recurrent reproach persisted in mainstream literary fiction well into the twenties, replicating the narrative pattern established by Freytag, Keller, and others. Modernist novels such as Franz Kafka's *The Trial* (1914–15) and Hermann Broch's *The Sleepwalkers* (1928–32), in contrast, did describe the autopoetic agency of bureaucratic "organisms."[91] As we will see in chapter 5, these texts dispensed with traditional modes of narration that were exclusively centered on "natural persons." The concept of "depersonation," however, which Alfred Döblin invoked against realist psychology in 1914, was not derived from the juridical debate about the depersonalization of organs controlled by an invisible aggregate person.[92] Instead, Döblin referred to medical theories of "possession and psychasthenia," a nervous disorder that was described and classified within the medical discussion about hypnosis and suggestion.[93] As we will see in the next chapter, tropes of the demonic were as central to that debate as they were to the juridical representation of invisible corporate bodies.

89. "Poetics of transfiguration": Thomé 1993, 282; on the hypnotic subtext of Keller's novel *Ursula* (1877), see Thomé (1993), 286 ff.

90. Niemann 1982, 96; see also 253.

91. Kafka, *The Trial* ([1914–15] 1990, 1998), 126/120.

92. Döblin, "An Romanautoren und ihre Kritiker (Berliner Programm)" [To novelists and their critics (Berlin program)] ([1914] 1989), 123.

93. Janet and Raymond, "Dépersonalisation et possession chez un psychasthénique" (1904).

III STAGING THE HYPNOTIC CRIME

These prearranged dramas are thus devoid of truth, unable to deceive the actor, the spectators, or the inventor. Joseph Delboeuf, "Die verbrecherischen Suggestionen" (1893–94)

Electra's deed arises from a sort of possession. Hugo von Hofmannsthal, *Aufzeichnungen aus dem Nachlaß* (1889–1929)

In 1887, the same year that Guy de Maupassant's *Le Horla* and Otto von Gierke's *Theory of Associations* came out, the French neurologists Jean-Martin Charcot and Paul Richer published *Les démoniaques dans l'art*. Assembling paintings from the Middle Ages and the early modern period, the doctors intended to provide a scientific explanation for the phenomenon of possession, thereby supplanting the medieval notion of a "perversion of the soul caused by the presence and the machinations of a *demon*."[1] The authors consequently interpreted the bodily postures of the possessed as corresponding to the stages of a "grand hysterical seizure." This project of "retrospective medicine" had already been prefigured in the first volume of Charcot's *Lectures on the Diseases of the Nervous System* (1877).[2] There, Charcot introduced "a celebrity in the annals of hystero-epilepsy"—the patient Augustine, who would later become an icon to the

---

1. Charcot and Richer 1887, v.

2. Charcot repeatedly referred to Émile Littré's scientific explanation of seemingly miraculous healings in Littré's "Un fragment de médecine rétrospective (Miracles de Saint Denis)" [A fragment of retrospective medicine (The miracles of Saint Denis)] (1869) as a model for his project.

surrealists—as "a *demoniac, a possessed*."[3] Charcot described Augustine as assuming the "most frightful postures" in seizures reminiscent of the "attitudes that history ascribes to the demoniacs."[4]

The Theatricality of "Grand Hysteria"

While ostensibly substituting medical science for religious doctrine, Charcot's neurological representation of hysteria nevertheless resorted to a supernatural concept in defining a "*demonic* variant" of the disease.[5] At the same time, Charcot invoked theatrical concepts, characterizing the *grande attaque hystérique* as a "drama" unfolding in four acts. According to Charcot, the "first part of the *drama* constituting the grand hysterical seizure," the "epileptoid period," was followed after a "short pause" by the "period of contortions and grand movements."[6] A predominance of this period marked the "demonic variant" of hysteria, and for its duration the hysterics were alleged to exhibit a physical strength that exceeded their age and sex—a phenomenon that in the Middle Ages had been considered a defining characteristic of demonic possession, thereby creating a distinction between the presence of a demon and simple insanity.[7] In addition to assuming specific contorted positions such as the famous "hysterical arc" (*arc de cercle*), the hysterics moved continually back and forth between different postures. The third period of "passionate attitudes," also described by Breuer and Freud in their *Studies on*

---

3. "Cas célèbre," "une démoniaque, une *possédée*": Charcot [1877] 1892/1877, 342/278*; emphasis in the original. On the surrealist celebration of Augustine, see, for instance, Aragon and Breton, "Le cinquantenaire de l'hystérie, 1878–1928" [The fiftieth anniversary of hysteria, 1878–1928] ([1928] 1988), 948.

4. Charcot ([1877] 1892/1877), 345/280*.

5. "Variété démoniaque": Charcot and Richer 1887, 102. For late-nineteenth-century responses to *Les démoniaques dans l'art* that ignore the appropriation of supernatural figures by medical theory and interpret, like Jan Goldstein, the "redefinition of the supernatural" as "a secularization in its intention and effect" (Goldstein 1982, 236), see Élie Méric, *Le merveilleux et la science* [The marvelous and science] (1888); and Jean Waffelaert, "Les démoniaques de la Salpêtrière et les vrais possédés du démon" [The demoniacs of the Salpêtrière and the true demonically possessed] (1888).

6. Charcot and Richer 1887, 95.

7. Ibid., 97. See also 102: "L'exagération et la prédominance de cette période constituent la variété démoniaque de la grande attaque hystérique."

Hysteria (1895), was characterized by visual hallucinations, dramatically experienced by the hysterics and "physically expressed in enactments of such verisimilitude that they [were] not even remotely rivaled by either the greatest actor or the most experienced model."[8] During the "final period," the patients gradually regained consciousness, but their ability to control their bodies was still impeded.

Charcot and his disciples diligently documented the succession of the precisely defined phases that constituted the *grande attaque hystérique* by means of sequential photography. As Charcot put it, referring to the "period of contortions and grand movements": "This whole portion of the seizure is . . . , if I am permitted to say so, incredibly beautiful and every single posture would merit documentation by the process of instantaneous photography."[9]

The theatricality of "grand hysteria" as described by Charcot was even more pronounced in his famous Tuesday Lectures, which took place in the amphitheater of the Salpêtrière Hospital before an audience of students, physicians, artists, and writers. There, Charcot induced hysterical attacks in his patients by exerting pressure on "hysterogenic" areas of their bodies (the lower abdomen, where the ovaries are located in women and the testicles in men).[10] Alongside this display of artificial attacks, Charcot emphasized how hysteria itself "imitated" other diseases in a sort of "neuromimesis."[11] On a third level of individual playacting by simulating patients, the "women afflicted with the grand neurosis" were alleged to exert "an admirable degree of cunning, wiliness and persistence" in "deceiving" their physicians.[12] Differentiating this willful dissimulation from "neuromimesis," Charcot stated:

8. Charcot and Richer (1887), quoted according to Schrenck-Notzing (1904), 77. See also Breuer and Freud, *Studien über Hysterie* ([1895] 1987/Freud 1953–74), 37/2:13.

9. Charcot ([1886] 1890/1889), 275/242*. On the use of photography in Charcot's nosography of hysteria, see Georges Didi-Huberman ([1982] 2003).

10. The theatricality of Charcot's Tuesday Lectures has been noted repeatedly in the history of medicine—see, for instance, Guillain [1955] 1959, 174–75: "The presentation of patients in a state of lethargy, catalepsy, somnambulism, as well as of patients in the process of having violent seizures, resembled more a theatrical than a scientific performance." See now also Felicia McCarren's study *Dance Pathologies* (1998), 159–71, which juxtaposes the theatricality of Charcot's Tuesday Lectures to Loïe Fuller's dance performances.

11. Charcot ([1886] 1890/1889), 16–17/14.

12. Charcot ([1877] 1892/1877), 281–82/230*.

I talk about simulation, not the *imitation* of one disease by another which we have just discussed, but the deliberate, intentional *simulation* in which the patients either exaggerate real symptoms or even create an imaginary group of symptoms. As everyone knows, the need to lie, sometimes to lie without practical purpose, by a kind of worship of *l'art pour l'art*, sometimes to lie in order to . . . *arouse pity* . . . , is a very common phenomenon, especially in hysteria. We shall encounter this factor at every step in the clinical observation of this neurosis.[13]

Charcot here reiterates the stereotypical connection between "women" and dissimulation, which he extends to male hysteria. At the same time, his description of hysterical simulation also draws on aesthetic categories. In the nineteenth century, the prevalent interpretation of Aristotle's *Poetics* considered the "arousal of pity" the central goal of tragedy, which thereby effected a catharsis in the spectator. The formula "l'art pour l'art," in turn, was appropriated from contemporary aestheticism and emphasized the artificial character of certain manifestations of hysteria, which could be separated from its true symptoms only with great difficulty. Yet while warning against the imaginary symptoms created by simulating hysterics, Charcot and Richer regarded the "grand seizure" a genuine display of hysteria, even though the "epileptoid period" performed a neuromimesis of epilepsy.[14]

The medical researchers working at the Salpêtrière thus considered the *grande attaque hystérique* as based on physiological natural laws. The Nancy school, in contrast, characterized this theatrical sequence as a "product of falsifying training."[15] As Bernheim emphasized, the grand hysterical seizure was not a genuine, authentic manifestation of a neurological disease but an artificial performance choreographed by the unconscious suggestion of the physician and enacted by the suggestible patient:

13. Charcot ([1886] 1890/1889), 17/12*.

14. The constitutive contingency of Charcot's careful and detailed nosography of "grand hysteria" or "hystero-epilepsy," which Charcot regarded as the most important form of hysteria, is also demonstrated by the fact that historians of medicine now explain the phenomenon of "neuromimesis," in which hysteria imitated epilepsy, by the accidental circumstance that epileptics and hysterics were housed in the same wing of the Salpêtrière (see, for instance, Gauld 1992, 308).

15. "Un produit de culture faussé": Bernheim ([1886a] 1888/1964), 127/90–91.

When one has seen how suggestible hysterics are . . . , one cannot reject the idea that imitation, effected by autosuggestion, plays a significant role in the genesis of these symptoms. A hysterical woman who has witnessed the sequence of a grand seizure in another patient will exactly repeat the series of phenomena that she has seen . . . , especially if she knows that . . . the observer [*observateur*] expects these phenomena in a certain order. . . . I now believe that the so-called classical attack of grand hysteria, which according to the Salpêtrière unfolds like a rosary in distinct, sharply defined stages, is an artifact [*une hystérie de culture*].[16]

According to Charcot's critics, the hysterical "grand seizure" as well as "grand hypnotism" were not physiologically given, "natural" facts documented by Charcot in a scientific nosography but "artificial construct[s]" created by the "factor of unconscious suggestion" in which the physician "produces himself that which he believes to observe objectively."[17]

Charcot and Richer had published the medieval paintings of the demonically possessed as "supplementary proof" that ostensibly supported their otherwise scientifically based nosography of hysteria.[18] Yet the very

16. Bernheim (1891/[1891] 1980), 168–69/124–25*. Bernheim similarly criticized Charcot's description of grand hypnotism with its three stages, lethargy, catalepsy, and somnambulism: "These stages do not exist. They are created by suggestion and constitute a suggested hypnotic neurosis" (167/123*).

17. "Kunstprodukt": Moll 1924, 89; "Factor der unbewussten Suggestion," "dass man selbst producirt . . . , was man durchaus objectiv zu beobachten meint": Armand Hückel, *Die Rolle der Suggestion bei gewissen Erscheinungen der Hysterie und des Hypnotismus* [The role of suggestion in certain phenomena of hysteria and hypnotism] (1888), 66. The same critique was formulated in Joseph Delboeuf's "De l'influence de l'imitation et de l'éducation dans le somnambulisme provoqué" [On the influence of imitation and education in induced somnambulism] (1886). Although Freud in his translator's preface (1888/1953–74) to the German edition of Bernheim's *De la suggestion* still maintained that Charcot's "symptomalogy of hysteria . . . [was] of a *real, objective* nature and not *falsified* by suggestion on the part of the observer" (vii/1:79), he agreed already in his review of Forel's *Hypnotism* with Bernheim's critique (cf. Freud [1889] 1987/1953–74, 127/1:94). Accordingly, Freud's obituary on Charcot also highlighted the "theatricality" (*das Theatralische*) of Charcot's lectures ([1893] 1952/1953–74, 29/3:18*). On the break between Freud and Charcot, see also Gelfand (1989).

18. "Preuve supplementaire": Didi-Huberman 1984, 127; see also Charcot and Richer 1887, vii: "ces documents . . . empruntés au domaine des arts, *confirment les autres preuves.*"

same paintings were also displayed on the walls of the Salpêtrière where they could serve as ever-visible stage directions for the performing patients.[19] The iconography of the demonic, instead of merely confirming Charcot and Richer's medical conception of hysteria, thus emerges as the actual cultural script, faithfully adapted by the neurologists in their elaborate choreography of "grand hysteria."

Hypnosis and Exorcism

While the iconography of demonic possession pervaded Charcot's medical nosography of the grand hysterical seizure, the therapy of hypnotism reproduced the religious ritual of exorcism that was likewise marked by a fundamental theatricality.[20] In his case history titled "Un cas de possession et l'exorcisme moderne" (1894), Charcot's disciple Pierre Janet gave a detailed description of his patient "Achille," who exhibited all of the symptoms that afflicted the demoniacally possessed of the Middle Ages—satanic laughter, glossolalia, contortions, and so on. Janet even asserted this parallel by quoting extensively from the *Mémoires de soeur Jeanne des Anges*, a diary written by a victim of the epidemic of demonic possession in Loudon, reedited in 1886 with comments by Tourette and an introduction by Charcot.[21] At the same time, Janet imitated practices of exorcism by directly addressing the demon possessing the patient. In the treatment of his patient, all of Janet's attempts to hypnotize Achille invariably failed: "Every method I applied in order to hypnotize Achille was unsuccessful; he answered me with insults and blasphemy, and the devil speaking through his mouth mocked my weakness." The physician therefore resorted to communication with the devil by means of automatic writing. Janet put a pencil in the right hand of his nearly unconscious patient, ordered him in a low voice to raise his left arm, and subsequently received an answer from Satan: "The hand had written, 'I

19. On the display of these paintings on the walls of the Sâlpetrière, see Guillain ([1955] 1959), 174–76.

20. On the theatricality of exorcism in the sixteenth and seventeenth centuries and on the appropriation of the religious ritual in Shakespeare's plays, see Greenblatt (1988), 94–128. For an anthropological analysis of the theatricality of exorcisms in Condar (Ethiopia) and Sri Lanka, see Leiris ([1958] 1996); and Kapferer ([1983] 1991).

21. See Gabriel Legue, ed., *Soeur Jeanne des Anges, supérieure des Ursulines de Loudon* (1886). In 1911, Hanns Heinz Ewers edited a German translation of the text (see Ewers 1911b).

do not want to.' This seemed to be an answer to my command; I had to continue. 'And why don't you want to?' I said to him in the same voice. The hand answered by writing, 'Because I am stronger than you.'—'Who are you?'—'I am the devil.'"[22]

According to Janet's account of his conversation with the devil, the doctor outwits his adversary, asking Satan to prove his superior strength by inducing in Achille that state of somnambulism that Janet himself had not been able to generate by means of hypnosis. After Janet has finally succeeded in thus producing a state of heightened suggestibility in Achille, the interrogation of the hypermnemonic patient reveals the real reason for Achille's possession: remorse for having been unfaithful to his wife, a notion that had been dissociated from the patient's waking consciousness and reemerged as a demon. In consequence, Achille's cure is effected through hypnotic suggestions that alter the memory of the traumatic cause of his neurosis:

> The memory of his guilt was modified by all kinds of *suggested hallucinations*. Finally even Achille's wife, *conjured up* at the right moment by a *hallucination* [*évoquée par hallucination*], granted complete absolution to her husband, who was more to be pitied than he was to be condemned.
>
> Even though these modifications took place only during somnambulism, they had a remarkable effect on the consciousness of the man after awakening. He felt relieved, liberated from that inner power (*puissance intérieure*) that had deprived him of the full control of his sensations and ideas.[23]

Janet's therapy functions as an elaborate simulation whose therapeutic effects rest on Achille's belief in his wife's apparition. While Janet did regard his therapy as a hypnosis that merely imitated the ritual of exorcism, the cure can also be read as an exorcism that postures as hypnosis. The "modern exorcism of hypnosis," as Janet himself put it, consisted of imaginary scenes, staged by the physician with his patient and perceived

22. Janet [1894] 1904, 386, 387.
23. Ibid., 404. The medical use of hypnosis to modify memory is also analyzed by Ian Hacking in his *Rewriting the Soul: Multiple Personality and the Sciences of Memory* (1995).

by the latter to be real.[24] The theatricality of this treatment remained tied to a therapeutic goal, since actor, patient, and spectator were identical.[25] But this structural difference to the cultural institution of theater disappeared in those hypnotic experiments that were enacted in order to demonstrate the possibility of criminal suggestions before a largely juridical audience.

Staging the Hypnotic Crime

While Charcot presented the demonic drama of "grand hysteria" in the amphitheater of the Salpêtrière, the medical researchers of the *école de Nancy* were enacting the spectacle of hypnotic crime. To recall Auguste Forel's previously quoted account of a staged murder under hypnosis: "Mr. H., simulating an injured person, fell to the floor. Then I explained to the hypnotized man that the fellow was not quite dead yet and that he should shoot him again, which he did without hesitation."[26] Liégeois, Bernheim, Forel, Schrenck-Notzing, and other physicians regarded these simulations as authentic proof of criminal suggestion. Tourette, in contrast, denounced such enactments as devoid of any scientific value.[27] The psychologist Hugo Münsterberg was equally doubtful, stressing the difference between real life and playacting: "It is true, I have seen men . . . shooting with empty revolvers . . . in laboratory rooms with doctors sitting by and watching the *performance*. But I have never become convinced that there did not remain a background idea of *artificiality* in the mind of the hypnotized and that this idea overcame the resistance, which would be prohibitive in real life. To bring an absolute proof of this conviction is hardly possible, as we cannot really kill for experiment's sake."[28]

The impossibility of enacting real murders allowed the opponents

24. Janet [1894] 1904, 379.

25. This point is also formulated by Bernheim—see his *De la suggestion* ([1886a] 1888/1964), 92/66*: "Thus he [a somnambulist] dreams through the drama that has been suggested to him . . . as if he were onstage, actor and spectator in one and the same person."

26. Forel (1895), 198–99.

27. Gilles de la Tourette (1887), 362 see also 372 and 375.

28. Münsterberg (1908), 223. The Belgian physician Joseph Delboeuf also lamented the impossibility of proceeding in a truly scientific way, which would mean instigating real murders under hypnosis: "Since, for a thousand reasons, one cannot conduct

of the *école de Nancy* to discredit the science of such "fake crimes" (*Scheinverbrechen*)—as Sigmund Freud called them—by equating their theatricality with the cultural institution of the theater.[29] The German psychiatrist Binswanger, for instance, insisted that such "observations" only demonstrated "the success of puerile show pieces [*kindliche Schaustücke*]."[30] But in Binswanger's view, these experiments did not at all demonstrate the plausibility of hypnotic crimes. Instead, the criticism formulated by Bernheim in regard to Charcot's artificial construct of *grande hystérie*— of mistaking staged performances for medical facts—also applied to the experiments conducted by the medical researchers from Nancy. As Binswanger put it:

> A wooden letter opener is put in the hand of a hypnotized woman and she is ordered to stab her alleged enemy; powdered sugar is used to poison beloved family members. . . . The patients . . . perform . . . these actions with greater or lesser reluctance, both in actual hypnosis and, under the influence of such criminal suggestions, for a shorter or longer period after the hypnotic state has ended. These actions are *invented* crimes of whose *purely theatrical significance [rein schauspielerische Bedeutung]* . . . the hypnotized patients are fully aware. No conclusions must be drawn from these experiments in regard to the possibility of *real* criminal suggestions.[31]

The critique that hypnotized subjects clearly distinguished between "real" and "invented" crimes was also advanced by Fuchs, Tourette, Münsterberg, and Delboeuf, who described "these arranged *dramas*" as "devoid of truth, unable to deceive the actor, the spectators, or the inventor."[32]

Bernheim therefore conceded the theatricality of the staged hypnotic crime for "certain somnambulists." But he contrasted those cases

---

experiments that result in dead bodies, the theoreticians of criminal suggestions limit themselves to feeble actions, which they compare to crimes" ([1893–94], 198).

29. Freud [1889] 1987/1953–74, 138/1:101–2*.

30. Binswanger (1892), 9.

31. Ibid., 9–10.

32. Delboeuf 1893–94, 192; see also Gilles de la Tourette 1887, 364, 372, 375; Freud [1889] 1987/1953–74, 138–39/1:101–2; Fuchs ([1890] 1895).

in which the somnambulist "knows that he is performing a *play*" to others where the somnambulists "have no power to resist and identify with
their role. In these latter cases, the subconscious being overcomes the
conscious being; the real conscience no longer exists, and these persons
do become criminals."[33]

In highlighting the issue of simulation, Bernheim succeeded in giving
his opponents' argument an unexpected twist. He admitted that medical experiments could not transcend the status of artificial enactments,
since it was impossible to commit real murders: "You see how divided
opinions are at present on this fundamental question, which for all too
obvious reasons has not been resolved yet by a *decisive* experiment."[34] Yet
instead of concluding that the staged hypnotic crime lacked scientific validity, Bernheim pointed to a complex mode of simulation that actually
supported his belief in the possibility of real hypnotic crimes. In these
second-order simulations as they were described by Bernheim, the hypnotized persons conceived of themselves as performing the suggested
actions only for the purpose of pleasing the hypnotist. But despite this
belief in their own freedom, they were actually incapable of resisting the
hypnotic commands. In Bernheim's words: "There are many persons who
imagine that they were under nobody's influence, because they remember hearing everything; they truly believe that they were simulating,
and it is sometimes difficult to convince them that they did not possess
the freedom *not* to simulate."[35]

This perfect immunization enables Bernheim to reveal the deceptive
semblance of "freedom" as a simulation of simulation. The status of simulation thereby becomes all-encompassing. The hypnotized mediums do
"not possess the freedom not to *simulate*." It therefore becomes impossible

33. Bernheim (1891/[1891] 1980), 139/103–4*. In similar terms, Bernheim also described the "agitation" of a female patient who posthypnotically executed a theft
suggested to her under hypnosis and consequently implored Bernheim not to expose
her to prosecution as an authentic proof for the possibility of hypnotic crimes: "This
was not a simulated emotion or the emotion of an actress. It was a real event" (1891,
143/105*); see also Bernheim, *L'hypnotisme et la suggestion dans leurs rapports avec la
médecine légale* (1897), 26: "Ce n'est certes pas une comèdie."

34. Bernheim (1891), 139/102*.

35. "Qu'ils n'étaient pas libre de ne pas simuler": Bernheim ([1886a] 1888/1964),
268/190*. Whereas Sigmund Freud's rendition of this passage is quite faithful (see
Bernheim [1886b] 1888, 173), the published English translation effaces Bernheim's
double negation.

to decide whether the staged hypnotic crime is only a performance devoid of any scientific value or, on the contrary, authentic proof of the possibility of real criminal suggestions—a proof that paradoxically consists of a second-order simulation. This undecidability, which also becomes a constitutive structural feature of Robert Wiene's film *The Cabinet of Dr. Caligari* (1919–20) (see below, 99), is a central concern of Arthur Schnitzler's literary production.

The Comedy of Hypnosis in Schnitzler

The inextricable entanglement of "truth and lie" marked Schnitzler's dramatic enactments of hypnosis on the stage of the Burgtheater in the same way as it pervaded his medical experiments at the Vienna policlinic.[36] Like numerous other medical researchers around the turn of the century, the young resident physician staged the "strange spectacle" of hypnotic crime:

> Then I also witnessed the execution of a posthypnotic command. Schnitzler had placed a slim little ruler on the windowsill of the vestibule. To the female patient on whom he was performing a tonsillectomy he issued the command: "You will now leave here, turn back at the Schottentor, return, pick up the dagger lying on the windowsill out in the vestibule, and use it to stab Dr. Hajek in the back!" The young woman left, but about twenty minutes later she returned, holding the ruler in her fist with every sign of frightful agitation, entering the room stealthily like a true murderess and searching for Dr. Hajek with guilty, furtive eyes. . . . This strange spectacle demonstrated all too clearly how a criminal emerges from a harmless person.[37]

Schnitzler further combined his therapeutic use of hypnosis in treating functional aphony—the loss of voice without evident impairment of the vocal organs—with the suggestion of fictional roles and situations: "You are a coach driver," "you are the ringmaster of Circus Renz."[38] His

---

36. Schnitzler ([1898] 1994), 215.

37. Salten ([1932–33] 1984), 55.

38. See Arthur Schnitzler, *Über funktionelle Aphonie und deren Behandlung durch Hypnose und Suggestion* [On functional aphony and its treatment by means of hypnosis and

patients enacted these scenes according to his directions, and Schnitzler excluded a "larger audience" from this playacting only when his colleagues maligned him for conduct.ng hypnotic "performances" (*Vorstellungen*) at the policlinic.[39]

The theatricality of these medical stagings was, however, perfectly clear to Schnitzler himself. In his review of Freud's translation of Bernheim's *De la suggestion*, Schnitzler explicitly pointed out that the hypnotized mediums enacted "poses" (*Posen*) borrowed from theater plays:

> A fairly humorous example . . . was observed by this reviewer in a rather skittish girl, F. T., who was able to *play* all kinds of *roles* in her somnambulism. I transformed her into an arctic explorer and stated that a polar bear was approaching, whereupon she took my arm and urged fearfully, "We had better leave!" . . . To be sure, the pose that shaped the enactment of certain roles was developed to an extraordinary degree in this person. For it could only be interpreted as the ability of enacting a pose, highly developed in the phase of somnambulism, and not as a departure from her own character when, as a queen, she refused to flee from a rebellion raging in her palace but rather exclaimed, every time that suggestion was attempted, "I remain strong! I shall not flee!" . . . It was the pose of the queen, probably familiar to her *from theater plays*.[40]

Thus it is not an unilateral adaptation of purely scientific research within drama but a reappropriation of somnambulist playacting when Schnitzler's one-act play *Asking Fate* (*Die Frage an das Schicksal* [1889]) features the hypnotic suggestion of roles. Whereas the physician Friedrich Fuchs criticized the "Comedy of Hypnosis" (1890) as lacking scientific value, Schnitzler's play adapted this medical "comedy" by representing the figure of Max, who hypnotizes Anatol's fiancée, Cora: "Well, I must tell you, I was stunned. Till now, I had considered the whole thing a fairy

suggestion] (1889e) and [1889a] 1984, [1889b] 1984. "Coach driver": Schnitzler [1889a] 1984, 40; "ringmaster": Schnitzler [1889a] 1984, 50. On this point, see also Thomé (1991), 58n38: "He [Schnitzler] suggested predominantly fictional situations to which the mediums reacted by playing suitable roles. . . . Behind this there is probably the fascination with . . . comedic role-play on the threshold of consciousness—themes that also have an impact on Schnitzler's later literary work."

39. Schnitzler ([1920] 1981), 313.

40. Schnitzler, "Rezension" ([1889c] 1991), 213n.

tale. But now, watching it, . . . seeing her fall asleep with my own eyes, . . .
watching her dance when you told her she was a ballerina, seeing her
cry when you told her that her lover had died, and seeing her pardon a
criminal when you made her a queen."[41] Yet in addition to replicating
the medial status of Schnitzler's play as enacted performance, the appropriation of hypnotic role-play simultaneously served to emphasize
the "comedy of our souls" on the level of dramatic plot.[42]

The medical researcher Fuchs traced the "comedy of hypnosis," where
"the great subjects only play a role," to the human "delight in deception."[43] In a parallel manner, Schnitzler's characters Max and Anatol
turn the "comedy of our souls" into an anthropological given, connect-
ing it to the stereotypical "enigma of women," who "'give themselves'
even when they give themselves."[44] When Anatol chooses to employ hypnosis as an allegedly "infallible means" to circumvent female deception
and "learn the truth," the result is the very same dilemma that marks
the medical enactments of hypnosis: it remains uncertain whether the
statements given by the somnambulist Cora are authentic, or whether
they are actually produced by Anatol's suggestions.[45]

Without doubting the veracity of testimony given by hypnotized subjects, André de Lorde's horror play L'acquittée (1913) presented the figure
of Madame Menard, who, after gaining legal acquittal, confesses under
hypnosis to having strangled several children.[46] But in his review of Hein-

41. Fuchs (1890); Schnitzler, *Die Frage an das Schicksal* ([1889d] 1993), 36.

42. "Comedy of our souls": Hofmannsthal [Loris, pseud.], "Einleitung" ([1892]
1993), 34.

43. "Comedy": Fuchs (1890), 7; "role": 10; "deception": 20.

44. "Enigma": Schnitzler ([1889d] 1993), 66; "give themselves": Nietzsche [1882–87]
1979, 291. Nietzsche's fragment ("Vom Probleme des Schauspielers" [On the problem
of acting]) also exemplifies the female "delight in deception" by invoking hypnosis: "Listen to physicians who have hypnotized females" (Nietzsche [1882–87] 1979,
290–91); see also Jacques Derrida, *Éperons: Les styles de Nietzsche* (1979), 68–69, on this
passage.

45. Michael Worbs's interpretation—"The fear connected to hypnosis is that
through it reality will be . . . uncovered behind semblance, the unconscious behind
the conscious" (1983, 226)—ignores the reduplication of the "comedy of our souls" in
hypnosis, which also produces mere simulations or semblance. "Learn the truth":
Schnitzler ([1889d] 1993), 39.

46. Compare de Lorde [1913] 1924, 178–79. On de Lorde's "theater of fear," see also
Gunning (1994). For a drama by de Lorde that is set in the Salpêtrière, see de Lorde
(1908).

rich Obersteiner's *Theory of Hypnotism* (1893), Schnitzler himself explicitly rejected the use of "hypnosis for the purpose of a forensic interrogation," claiming that it only produced further playacting, in which truth and lie are inextricably entangled.[47] Max's misogynist equation of this dilemma with women—"One thing is clear to me: that women lie even under hypnosis"—naturalizes the link of simulation and women in the same way as Emil du Bois-Reymond's statement: "Mulieri ne mortuae quidem credendum est" [Even a dead woman is not to be believed].[48] The metatheatrical reduplication of the "comedy of hypnosis" on the stage of the Burgtheater, however, simultaneously highlights the fundamental theatricality inherent in the medical enactments of hypnosis, which oscillate between a simple and a second-order simulation.

A similar impasse forms the center of Schnitzler's one-act play *Paracelsus* (1898), which opened on the first of March 1899 at the Vienna Burgtheater. Here again it remains uncertain whether the suggestions implanted in Justina's mind by the physician Paracelsus bring the truth to light or whether they merely (re)produce a play. Bernheim's insight into the possibility of "retroactive hallucinations"—"It is possible to suggest to such people [somnambulists] that at a certain time in the past they witnessed or committed some act, and the image thus created in their brain will become a lifelike memory which dominates them and which they consider an irrefutable reality"—finds an explicit adaptation in Schnitzler's play.[49] Not only does Paracelsus suggest to Medardus that he traveled in distant lands—a "dream" of which the latter "would forever *swear* that it was true."[50] In addition, Paracelsus suggests to Justina that

47. Compare Schnitzler, "Rezension von Heinrich Obersteiner, *Die Lehre vom Hypnotismus*" [Review of Heinrich Obersteiner, *The Theory of Hypnotism*] ([1893] 1991), 316: "He [Obersteiner] . . . finally makes many apt comments about the . . . forensic importance of hypnotism, which latter he rightly finds only in the field of criminal law, but not, like other authors, in that of civil law. And everybody will also agree with his objections against the proposal, made some time ago, to use hypnosis for the purpose of a forensic interrogation."

48. "Women lie under hypnosis": Schnitzler ([1889d] 1993), 48; "mulieri": du Bois-Reymond, "Gutachten über Hypnose und Suggestion" [Expert opinion on hypnosis and suggestion] (1892), 13.

49. Bernheim [1886a] 1888/1964, 232/164*.

50. Schnitzler [1898] 1994, 195. On the possibility of false testimonies in court as a result of such retroactive hallucinations, see also Bernheim ([1886a] 1888/1964), 237–38/168–69.

she cheated on her husband, Cyprian, with Squire Anselmus. Bernheim had described such a hypnotically implanted false memory as "imposing itself upon the imagination" of the hypnotized subject "with all the clarity of real experience . . . , like a *dramatic scene* forcefully sketched by the writer."[51] The medical assumption, which is formulated in theatrical terms, is powerfully enacted in Schnitzler's play, where Justina cannot resist the liveliness of Paracelsus's suggestions:

> CYPRIAN: You're dreaming. You are innocent!
> JUSTINA: Would it were true! But I feel horror when I look at myself. In his arms I see myself and feel his kisses scorch my neck and lip and cheek.[52]

Cyprian, who at this point still strives to convince Justina of her "innocence," also starts doubting his wife's faithfulness when Paracelsus insinuates: "And what if it were the truth after all, a truth I only stirred up in her heart? . . . Who will ever tell us whether what she dreams of was not also experienced?" It remains uncertain whether the retroactive hallucination suggested to Justina by Paracelsus is indeed a hallucination or, on the contrary, a true event that Justina can recall only in hypnotic hypermnesia: "Dream and waking, truth and lie, flow into each other. Certainty is nowhere. . . . We are always playacting."[53]

Schnitzler's play transfers Bernheim's medical description of "retroactive hallucinations," which lodge in the consciousness of the hypnotized subject like a "dramatic scene," onto the stage of the Viennese Burgtheater. The play also invokes a therapeutic adaptation of hypnosis when Paracelsus remarks, "Are you afraid of *memory*? There is no better way of removing its horrifying power than to *awaken it to life*." In their *Studies on Hysteria* (1895), Josef Breuer and Sigmund Freud had represented

51. Bernheim [1886a] 1888/1964, 238/169*.

52. Schnitzler [1898] 1994, 205.

53. Ibid., 206–7, 215. For an analysis of the current memory wars waged in the United States about the status of hypnotically recovered memories of sexual abuse in childhood, see Showalter 1997, 144 ff. Showalter also calls attention to the fact that the majority of people who consider themselves victims of alien abduction regained the memory of that trauma under hypnosis: "Only when the abductees talked with ufologists who knew the metanarratives did patterns emerge. All the abductees had lost their memories and had to be treated with hypnosis" (191).

the cathartic reawakening of memory in similar terms: "We found . . . that the individual hysterical symptoms immediately and permanently disappeared when we had succeeded in *awakening* [*erwecken*] the *memory* of the causal event to complete lucidity, thereby also calling up its accompanying affect, and when the patient had described that event in the greatest possible detail and had put the affect into words."[54] While *Paracelsus* cites the *Studies on Hysteria*, Freud refers to Schnitzler's play in his *Fragment of a Hysteria Analysis* (1905).[55] At the same time, Schnitzler's dramatic adaptation of the "talking cure" in *Paracelsus* points to the underlying theatricality of Freud's cathartic method.[56]

Transference and Conjuring in the Talking Cure

Freud had hoped to break with suggestive practices when he took up the technique of free association in 1895, remarking that "psychoanalysis proper" began "with the renunciation of hypnosis as a tool."[57] But this transition from performance to narration was not completely successful.[58] For despite the attempt "to bypass hypnosis," suggestion did retain a constitutive role for the therapeutic effects of analysis, while Freud's etiology of hysterical symptoms simultaneously replicated Charcot's and Janet's invocation of figures of demonic agency.[59]

Freud's reliance on tropes of the supernatural can be observed al-

54. Schnitzler ([1898] 1994), 192. Breuer and Freud ([1895] 1987/Freud 1953–74), 30/2:6*. This parallel between *Paracelsus* and the *Studies on Hysteria* is also highlighted by Michael Worbs (1983, 230–31). Worbs's instructive study *Nervenkunst* [Nerve art] concentrates, however, on the telos of later psychoanalytical insights that, according to Worbs, were anticipated "by the poet's . . . divinatory intuition" (1983, 232). Consequently, Worbs does not analyze the theatricality of the medical research into hypnosis.

55. Compare Freud ([1905] 1971/1953–74), 119n1/7:44n1.

56. "Talking cure": Breuer and Freud ([1895] 1987/Freud 1953–74), 50/2:30.

57. Freud [1917] 1948/1953–74, 302/16:293*. See also Freud [1914b] 1946/1953–74, 54/14:16: "The history of psychoanalysis proper, therefore, only begins with the new technique that dispenses with hypnosis."

58. See also Borch-Jacobsen (1989), 97, on this point. On Freud's individualization of his "case histories," which 'read like novellas" (Breuer and Freud [1895] 1987/Freud 1953–74, 180/2:160*), see Marcus (1985); Thomé (1993), 190 ff.; and others.

59. "To bypass hypnosis": Breuer and Freud ([1895] 1987/Freud 1953–74), 284/2:268.

ready in his early essay "A Case of Hypnotic Healing, with Remarks on the Genesis of Hysterical Phenomena through the Counter-Will" (1892), in which he developed an explanation for the emergence of hysterical phenomena that resembled Janet's medical case history of Achille. Emphasizing the "demonic trait" of hysteria, Freud described a complex process in which "distressing antithetic ideas" that ran counter to the conscious will of the subject were dissociated from the waking consciousness.[60] These "inhibited intentions," however, did not simply disappear. Instead, they continued to dwell in a "shadowy realm," leading "an unnoticed existence . . . until stepping forth as *specters* to *seize possession of the body* that had otherwise served the dominant ego-consciousness."[61]

A similar account of demonic possession reemerged thirty years later in Freud's analysis of "A Seventeenth-Century Demonological Neurosis" (1923). There, Freud set out to supplement Charcot's retrospective diagnosis of hysteria in visual "representations of possession" by "retracing" the neurosis in case histories, shifting from a nosography of the visible "manifestations" of hysteria to a psychological reading of the "subject-matter of the neurosis."[62] Turning against a purely somatic medicine that acknowledged only physiological findings, Freud affirmed the validity of medieval notions of demonic agency:

> The demonological theory of those dark times has won in the end against all the somatic conceptions from the period of "exact" science. The states of possession correspond to our neuroses, and, in order to explain them, we resort once again to psychic powers [*psychische Mächte*]. To us, the demons are evil and reprehensible wishes, derivatives of instinctual impulses that have been repudiated and repressed. We only renounce the projection of these *psychic beings* [*seelische Wesen*] into the external world which the

60. "Dämonischer Zug": Freud (1892–93/1953–74), 127; the English standard edition of Freud's works only contains an abridged version of this essay in which this passage is missing; "peinliche Constrastvorstellungen": ibid., 106/1:121.

61. Ibid., 127. See also Breuer and Freud [1895] 1987/Freud 1953–74, 16/2:251*: "The dissociated psyche is the *demon* by which the naive observation of early superstitious times believed the patients to be possessed. It is true that a spirit foreign to the patient's waking consciousness holds sway in him; but the spirit is in fact not a foreign one but a part of his own psyche" (emphasis in the original).

62. Freud [1923] 1940/1953–74, 317/19:72*.

Middle Ages carried out; we regard them as having arisen in the patient's inner life, *where they have their abode.*[63]

In this passage, Freud appears to replace the supernatural interpretation of possession with a natural explanation that "believes, not in the devil,... but in psychoanalysis."[64] Yet in ascribing a life to the "psychic beings" of evil and reprehensible wishes, Freud relies—like Gierke in his juridical animation of the invisible corporate organism—on the rhetorical strategy of prosopopoeia. It is thus the displacement, not the dismissal, of demonic figures that allows for Freud's insight into the psychological mechanism of dissociation.[65]

But not only Freud's etiology of hysteria draws on tropes of supernatural agency, which simultaneously pervade representations of invisible corporate bodies and the literature of the fantastic. In addition, Freud's therapy also remains indebted to the "modern exorcism of hypnosis" as it was enacted by Janet.[66] Similar to Janet's staging of imaginary scenes, Freud's conjuring of demons, which after the cathartic abreaction vanish "like a ghost that has been laid to rest," rests on a theatrical performance by patient and doctor.[67] Breuer and Freud's notion of a "cathartic

63. Ibid., 317–18/19:72*. See also Freud [1919] 1982/1953–74, 266/17:243: "The Middle Ages quite consistently ascribed all such maladies to the influence of *demons*, and in this their psychology was *almost correct.*"

64. Freud [1923] 1940/1953–74, 345/19:98*.

65. A remarkably positive account of medieval demonology is also to be found in Freud's obituary on Charcot—see Freud [1893] 1952/1953–74, 31/3:20:

No one should object that the theory of a splitting of consciousness as a solution to the riddle of hysteria is much too remote to impress an unbiased and untrained observer. For, by pronouncing possession by a demon to be the cause of hysterical phenomena, the Middle Ages in fact chose this solution; it would only have been a matter of exchanging the religious terminology of that dark and superstitious age for the scientific language of today. Charcot, however, did not follow this path towards an explanation of hysteria, although he drew copiously upon the surviving reports of witch trials and of possession, in order to show that the manifestations of the neurosis were the same in those days as they are now.

66. Janet ([1894] 1904), 379.

67. Breuer and Freud [1895] 1987/1953–74, 297/2:281. The language of the supernatural within the *Studies on Hysteria* also comes to the fore in the following statement: "Her troubles disappeared as *though by magic*" (198/2:178); and 66/2:46, on the

method" emerged from a reciprocal exchange between medicine and classical philology that engendered a rereading of the Aristotelian theory of tragedy.[68] Accordingly, the curative, cathartic repetition of the originary, traumatic scene presented itself as a theatrical "reproduction"—an abreaction, in which "the psychical process that had originally taken place . . . must be repeated as vividly [*lebhaft*] as possible."[69]

Even after the transition from the cathartic method to free association and analysis, there remained a constitutive residue of demonic possession in the talking cure—the transference between patient and analyst that functioned as an equivalent or "counterpart" to the hypnotic "rapport."[70] Just as Janet cured his patient Achille by conjuring the apparition of his forgiving wife, a successful analysis depends on that moment of transference in which the patient "sees" (*erblickt*) in the analyst "the return—*reincarnation*—of an important figure from his childhood."[71]

In his essay "Remembering, Repetition, Working Through" (1914), Freud therefore referred to the therapeutic restaging of the past as a

---

"*miraculous [wunderbar]* fact that from the beginning to the end of the illness all the stimuli arising from the secondary state, together with their consequences, were permanently removed by being given verbal utterance in hypnosis."

68. While Breuer adapted Jakob Bernays's interpretation of catharsis as a "discharge" (*Entladung*), first developed in Bernays's *Zwei Abhandlungen über die aristotelische Theorie des Dramas* [Two treatises on the Aristotelian theory of the drama] (1880), the philologist Alfred Berger, in turn, invoked Breuer and Freud's medical therapy in order to illustrate how tragedy affected its audience: "The cathartic treatment of hysteria described by the physicians Dr. Josef Breuer and Dr. Sigmund Freud is very well suited to elucidate the cathartic effect of tragedy" (Berger, "Wahrheit und Irrtum in der Katharsistheorie des Aristoteles" [Truth and error in the catharsis theory of Aristotle] [1897], 81). On Breuer's adaptation of Bernays, see also Langholf (1990), 10–11.

69. "Reproduction": Breuer and Freud [1895] 1987/Freud 1953–74, 33/2:11; "as vividly as possible": 30/2:6.

70. "Gegenstück": Freud [1921] 1974/1953–74, 118n2/18:126*. On "transference" as a "residue" of demonic possession in analysis, see also Mannoni 1980, 49–50: "Le transfert est ce qui nous reste de la possession, et on l'obtient par une série des soustractions. On élimine le diable, restent les convulsionnaires. On élimine les réliques, restent les 'magnétisés' de Mesmer. . . . On élimine l'hypnose, il reste: le transfert." See also Terry Castle: "A successful analysis, ostensibly, is a kind of exorcism" (1995, 187).

71. Freud, "Abriss der Psychoanalyse" [1938] 1950/1953–74, 100/23:174*; for a more detailed analysis of the relationship between the suggestive production of visual hallucinations and the new medium of film, see chap. 4, "Bernheim, Caligari, Mabuse."

"conjuring": "Repeating, as it is induced in analytic treatment according to the newer technique . . . implies *conjuring up* a piece of real life."[72] In this "conjuring" or transference, the patient engages in a performance of (imaginary) scenes, a reenactment of an old drama, which the patient "is *reproducing* tangibly, as though it were happening in the present."[73]

Hofmannsthal's *Electra*

Therapy as drama, however, could not find a direct equivalent in drama as therapy, since the structural difference between catharsis of the spectator (Aristotle, Bernays) and catharsis of the actor (Breuer and Freud) prevented an immediate adaptation of theatrical medicine on the stage of the theater. Yet when writing the tragedy *Electra* (1903), Hugo von Hofmannsthal did read the "strange book on hysteria authored by the Doctors Breuer and Freud," as he described it in one of his letters.[74] The play had its opening night on October 30, 1903, directed by Max Reinhardt and featuring the famous actress Gertrud Eysoldt in the leading role. Hofmannsthal's adaptation of Breuer and Freud's treatise is evident when the figure of Clytemnestra invokes the cathartic effect of language, asking her daughter for "an antidote to dreams": "Do you have no other words to comfort me? . . . How one pronounces a word and a sentence, much depends on that."[75] Even though Hofmannsthal's conservative conception of drama prohibited the enactment of hypnosis onstage, the

72. Freud [1914a] 1946/1953–74, 13–14,12:153. See also Freud, "Die Frage der Laien-analyse" [The question of lay analysis] [1926] 1948/1953–74), 258/20:227*: "To send the patient away as soon as the inconveniences of his transference-neurosis make their appearance would not make sense. . . It would be as though one had conjured up spirits and run away from them as soon as they appeared. Sometimes, it is true, nothing else is possible . . . , but one must at least have struggled with the evil spirits to the best of one's strength."

73. Freud [1926] 1948/1953–74, 258/20:226*.

74. Hofmannsthal, *Briefe* [Correspondence] ([1900–1909] 1937), 384. Marianne Schuller's interpretation of the relationship between the *Studies on Hysteria* and *Electra* as a "*dramatization* of the novella form" (1989, 464) ignores the fundamental theatricality of the cathartic method—cf. also Borch-Jacobsen (1989), 97: "If Freud and Breuer described the *stories* of their patients as *cathartic*, it is because these *stories* were in fact *dramas* that were played out, acted, mimed."

75. Hofmannsthal [1903] 1979, 202; see also 203: "But you have words. You could say much that would help me."

theatricality of medical research into hysteria and hypnosis did become a constitutive force in Hofmannsthal's play.[76]

Electra alludes to external suggestions that cause a dissociation of Clytemnestra's consciousness, when she remarks to her mother: "You are yourself no longer. . . . What they [the confidantes] hiss into your ears, *tears* your mind *apart* again and again; thus you walk *in a haze*, forever as *in a dream*." At the same time, Hofmannsthal's stage direction, "[Clytem-nestra's] eyelids appear exceedingly large, and it seems to be costing her a terrible effort to keep them open," emphasizes the somnambulist's open eyes and corresponds to Charcot's reading of Lady Macbeth: "You see, her eyes are open."[77] The bodily iconography of somnambulism also extends to the figure of Electra, who is "startled, *like a sleepwalker* hearing his name called."[78]

The medical discussion about hysteria, hypnotism, and crime per-vades Hofmannsthal's tragedy not only in the makeup and the bodily movements of the characters but also on the level of dramatic action. The somnambulist Electra constantly evokes the murder of Clytemnestra: "No, you [Chrysothemis] and I . . . must . . . slay the hag." This "deed" is never executed by Electra. Chrysothemis's exclamation—"Murder her *sleepingly* and then live on!"—nonetheless ascribes a murder committed

76. Hofmannsthal's reticence to represent hypnosis onstage finds a parallel in his critique of Regnard's play *The Gambler*, where Hofmannsthal affirms that a hys-terical seizure cannot be represented directly: "The actual activity of the gambler is after all gambling, along with whatever goes on inside him while he is engaged in it; but this cannot be represented just as, for instance, the hysterical seizure of the hysteric" ("Aufzeichnungen aus dem Nachlaß" [1889–1929] 1980, 525). See also Worbs (1983), 293: "The hysterical seizure itself—here Hofmannsthal's concept of drama for once coincides with Freud's conservative aesthetic concept—cannot be represented onstage. Hence it is very difficult to recover the four stages of the grand hysterical seizure in *Electra*."

77. "His eyes were open. In *Macbeth* there is a very significant observation on som-nambulism. The doctor sees Lady Macbeth rise and begin her somnambulist activity; he turns to the other characters on stage and, supposing them better informed than they are in fact, exclaims: 'Look, her eyes are open'" (Charcot [1887] 1987, 39). See also Charcot [1887] 1987, 42: "Shakespeare says in his Macbeth scene, 'Her eyes are open.' This is an important observation by a writer who was not physician. One could say that he wanted to give the physicians of his time a short medical lesson. . . . When Tuke outlined for his fellow physicians the important features of somnambulism, he emphasized: 'Are the eyes open?'"

78. Hofmannsthal [1903] 1979, 199, 198, 192.

in spontaneous somnambulism to Electra, which also seems implied by Hofmannsthal's retrospective interpretation in his *Notes*, where he states: "Electra's *deed* arises from a kind of *possession*."[79]

Without ever being realized, the murder of Clytemnestra at the hands of a sleepwalking Electra thus becomes precondition and telos of the dramatic plot. In the end, it is Orestes who, withdrawn from the audience's sight, kills Clytemnestra backstage, while Electra—instead of committing the "deed"—suffers a hysterical seizure that concludes the action onstage: "She has *thrown her head back* like a maenad. She throws out her knees, stretching her arms out; it is a nameless dance in which she strides ahead."[80]

It has often been emphasized that Hofmannsthal's stage direction for this "dance" corresponds to the description of a hysterical seizure in Breuer and Freud's *Studies on Hysteria*: "She cried out, . . . her face flushed, she *thrust her head back*, shut her eyes, her torso bent backwards."[81] But the peculiar equivalence of seizure and murder that can be observed in Hofmannsthal's play stages above all Charcot's essay "Hypnotism and Crime" (1890), according to which a hysterical attack often takes the place of a hypnotic crime. Firmly rejecting the possibility of hypnotic crimes, Charcot asserted: "As I know very well from repeated experiments, a fit of hysteria will in most cases be the end of the matter."[82]

In stark contrast to Michael Worbs's reading of Hofmannsthal's tragedy, Electra by no means "takes the word as replacing the deed . . . just like psychoanalysis."[83] Instead, Electra performs a hysterical attack instead of a somnambulist crime—just like Charcot's patients. Even though the play does not represent a murder under hypnosis onstage, the medical debate about hypnotic crimes does function as a central point of reference for *Electra*. The ending of the tragedy in Electra's hysterical seizure faithfully reproduces Charcot's medical experiments in the Salpêtrière where his patients performed the *grande attaque hystérique* instead of theatrical fake crimes.

79. Ibid., 214, 228, 215; Hofmannsthal [1889–1929] 1980), 620–21.

80. Hofmannsthal [1903] 1979, 233, 228.

81. Breuer and Freud [1895] 1987/1953–74, 156/2:137*. This parallel between *Electra* and the *Studies on Hysteria* has been pointed out repeatedly—see, for instance, Schneider (1985), 221. On the turn-of-the-century perception of Electra as a hysteric, see Worbs (1983), 269–72.

82. Charcot (1890), 164.

83. Worbs (1983), 291.

The surreptitious appropriation of contemporary medical research into hysteria and hypnosis within Hofmannsthal's dramatic work can also be observed in *Life, a Dream* (1904), an early version of *Der Turm* (The tower). There, Clotald, an adviser to the king, employs "the evil arts of speech that . . . *cut into the soul*, with the wicked, cold word," in order "to *rule* the king's spirit . . . *from within*." Indeed, Clotald boasts of his power to control the slumbering Sigismund: "I enjoy whispering to people who talk in their slumber. Immersing them deeply, ever more deeply into their dreams—that is my pleasure. . . . It suits me to use them like pets when I am the only one awake."[84]

Yet Clotald's suggestive power over the somnambulist Sigismund, who can no longer distinguish between dream and waking, pervades the play without ever becoming directly palpable. In contrast to Schnitzler's plays *Anatol* and *Paracelsus* or Beer-Hofmann's pantomime *Pierrot Hypnotist* (1892), neither *Life, a Dream* nor *Electra* features a direct enactment of hypnosis onstage—a remarkable restraint in the dramatic representation of somnambulism, whose visual presence in *Electra* is established mostly by an extraordinary proliferation of stage directions and scene annotations within a play that after its opening night was rarely performed.[85]

Hofmannsthal's notable reticence in the dramatic enactment of hypnosis points to his conservative conception of drama and the structural difference between catharsis of the actor (Breuer and Freud) and catharsis of the spectator (Aristotle). But in addition, around 1900, a newly emerging, competing medium also rendered it increasingly difficult to enact the process of hypnosis onstage or to aim openly for a hypnotic effect on the drama's audience. Hofmannsthal's *Stage Annotations to Electra* do hint at the tragedy's intended hypnotic influence on its spectators: "The sets are completely devoid . . . of those pseudo-antique banalities that are more apt to induce sobriety than to create *a suggestive*

84. Hofmannsthal, *Das Leben ein Traum* ([1904] 1979), 195, 203, 204.

85. The visual emphasis on hypnotic and hysterical body motions becomes even more evident in Hofmannsthal's pantomime *Der Schüler* [The pupil] ([1901] 1979) and that of Beer-Hofmann, *Pierrot Hypnotiseur* ([1892] 1984). In addition to these pantomimes, the new medium of "sleep dance" (Schrenck-Notzing 1904) also centered on the hypnotized body. On the boom of dance under hypnosis, which celebrated trance as an allegedly "authentic" or "natural" bodily expression, see also Baxmann 1991 and Brandstetter 1992.

effect."[86] But Hofmannsthal is not able to affirm aggressively the play's suggestive power. Hermann Bahr's *Dialogue on the Tragic* (1904), in turn, projected the hypnotic impact of tragedy, which Bahr deduced from Breuer and Freud's *Studies on Hysteria*, back on to antiquity.[87] Even within the radical theater projects of the avant-garde, which were not constrained by conservative conceptions, the dramatic appropriation of hypnosis remained surprisingly marginal. Antonin Artaud drew on religious rituals and medical therapies to invigorate what he considered an ossified, lifeless theater of words. He thus promoted a theater that was meant to function "like a renewed exorcism," "with a bodily impact on the mind."[88] But the theater of cruelty, "in which bodily, violent images crush and *hypnotize* the nervous system of the spectator," remained a utopian project.[89] Instead it was the medium of cinema—the "substitute for dreams" as it was called by Hofmannsthal—that became the most prevalent cultural appropriation of hypnotism.[90] In his psychological study *The Photoplay* (1916) Hugo Münsterberg accordingly invoked the explicit analogy of the "hypnotizer whose words awaken in the mind of the hypnotized person ideas which he cannot resist" in order to compare the suggestive power of drama and film:

> The *spellbound* audience in a theater or in a picture house is certainly in a *state of heightened suggestibility* and is ready to receive suggestions. One great and fundamental suggestion is working in both cases, inasmuch as the drama, as well as the photoplay, suggests to the mind of the spectator that this is more than mere play, that it is life which we witness. But if we go further and ask

86. Hofmannsthal, "Szenische Vorschriften zu Elektra" (in *Elektra* [1903] 1979), 240.

87. See Bahr (1904), 17 ff., esp. 23: "Tragedy indeed has no other goal than these two physicians [Breuer and Freud]."

88. "Comme des exorcismes renouvelés": Artaud [1932–38] 1964, 106; "efficacité physique sur l'esprit": 56; cf. also ibid., 96: "I propose to return within theater to that elementary, *magical* concept that has been taken up again by modern psychoanalysis and that consists in the patient's having to assume, for the purpose of healing, the external posture of that condition to which we want to return him."

89. "Un théâtre où des images physiques violentes broient et hypnotisent la sensibilité du spectateur": ibid. 99.

90. See Hofmannsthal, "Der Ersatz für die Träume" (1921).

for the application of suggestion in the detailed action, we cannot overlook the fact that the theater is extremely limited in its
means.[91]

According to Münsterberg, film's superiority over the theater rested on
the possibility of editing, which allowed for an indirect representation
or suggestion of scenes that could not be represented onstage. Cinematic
montage thus rendered even Reinhardt's revolving stage "slow and
clumsy."[92] But as the next chapter will show, the hypnotic power of the
new medium was also enacted by the cinematic devices of the close-up
and the point-of-view shot.

91. Münsterberg [1916] 2002, 97. See also Moll 1924, 563: "Film has a power of suggestion quite different from that of theater." On Bernheim's definition of hypnosis
as a state of "increased suggestibility," see above, 23–24.
    92. Münsterberg [1916] 2002, 98, 59.

IV BERNHEIM, CALIGARI, MABUSE: CINEMA AND HYPNOTISM

Stunning, too, the manner in which Mabuse's hypnotizing gaze forces not only his victims but also the audience under its power. Eugen Tannenbaum, *Berliner Zeitung am Mittag*, March 23, 1922

In February 1920, numerous posters appeared throughout Berlin, addressing the city dwellers with the forceful exhortation: "You must become Caligari" (*Du musst Caligari werden*). The enigmatic slogan, also printed in several newspapers, was soon revealed to be part of an innovative advertising campaign for a new film. The movie, directed by Robert Wiene, was just completing the last stages of production at the Decla Company, and immediately after its release, *The Cabinet of Dr. Caligari* was acclaimed a masterpiece of German Expressionist cinema; its plot, unknown to the public at that time, centered on a showman and hypnotist who forces a somnambulist to submit to his will, compelling the docile medium to commit several murders.

Yet on the posters and in the newspaper ads, no mention was made of the film's title, plot, or even the fact that the campaign was meant to advertise a film. Instead, only a hypnotic vortex-like spiral and a note with the date and place of the opening night accompanied the mysterious command that called for each passerby to transform him- or herself into Caligari. The almost coercive interpellation "You must" foregrounded and simultaneously enacted the "suggestive" or "hypnotic" power of advertising, which was still a fairly new mode of shaping social behavior.

Just a few years earlier, the American psychologist Walter D. Scott had described the "*influencing* of human minds" as "the one function of advertising." According to Scott, a successful promotional campaign relied less on conveying information than on "suggestion"—a process that, instead of appealing to rational faculties, was based on surreptitiously implanting an idea in a susceptible mind without raising contrary or inhibiting thoughts. As Scott asserted: "The most perfect working of suggestion is to be seen under hypnosis. . . . There is no possible criticism or deliberation and so we have the extreme case of susceptibility to suggestion."[1]

In this conceptualization of advertising, Scott invoked the medical theories of hypnotism and suggestion as they had been developed by Hippolyte Bernheim and the Nancy school. Yet around 1900, hypnosis was not merely linked to advertising; indeed, structural affinities also connected hypnotism with the newly emerging medium of cinema. Accordingly, numerous films—such as *The Criminal Hypnotist* (1909, dir. D. W. Griffith), *Svengali* (1914, dir. Jacob Fleck), *Spellbound* (1916, dir. Harry Harvey), *Die Augen der Mumie* (The eyes of the mummy [1918, dir. Ernst Lubitsch]), *Hypnose* (Hypnosis [1919]), and *Sklaven fremden Willens* (Slaves of a foreign will [1920])—appropriated the medical, legal, and literary tales of hypnotic crime. After the turn of the century, the scientific interest in hypnosis was initially superseded by the emergence of psychoanalysis and a renewed concentration on physiology within medical research. The *Journal of Hypnotism* (*Zeitschrift für Hypnotismus*), which was edited by Auguste Forel and his disciple Oskar Vogt, was renamed the *Journal for Psychology and Neurology* (*Journal für Psychologie und Neurologie*) in 1902.[2] But during World War I, hypnosis and suggestion had an unexpected resurgence in the treatment of war neuroses and shell shock. Auguste Forel's and Albert Moll's medical treatises about hypnotism, first published in the 1880s, thus went through several new editions between 1918 and 1924.[3]

1. Scott, *The Psychology of Advertising* ([1908] 1917), 2, 82.

2. The waning medical interest in the issue of hypnotic crimes also led to a change in the subtitle of Forel's textbook, which after its 4th edition in 1902 no longer listed the "significance of hypnotism for criminal law" (see bibliography). On the changes in the 5th edition from 1907, see above, 28 n. 35.

3. Compare Forel 1918, 1919, 1921, 1923; Moll 1924; see, esp., Moll (1924, 34): "A notable upsurge in hypnotism took place in the wake of the World War. A large number of physicians have used hypnosis with great success in the treatment of war neuroses." See also Ruth Leys's *Trauma* (2000), 93–100, on the "revival of hypnosis"

Simultaneously, late-nineteenth-century tales of hypnotic crime found an equally popular sequel within the postwar literature of the fantastic, in texts such as Gustav Meyrink's *The White Dominican* (1921), Cätty Bachem-Tonger's *Under the Spell of Hypnosis* (1922), Otto Soyka's *The Smith of Souls* (1921), and Hans Dominik's *The Power of the Three* (1922).[4]

The Cabinet of Dr. Caligari

Although neglected by most historiographies of Weimar cinema, the intense medical debate about the possibility of hypnotic crimes was also constitutive for Robert Wiene's famous film *The Cabinet of Dr. Caligari*, which opened on February 26, 1920, at the Marmorhaus in Berlin. The first frame of the film shows, in a medium shot, two men with parched white faces, sitting on a bench. As if referring to his own status as a ghostly phantom on the cinematic screen, the older man says to Francis: "There are ghosts [*Geister*]—they are all around us."[5] A woman dressed in white becomes visible, gliding past the two men in a somnambulist trance. Referring to the almost spectral apparition, Francis calls her his "bride," continuing: "What I have experienced with her is much stranger still than what you have experienced—let me tell you about it." And the camera cuts to a film set built of papier-mâché, representing a small town with narrow winding streets.

From the very beginning, the film emphasizes that the moving images on the cinematic screen are a simulation akin to a "phantom" or

during World War I. For medical and legal texts on hypnotism from this period, see also Wagner-Jauregg (1919); Sanders (1921); Többen (1921–22); Bacmeister (1922); Seeling (1922, 1928); Moll (1928); Lucas (1930).

4. Soyka, *Der Seelenschmied* (1921b); Meyrink, *Der weisse Dominikaner* (1921); Bachem-Tonger, *Im Banne der Hypnose* (1922); Dominik, *Die Macht der Drei* ([1922] 1954). There was also a close connection between the representation of hypnotism and the figure of being possessed by another person, a process that not only is described in Strobl's *Umsturz im Jenseits* [Rebellion in the beyond] (1920) or Spunda's *Devachan* (1921) but also constitutes a central narrative concern in Gustav Meyrink's *Das Wachsfigurenkabinett* [The house of wax] (1908), *Walpurgisnacht* [Walpurgis night] (1917), and *Der Engel vom westlichen Fenster* [The angel of the west window] ([1927] 1975) as well as in Robert Wiene's film *Orlacs Hände* [The hands of Orlac] (1926).

5. Intertitles of the film are quoted according to the reproduction of the original intertitles by the Stiftung Deutsche Kinemathek (Wiene [1919], Z).

a "vision."[6] Furthermore, the internal plot is marked as the (unreliable) narration of Francis, who is one of the protagonists of his own story. The pronounced artificiality of the set, in which both frame and internal plot unfold, undercuts realist conventions. Painted shadows, dagger-shaped windows, a pale sky against which bare trees stand out in bizarre shapes—these visual markers of instability create a cinematic space of paranoia and distrust. In the critical responses to the film, Wiene's *Caligari* was therefore instantly hailed as a powerful cinematic instantiation of Expressionism.[7] But while "le Caligarisme," as the visual style of the film was called in France, certainly undertook borrowings from Expressionist art, its eclectic mise-en-scène amalgamated high art and mass culture, thereby appealing to a broad audience and ensuring the commercial success of the movie.[8] At the same time, the strangely distorted spaces of the film set appear as a materialization of the visual hallucinations that Bernheim induced by means of verbal suggestion in his hypnotized patients, "populating" their "imagination" with "phantoms and chimeras."[9]

In a further reference to its own status as a spectacle, the film introduces the showman Caligari, who exhibits a clairvoyant somnambulist at the fairground in the small town of Holstenwall. Aside from featuring freak shows and cabinets displaying somnambulists, the fairground was also the site of the early "cinema of attractions," which often toured in a tent from town to town.[10] According to Hugo Münsterberg's *The Photoplay: A Psychological Study* (1916), these circus-like performances centered on the "perfection" of the cinematic "apparatus," thus capturing the "attention" of the "spellbound" audience.[11]

---

6. Thomas Mann, *Der Zauberberg* [The magic mountain] ([1924] 1989), 336, 335.

7. See "Robert Wienes *Das Cabinet des Dr. Caligari*" ([1920] 1995); Flüggen, "Münchener Erstaufführungen" (1920).

8. Recent scholarship has shown that the designers of the film set—Hermann Warm, Walter Reimann, and Walter Röhrig—had no direct relation to the avant-garde journal *Der Sturm*, as Siegfried Kracauer had claimed in his influential interpretation of the film; see Kracauer (1947), 68; Kasten (1990), 43–44; Elsaesser, *Weimar Cinema and After* (2000), 36–51.

9. Bernheim 1891/1892, 50/37*.

10. See Gunning, "The Cinema of Attractions" ([1986] 1990).

11. Münsterberg [1916] 2002, 57. See also ibid., 152: "To a certain degree the mere technical cleverness of the pictures even today holds the interest *spellbound* as in those early days when nothing but this technical skill could claim the attention."

The film shows Caligari on the fairground, advertising the exhibition of his somnambulist medium by assuring the crowd before his little tent: "Before your eyes, Cesare will rise from the rigor of death."[12] Displaying the somnambulist to the audience inside his "cabinet," Caligari transposes Cesare from the state of "lethargy," in which the hypnotized persons present "the appearance of a corpse before the onset of rigor mortis," into the state of somnambulism.[13] As if quoting Tourette's description of the third stage of "grand hypnotism," the sleeper is represented as "a true *automaton* . . . , obeying all expressions of his magnetizer's will."[14] In a close-up, the camera shows the somnambulist's face as he slowly opens his eyes (figs. 2 and 3). Cesare's wide-open eyes recall Hofmannsthal's stage direction from *Electra*: "[Clytemnestra's] eyelids appear exceedingly large, and it seems to be costing her a terrible effort to keep them open."[15] The representation of Cesare's awakening simultaneously corresponds to Charcot's medical nosography of "grand hypnotism," which emphasizes the sleepwalker's open eyes, in artificial as well as in spontaneous somnambulism.

The film cuts to a medium shot, showing Cesare's complete body as he begins to move his arms and legs. The androgynous medium slowly steps forward, like a puppet that is held by invisible strings. His peculiar motions correspond to Haller's "automaton-like" walk in Max Mack's *The Other* (1913), the first film adaptation of Paul Lindau's drama from the late nineteenth century, which centered on the story of a district attorney who, in a state of somnambulism, commits crimes that he would abhor while awake.[16] The original screenplay for Wiene's *Caligari* describes the sleepwalker's movements in the following terms: "Caesare [*sic*] stands motionless for several more seconds. . . . Something like a shudder quite subtly and remotely shows on his face! . . . His arms, pressed to his body, rise forward, *as if automatically*, in small, distinct intervals, as though they wanted to catch hold of something."[17] Under Caligari's suggestive

12. Wiene, intertitles (in *Z* [1919]).

13. The quote is from Gilles de la Tourette, *L'hypnotisme* (1887), 91.

14. Ibid., 96.

15. Hofmannsthal, *Elektra* ([1903] 1979), 198.

16. Lindau, *Der Andere* (1893), 58. On the positive medical reception of Lindau's play in the nineteenth century, see above, 33. On the appropriation of hysterical, epileptic, and somnambulist body movements within early film comedy, see also Ruth Rae Brown, "From Charcot to Charlot" (2001).

17. Mayer and Janowitz, "Das Cabinett des Dr. Calligaris" ([1919] 1995), 65.

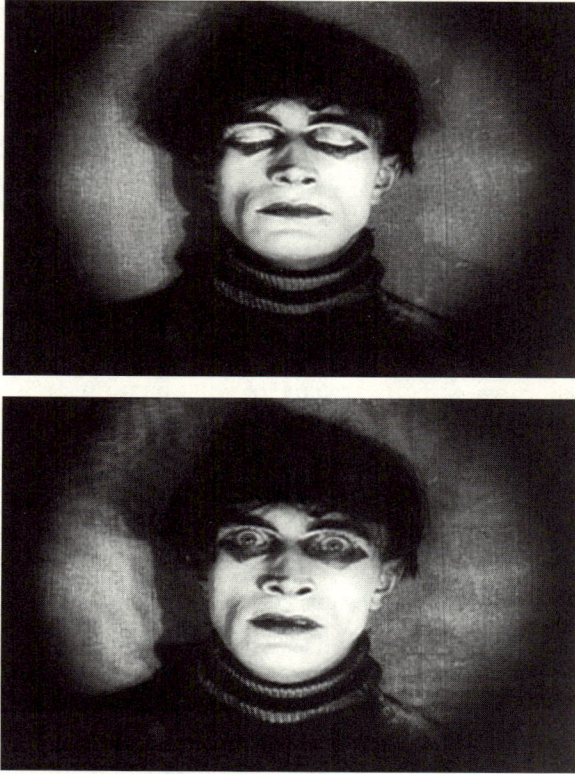

FIGURES 2 AND 3. Transition from lethargy to somnambulism: Cesare's wide-open eyes correspond to Charcot's
medical nosography of "grand hypnotism." From Robert
Wiene, *The Cabinet of Dr. Caligari* (1919–20).

influence, Francis's friend Alan, who "concentrates, as if *spellbound*, on
Cesare's awakening," poses the question of how much longer he has to
live.[18] "Till dawn," pronounces the clairvoyant medium.

A chain of mysterious crimes ensues, perpetrated not by the original
suspect but by Caligari's somnambulist medium, Cesare. Francis pursues
the fleeing showman to an insane asylum, discovering with dismay that
Caligari and the director of the institution are one and the same. While
Dr. Caligari sleeps (shown in a strangely disorienting high-angle shot),
Francis and three physicians from the mental asylum search the director's office. In a cabinet they find a book on his "special field of study." The

18. Ibid., 65.

title page is shown on the screen and reads: "Somnambulism: A Compendium Edited by the University of Uppsala. Published A.D. 1726." Francis skims through the volume and comes across the following story, which is displayed on title cards:

> The Cabinet of Dr. Caligari.
> In the year 1703, a mystic by the name of Dr. Caligari along with a somnambulist called Cesare appeared at various country fairs in the small towns of northern Italy. For months, he wreaked panic in town after town, through murders that were always perpetrated under the same circumstances—for he compelled a somnambulist, whom he had entirely subjected to his will, to carry out his monstrous designs. By means of a puppet figure, modeled in the exact likeness of Cesare and placed in the chest when Cesare was away, Dr. Caligari was able to disperse any suspicion which fell on the somnambulist.

As in Max Mack's film *The Other* (1913), medical evidence supporting the possibility of hypnotic crimes is introduced in Wiene's *The Cabinet of Dr. Caligari* by means of a scientific book, which is read by one of the protagonists.[19] The story within the story, which seems to provide an explanation for the previous plot turns, appropriates the "fantastical stories" in which late-nineteenth-century medical research conjured the unlimited power of hypnotic suggestion.[20] Next to the scientific treatise on somnambulism, Francis and the three doctors find a diary in the di-

19. In the very first scene of Max Mack's *Der Andere* (1913), the medical councillor, Feldermann, gives to the public prosecutor, Hallers, a book that describes how, "as a result of a fall, a serious disease" or "as a result of overexertion," a "double being" might arise in a person—"along with the healthy element a morbid one. The one does not know of the other. In *a kind of twilight haze [in einer Art Dämmerungszustand]*, the morbid element is capable of committing acts of which the healthy one does not have the slightest inkling" (Mack [1913], intertitles [app. A]). Compare also p. 4 of the program notes: "Lindau . . . shows us an attorney who, *in a kind of somnambulist dream state* becomes a robber, a burglar, and a thief" (program notes from the film's opening, Stiftung Deutsche Kinemathek, Berlin); and Alfred Klaar, "Paul Lindau as a Film Dramatist" ([1913] 1992), 344: "Signs of such a double life are amply documented in records of hypnosis and suggestions that continue to operate through a normal state of consciousness."

20. "Fantastical stories": Gilles de la Tourette, *L'hypnotisme* (1887), 183.

FIGURE 4. The director of the insane asylum succumbs to the compulsive idea: "You must become Caligari" [Du musst Caligari werden] (from Robert Wiene's *The Cabinet of Dr. Caligari* [1919–20]).

rector's office. In interspersed flashbacks we are shown how the director of the insane asylum develops the "compulsive idea" to transform himself into the historical figure of Caligari: "You must become Caligari"—an autosuggestion that is repeatedly superimposed in writing on the actual filmic image (fig. 4).[21]

While writing in silent film is commonly restricted to the intertitles, it here intrudes on the cinematic image, a visual demonstration of the power of the director's compulsive idea to produce sensory hallucinations and to determine his actions. The episode in which the doctor succumbs to the compulsion to become Caligari thus contains the nucleus of the ad campaign that exhorted inhabitants of Berlin, in the weeks before the film's release, "Du musst Caligari werden." At the same time, the obsession the director falls victim to can also be linked to a literary text from which the film's script may have been adapted: the protagonist of Wilhelm Walloth's novel *Under the Spell of Hypnosis* (1897) has surprising parallels to Dr. Caligari. Walloth's text centers on the figure of Dr. von Haffner, who cannot stop pondering the question of whether "a

21. "Compulsive idea" (*Zwangsvorstellung*): Wiene, intertitles (in Z [1919]).

skilled hypnotist could force even the most virtuous person to commit
the biggest crime." After the idea of resolving the uncertainty by means
of an actual murder enters Haffner's mind, his "constant dwelling on
this sinister plan" turns into an "autosuggestion," which—like Caligari's
compulsive idea—seizes control of his actions with "compelling force"
(mit triebartiger Gewalt), turning him into a criminal.[22]

In addition to these late-nineteenth-century tales about the unlimited power of suggestion, Wiene's The Cabinet of Dr. Caligari also adapts
the "strange spectacle" of artificial hypnotic crimes, staged by numerous
physicians with blank cartridges and wooden daggers in order to prove
the possibility of criminal suggestions (see above, 73).[23] The intense debate about the status of these medical simulations is appropriated by
the narrative structure of the film. Its closing scenes reveal the narrator
and protagonist Francis to be an inmate of the insane asylum run by the
Caligari figure. Francis's story may thus be the paranoid hallucination of
a madman. In the film's last shot, the director of the insane asylum as-
sures the spectator, directly addressing the camera: "At last I understand
his delusion; he thinks that I am that mystical Caligari!—And now I also
know the way to his cure."[24]

This unresolvable conflict between frame and Francis's narration
is by no means a glorification of totalitarian power, transforming an
originally subversive or "revolutionary" screenplay into a "conformist"
affirmation of authority as Siegfried Kracauer asserted in his influential
study From Caligari to Hitler (1947).[25] Instead, the tension between frame
and internal story functions as a metacommentary on the medical "fake
crimes," whose status as either authentic evidence for the possibility of
criminal suggestions or scientifically worthless "showpiece" remains
equally undecidable.[26] But before further exploring the ways in which
the narrative structure of Caligari replicates the ambiguous status of the

22. All quotations from Wilhelm Walloth, Im Banne der Hypnose: Ein psychologischer
Roman [Under the spell of hypnosis: a psychological novel] (1897), 155 and 240.

23. "Strange spectacle": Salten, "Über Schnitzlers hypnotische Versuche" [On
Schnitzler's hypnotic experiments] (1932), 55.

24. Wiene, intertitles (in Z [1919]).

25. Kracauer 1947, 67.

26. "Scheinverbrechen": Freud, "Rezension von A. Forel, Der Hypnotismus" ([1889]
1987/1953–74), 138/1:101–2"; "Schaustück": Binswanger, "Gutachten über Hypnose
und Suggestion" (1892), 9.

medical experiments with criminal suggestion, it seems necessary to address Kracauer's arguments, which have shaped the interpretation of the film for several decades.[27]

Kracauer, who researched his "psychological history" of Weimar cinema during World War II, conceptualized the figure of Dr. Caligari as an allegorical "premonition" of Hitler, thereby adopting a teleological perspective that erases historical contingency. Twenty-five years after the release of *Caligari*, Thomas Mann's narrative *Mario and the Magician* (1930) and Fritz Lang's film *The Testament of Dr. Mabuse* (1932–33) did allude to totalitarian fascism in their representation of hypnotic omnipotence; but Wiene's film was produced in 1919, not in the 1930s when the rise of National Socialism was imminent. Kracauer thus ascribed a prophetic "vision" to the authors of the screenplay, Hans Janowitz and Carl Mayer—an assumption he sought to justify by relying on an unpublished account of the film's production history, written around 1939 by the exiled Janowitz, who then, in hindsight, presented his script as a critique of totalitarian tyranny.[28] The recovery of the original film script in 1976, however, disproved a number of claims made by Janowitz. For while it still holds true that the frame, which makes Francis an inmate of the insane asylum, was not part of the original screenplay but added later by Wiene, the script did contain a framing device from the very beginning.[29] At one point, the screenplay even hints at the possibility that Francis, the narrator, may be insane, when Francis himself questions his sanity upon realizing that the showman Caligari and the director of the asylum are one and the same: "I felt as if I myself had lost my mind."[30] Wiene's editorial intervention merely emphasized an ambiguity already inherent in the original screenplay. Simultaneously, the film's paradoxical narrative structure appropriates contemporary concerns about the danger of criminal suggestion, thereby transforming the peculiar status that marked the medical spectacle of staged hypnotic crimes into a conflict between internal story and frame.

Within the internal story, Caligari realizes Delboeuf's dream of the real, truly scientific experiment "that end[s] with dead bodies" and must

27. See, for instance, Eisner [1952] 1969, 18; Murray 1990, 26–27.
28. Kracauer 1947, 72, 73. Excerpts of Janowitz's manuscript were published in 1990—see Janowitz [1937] 1990.
29. See Mayer and Janowitz [1919] 1995, 51; Robinson 1997, 60.
30. Mayer and Janowitz [1919] 1995, 98.

be regarded as unquestionable proof of the limitless power of hypnosis.[31] In the diary that Francis finds next to the scientific study on somnambulism in Dr. Caligari's office, the director of the asylum jubilantly
describes the long-awaited "admission of a somnambulist" as allowing
him to finally execute a real-life experiment: "Now I shall solve the psy-
chiatric riddle of that Caligari!! Now I shall fathom whether it is true
that a somnambulist may be forced to commit acts that he would never
commit in a waking state, that indeed he would loathe. . . . Whether it is
true that the sleeper can be driven to the very act of murder."[32]

Medical experts from the late nineteenth century were not able to
determine with any certainty whether hypnotic crimes were possible
because their scientific experiments could not transcend the status of
simulation (cf. 75, above). As Hippolyte Bernheim put it in his lectures:
"You see how divided opinions are at present on this fundamental question, which for all too obvious reasons has not been resolved yet by a
decisive experiment."[33] Hugo Münsterberg similarly wrote: "To bring an
absolute proof of this conviction is hardly possible, as we cannot really
kill for experiment's sake."[34] The director of the asylum, in contrast, conducts a truly "decisive experiment" by forcing Cesare to commit actual
murders, thereby resolving the all-important question of whether "it is
true the sleeper can be driven to the very act of murder."[35] In this manner, Dr. Caligari implements the kind of real-life experiment that had
long existed as a paranoid fantasy of the neurologists and even under-
pinned the strange interpretation of an accident at the Salpêtrière: when
Tourette was attacked and seriously injured by a female patient in 1892,
a rumor immediately circulated, denied by both the *Revue de l'hypnotisme*
and the *Zeitschrift für Hypnotismus*, that the incident constituted a real
hypnotic crime, designed to prove to the skeptic Tourette that criminal
suggestions were indeed possible: "The assassination attempt committed

31. The quote is from Delboeuf, 'Die verbrecherischen Suggestionen" (1893–
94), 198.

32. Wiene, intertitles (in Z [1919]).

33. Bernheim 1891/1892 139/102*.

34. Münsterberg, "Hypnotism and Crime" (1908), 223.

35. The reference to the truly scientific experiment also comes to the fore in
Mayer and Janowitz's screenplay, where the director of the insane asylum develops
the "compulsive idea": "You must become Calligaris and send the somnambulist out
to commit murder. This is the only way in which you can serve science" (Mayer and
Janowitz [1919] 1995, 105).

against Mr. Gilles de la Tourette has given rise to a great variety of commentaries. It has been said that our esteemed colleague was the victim of a 'criminal suggestion' intended to convince him that it is feasible to implement similar suggestions."[36]

But the "absolute proof . . . of really kill[ing] for experiment's sake," enacted by Caligari in having the municipal secretary and Alan murdered by his somnambulist medium Cesare, is called into question again, since frame and narration denounce each other as paranoid hallucination.[37] While the medical performance of the staged hypnotic crime oscillates between a simple and a second-order simulation (see 75, above), Wiene's *The Cabinet of Dr. Caligari* leaves open the question whether Francis or Caligari is insane. Francis's assertion—"All of you think—I am mad—! That is not true. It is the director who is mad!"—is no less credible than the director's assurance that he will cure his patient. The conflict between frame and narrative, which mutually contradict each other, can therefore not be resolved in favor of a coherent interpretation that would efface this structural uncertainty. Contrary to the implications of Kracauer's reading of the film, there are no visual indications that would lend more credibility to the world of the frame than to the internal story. Instead, the tension between frame and narrative reproduces the ambiguous status of the medical "fake crimes" from which the film emerges.

At the same time, the paradoxical narrative structure of Wiene's film can also be read as a self-reference to the "peculiar oscillation" in which, according to Münsterberg, the spectators of early cinema alternated between the insight into the mediality of the filmic projections and an intermittent suspension of disbelief.[38] As Münsterberg wrote in regard to the cinematic simulation of depth and motion, describing a "conflict" between the viewer's perception and knowledge: "We certainly see the

36. "Mittheilung vermischten Inhalts" (1893–94), 176. Similar debates ensued in November of 1920 after a failed "attempt" on the life of the physician Julius Wagner-Jauregg, who practiced in Vienna. Wagner-Jauregg interpreted the failure of the hypnotic crime of which he was the intended victim as evidence for the "limited power of hypnosis," which could not be used to criminal ends: "Mr. J. Wagner (welcomed with lively applause) remarks that the author of the 'assassination attempt' proved the truth of an assertion made for years by the speaker, namely, that no hypnotic crime has hitherto really taken place" (Hofer 1920, 2077–78).

37. The quote is from Münsterberg, "Hypnotism and Crime" (1908), 223.

38. Münsterberg 1916, 110.

depth, and yet we cannot accept it."[39] In formalist film theory, this "peculiar complex state" in which the viewer, despite better knowledge,
concedes a certain reality to the moving images on the cinematic screen
has often been compared to Freud's conception of the "disavowal," by
which the fetishist allows two mutually exclusive assumptions to co-
exist side by side.[40] But instead of psychoanalytic theory, Bernheim's representation of suggestion, especially his description of visual film-like
hallucinations produced by hypnotic suggestion, seems to offer a more
pertinent parallel: just as the audience of Wiene's *Caligari* alternates
between believing in Francis's normalcy and Caligari's, and just as the
status of the filmic image oscillates between illusion and reality in the
mind of the viewers, so Bernheim's patients surrender to the vividness of
the suggested hallucinations while simultaneously understanding their
illusory character: "The hallucinations generated by suggestion can be
as clear as reality; the hypnotized subject, *even though he knows* that it is
a hallucination, cannot escape it."[41]

Wiene's filmic representation of hypnotic crimes thus reveals itself
as a complex appropriation of the medical debate about criminal suggestions. The undecidability that marks the medical spectacle of hypnotic
fake crimes is transformed into a conflict between the internal story and
the frame. In addition, the film's paradoxical narrative structure can also
be read as a reference to cinema's suggestive power, which is enacted
even more compellingly in Fritz Lang's *Dr. Mabuse, the Gambler* (1922).

Dr. Mabuse, the Gambler

Norbert Jacques's novel *Dr. Mabuse, the Gambler* was initially published
between September 25, 1921, and January 29, 1922, in the *Berliner Illustrirte Zeitung*. Printing the serial novel brought the newspaper its highest

39. Ibid., 70. For a compelling critique of the stereotype that the "primitive"
viewer of the early years actually believed in the reality of the cinematic images, see
Gunning, "'Primitive' Cinema: A Frame-up? Or, The Trick's on Us" (1990), and Gunning, "An Aesthetics of Astonishment: Early Film and the (In)Credulous Spectator"
(1995c). Compare also Tsivian 1994, 145 ff.

40. "Peculiar complex state": Münsterberg 1916, 71. Freud, "Fetischismus" [Fetish-
ism] ([1927] 1948/1953–74), 316/21:153; Christian Metz, *The Imaginary Signifier* ([1977]
1982), 72 ff.

41. Bernheim, *De la suggestion* ([1886a 1888/1964), 57/40*.

circulation since its foundation in 1892. When the book version appeared in February of 1922, it became one of the greatest successes of the Ullstein Publishing Company. The number of copies sold exceeded half a million—then a staggering number.[42] Fritz Lang's adaptation of Jacques's novel was equally popular, but the transition from literary to filmic representation simultaneously allowed for a metacinematic commentary on the parallel between the visual simulations of cinema and the hypnotic suggestion of visual hallucinations as practiced by Bernheim and other physicians.

In contrast to Wiene's *Caligari*, Fritz Lang's *Dr. Mabuse, the Gambler* does not introduce the scientific theories of hypnotism by displaying a book read by one of the protagonists. Instead, Mabuse, in one of his numerous disguises and roles, gives a lecture titled "Psychoanalysis as a Factor in Modern Therapeutics." In this lecture Mabuse equates transference between patient and analyst with hypnotic rapport, affirming: "If I succeed in establishing the *contact* between physician and patient in such a way as to completely *exclude all disturbing external influences*, then I harbor the firm conviction that in the future 80% of all nervous diseases will be cured through psychoanalysis."[43]

In her review "A Film and Psychoanalysis" (1922), Margit Freud correctly pointed out that the film "suspends, as it were, the differences among suggestion, hypnosis, and psychoanalysis." Yet Fritz Lang's and Norbert Jacques's perverse readings of psychoanalysis rightly show that analytic therapy does not constitute "the opposite of hypnosis," as Margit Freud claimed.[44] Instead, Sigmund Freud himself considered "transference," in which the patient's "unconscious thoughts refer to the physician," to be the functional equivalent or "counterpart" to hypnotic rapport.[45] And already twenty-five years earlier, Freud's essay "Psychic Treatment" had aptly characterized the tie between hypnotized subject

42. Compare Günter Scholdt, "Mabuse, ein deutscher Mythos" [Mabuse, a German myth] (1994), 372.

43. Lang's *Dr. Mabuse, der Spieler*, intertitle (see app. A). The whole sequence is missing in most American video and DVD versions of the film currently in circulation. Only the 270-minute version by the Friedrich Wilhelm Murnau-Stiftung and distributed by Kino Video contains this scene.

44. Margit Freud, "Ein Film und die Psychoanalyse" ([1922] 1994), 343 and 344.

45. Freud, "Massenpsychologie und Ich-Analyse" [Mass psychology and ego analysis] ([1921] 1974), 118 n. 2/18:126*.

and doctor as the medium's "exclusive concentration" on the hypnotist.[46] However, the elimination of "disturbing external influences" renders not only the therapeutic effects of suggestion possible; Mabuse's employment of hypnosis for criminal ends is also based on an "exclusive concentration" that generates an overwhelming rapport between the hypnotist and his hypnotized medium—a process powerfully enacted in the fourth hypnosis scene of the film.

In the course of a poker game, Mabuse hypnotizes the disguised district attorney Wenk by means of a pair of Chinese spectacles and the magical formula "TSI NAN FU."[47] Just as Lang's previous film *The Spiders* (1919) does, *Dr. Mabuse, the Gambler* thus exoticizes hypnosis by presenting it as derived from non-Western forms of magic. In a shot/reverse shot, the camera shows Wenk's stack of money and, in an iris, Mabuse's shiny spectacles before cutting to close-ups of Wenk and of Mabuse that announce the "battle of the wills" that is to follow.[48] After this face-off, the camera predominantly assumes the perspective of Wenk, with whom Mabuse establishes "contact." A wide shot shows Wenk arranging his money while a strange black masking encloses him from both sides, signaling how Mabuse concentrates his energy on the already-somnolent opponent. The film cuts to an extreme close-up of Mabuse's eyes, which invade and dominate Wenk's (and the spectator's) field of vision completely (fig. 5). A point-of-view-shot follows, showing Wenk's hand of cards, and suddenly the words "TSI NAN FU" appear in writing on top of the cards—similar to the compulsive idea that seizes possession of Dr. Caligari in Wiene's film. After a short cut to Mabuse's assistant Hawasch, who admonishes his comrade Spoerri to pay attention, there follows another shot of Mabuse. The background around Mabuse's brightly illuminated head (fig. 6) gradually fades out (fig. 7)—a powerful visualization of how Mabuse succeeds in eliminating "disturbing external influences." Mabuse's piercing gaze

46. "Alleinschätzung": Freud, "Psychische Behandlung" [Psychic treatment] ([1890] 1942/1953–74), 307/7:296*. Freud's essay, which was written in 1890 and first published in 1905, asserts that a definite hypnotic change can be brought about in "some eighty percent of subjects" (305/7:294), a claim echoed in Mabuse's lecture that affirms "in the future 80% of all nervous diseases will be cured through psychoanalysis."

47. In the early twentieth century, Tsi-Nan-Fu was the colonialist name for the capital of Shandong.

48. I borrow this phrase from Tom Gunning's reading of this sequence. See his *The Films of Fritz Lang* (2000), 109–10.

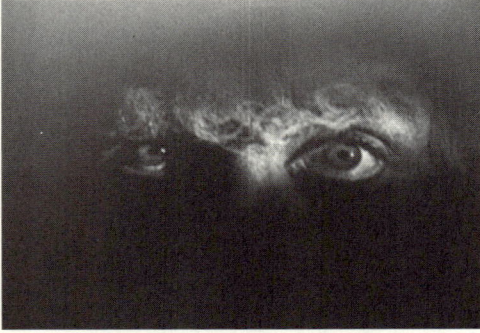

FIGURES 5–8. Hypnotic sequence from Fritz Lang's *Dr. Mabuse, the Gambler:* point-of-view shots and camera movement enact the suggestive power of the cinema.

is fixed on the camera, while his head seems to move slowly forward in space, growing larger and larger until it takes up and controls the entire screen (fig. 8). The hypnotic command "YOU TAKE!" appears as an intertitle that also increases in size and becomes progressively more compelling.

Fritz Lang's reliance on point-of-view-shots forces the spectator to identify with Mabuse's hypnotized victim. The cinematic representation of hypnosis is thus transformed into a celebration of the hypnotic power of cinema—an effect not only pointed out by Raymond Bellour, but emphasized as well in the first reviews of the film after its opening night on April 27, 1922.[49] Eugen Tannenbaum, for instance, wrote in the *Berliner Zeitung*: "Stunning, too, the manner in which Dr. Mabuse's hypnotizing gaze forces not only his victims but also the audience under his power."[50] And the *Neue Zeit* emphasized in similar terms: "Downright *fascinating* the struggle between Mabuse and the district attorney. Mabuse's face becomes larger and larger, literally *hypnotizing* the audience."[51]

It is Lang's combination of camera perspective and movement that renders possible the "transfer of [Mabuse's] power of suggestion directly onto the audience"—by elevating Mabuse's eyes to the sole center of the viewer's attention.[52] In this manner, the film employs a specifically cinematic mode of representing the hypnotized subject's "exclusive concentration" on the hypnotist. An anticipation for this cinematic mode of not just representing but enacting hypnosis is to be found in Louis Feuillade's *Les yeux qui fascinent* (1916).[53] The film came out as the sixth part of Feuillade's famous serial about Irma Vep and a criminal organization called *Les Vampires*, introducing an antagonist to the gang, the criminal Moreno, who is characterized by an intertitle as endowed with a "terrible hypnotic power." Right before this linguistic invocation of Moreno's suggestive capabilities, a medium-close shot shows Moreno staring into the

49. Compare Bellour 197c, 101: "These point-of-view-shots seem perpetually to reinscribe within the filmic system the hypnotic power concentrated in the character of Mabuse, that sovereign and theoretical figure in whom Lang concentrated all the power of vision, . . . thus attributing to him the strictly hypnotic power of the cinematographic apparatus."

50. Tannenbaum [1922] 1994, 294.

51. "Dr. Mabuse, der Spieler" ([1922b] 1994), 317.

52. The quote is from "Dr. Mabuse, der Spieler" ([1922a] 1994), 314.

53. "Alleinschätzung": Freud [1890] 1942/1953–74, 305. On Lang's use of a moving camera in this sequence, cf. also Rudolf Arnheim, *Film als Kunst* [Film as art] ([1932] 1979), 124.

FIGURE 9. Moreno's hypnotic gaze forces the audience under his spell (from Louis Feuillade's *Les yeux qui fascinent* [1916]).

camera, directly addressing the audience with his hypnotic gaze (fig. 9). The shot lasts for a few seconds. But the subsequent hypnosis of Moreno's helpless victim Laure is shown only in profile, creating a complicity between the spectator and Moreno by placing the camera on an axis with the hypnotist. In contrast to Lang's film with its extended point-of-view shots, Feuillade thereby precludes the spectator from identifying with Moreno's hypnotized subject.

Lang's masterful representation of Mabuse's hypnotic powers may have also responded to Hugo Münsterberg's call for a representation of hypnosis that in itself exerted a suggestive influence. In *The Photoplay: A Psychological Study* (1916), the German-born psychologist who taught at Harvard University conceived of the close-up as the cinematic equivalent to the mental act of attention. As Münsterberg stated: "The detail which is being watched has suddenly become the whole content of the performance, and everything which our mind wants to disregard has been suddenly *banished from sight*. . . . The close-up has objectified in our world of perception our mental act of attention."[54] In similar terms, the French film theorist Jean Epstein remarked in 1921: "The close-up limits

54. Münsterberg, *The Photoplay* ([1916] 2002), 87. On attention around 1900, see also Jonathan Crary, *Suspensions of Perception: Attention, Spectacle, and Modern Culture* (1999).

and directs attention." Yet Epstein went even further, explicitly ascribing to the "intensifying agent" of the close-up a hypnotic effect on the spectator: "A head suddenly appears on screen and drama, now face to face, seems to address me and swells with an extraordinary intensity. *I am hypnotized.*"[55]

Seemingly prefiguring Epstein's conceptualization of the close-up and Lang's visualization of how the hypnotized Wenk centers his attention exclusively on Mabuse, Münsterberg described how in a close-up "everything else has *really faded into darkness.*"[56] In addition, Münsterberg also made specific suggestions for a filmic enactment of hypnosis. "If we see on the screen a man hypnotized in the doctor's office," he wrote, "the patient himself may lie there with closed eyes, nothing in his features expressing his emotional setting and nothing radiating to us."[57] Yet, as Münsterberg emphasized, a whole new range of possibilities would open up as soon as the camera work exploited the visual capabilities of the photoplay rather than simply engaging in a "slavish imitation" of theater: "But if now only the doctor and the patient remain unchanged and steady while everything in the whole room begins at first to tremble and then to wave and to change its form more and more rapidly so that a feeling of dizziness comes over us and an uncanny, ghastly unnaturalness overcomes the whole surrounding of the hypnotized person, *we ourselves become seized by the strange emotion.*"[58] In 1916, Münsterberg projected that such a cinematic representation of hypnosis, one that hypnotized the audience, would occur sometime in the "future" of motion pictures. In

55. Jean Epstein, "Magnification" (1921), 235, 239, 235. See also 238: "The director suggests, then persuades, then hypnotizes. The film is nothing but a relay between the source of nervous energy and the auditorium which breathes its radiance."

56. Münsterberg [1916] 2002, 87. See also 85: "While the attended impression becomes more vivid, all the other impressions become less vivid, less clear, less distinct, less detailed. They fade away. We no longer notice them."

57. Ibid., 108.

58. Ibid. Rudolf Harms's *Philosophie des Films* [Philosophy of film] (1926) similarly regarded hypnosis as a specifically filmic subject: "Cinematic representations of hypnosis in which the hypnotist s eyes, first shown in normal size and distance, grow to gigantic dimensions toward the spectator, forcing him under their spell; intertitles, first shown in normal size, suddenly increasing and expanding until ... taking up the entire space of the screen and screaming soundlessly; these are realms specific only to film as a distinct art, which film must show, because it can do so" (116).

fact, though, it was only six years later that Lang's *Dr. Mabuse, the Gambler* powerfully enacted the spellbinding power of cinema.

Drawing on Lang's *Mabuse*, the influential film theoretician Raymond Bellour has postulated a seemingly universal relationship between cinema and hypnosis, defining filmic representations of hypnosis as "manifestations . . . of a fundamental relationship between the cinematographic and the hypnotic apparatus."[59] It is true that Lang's *Dr. Mabuse, the Gambler* points to a structural affinity between cinema and hypnosis. However, in appropriating contemporary medical theories of suggestion, the film testifies not to a timeless but to a historically specific interrelation of hypnotism and the motion picture around 1900. While the formalist parallel between hypnotic and filmic simulation is more powerful than the frequently strained analogy of film and the dream, Bellour's abstract mode of argumentation threatens to erase the historical particularity that marks the interaction between hypnotism and the emergence of cinema.[60] For it is in the late nineteenth and early twentieth centuries that the visual medium had a startling newness, allowing for an amplification of its (alleged) power and impact. Conversely, the medical debate about the power of hypnotic suggestion reached its peak around the same time, between 1885 and 1900, and then again in the years following World War I. In order to analyze the contingent but nonetheless mutually constitutive interrelation that links hypnotism and cinema's emergence and cultural appropriation, we will therefore trace the intermedial exchange among medical representations of suggestion, cinematic enactments of hypnosis, and medical conceptualizations of film, combining a formalist analysis attuned to the visuality of filmic images with a close reading of medical and psychological texts.

59. Compare Bellour 1979, 101: "These fictionalized filmic representations are the *manifestations* . . . of a *fundamental* relationship between the cinematographic and the hypnotic apparatus." Compare also Bellour and Kermabon 1988.

60. It is the abstraction of his argument that allows Bellour to formulate a surprisingly similar interpretation of Jacques Tourneur's *Curse of the Demon* (1957), a film from the second half of the twentieth century—see Bellour, "Believing in the Cinema" ([1986] 1990). On the resemblance of film to dreams, see Bellour 1979, 101: "In the film as in hypnosis one is at a level of simulation which allows for a more exact comparison between the cinematic effect and the hypnotic process than between the cinematic effect and the dream." For a detailed analysis of the analogy of film and the dream, see Metz [1977] 1982, 101 ff.

The Hypnotic Production of Visual Hallucinations as Cinema

A cultural history of media and the sciences uncovers within medical discussions of hypnotism an implicit conceptualization of film. Scientific textbooks on suggestion not only warned against the terrifying specter of hypnotic crime; they simultaneously offered a film theory *avant la lettre*, already formulated at the end of the nineteenth century. In describing the relationship between hypnotic sleep and amnesia in the waking state, Hippolyte Bernheim thus employed the curious notion of a "nervous light" in order to elucidate the mental processes of suggestion. As Bernheim put it in 1885, the amnesia that ensues after awaking from hypnosis can be explained in analogy to the disappearance of images that are no longer illuminated:

> So what happens at awakening? The hypnotized subject retrieves full possession of himself. His previously concentrated nervous activity spreads once again over the entire upper region of his brain.... The impressions perceived during sleep have now disappeared; they were received, with a great expenditure of nervous energy, *of a nervous light, if I may use the expression*, and now that the *brightness of this light* has decreased, they are no longer sufficiently *lit*; they are *latent like an insufficiently illuminated image*. ... The nervous energy, previously concentrated on certain regions of the brain, has now spread everywhere; as a result of the change in the *distribution of the light* the earlier impressions are *illuminated* less; a new state of consciousness has been engendered.[61]

This figure of a "nervous light" lacks a conceptual equivalent within Bernheim's medical text and seems derived from the cultural knowledge about the projection of images that nine years later allowed the brothers Lumière to present the cinematograph to an astounded audience. Ac-

---

61. Bernheim [1886a] 1888/1964, 207/147*. The same analogy appears in Bernheim's *Hypnotisme, suggestion, psychothérapie: études nouvelles* (1891/1892): "With their eyes open, everything fades away. The image ceases to be clear [*éclairée*]; it is now invisible to the consciousness, to the mental eye. ... The light of attention is cast outward [*l'attention diffuse la lumière au dehors*], the memory of the suggestion is extinguished" (130–31/97*).

cording to Bernheim, in our waking state we cast "the light of attention outward," so that the images received through the sensory organs are "illuminated."[62] The state of hypnosis, in contrast, is described by Bernheim as an illumination of internal mental images, which "populate" the imagination of the somnambulists as "phantoms and chimaeras."[63] The amnesia in which the "impressions perceived" under hypnosis are no longer remembered thus corresponds to the disappearance of the projected moving images as soon as the cinematic screen is no longer sufficiently lit—a description of mental processes in anticipated cinematographic terms that seems even more pronounced in Bernheim's representation of memory as the "seeing . . . of images that become alive before our eyes, often as clear as reality."[64]

Thirty years later, the prefiguration of a visual medium like film within Bernheim's representation of amnesia and memory was transformed into an explicit comparison between the workings of the human psyche and cinematic modes of representation when Münsterberg's study *The Photoplay* (1916) defined the cinematic flashback as "an objectivation [*sic*] of our memory function."[65] Similarly, medical textbooks about hypnotism from the 1910s and 1920s expressly emphasized the equivalence between watching a film and the hypnotic recall of a past event. As Anton Kaes has pointed out in his compelling juxtaposition of *Dr. Caligari* to contemporary medical notions of shell shock, the psychoanalytic theorist Ernst Simmel in 1918 compared the hypnotic recovery of memory to the watching of a film: "The experience can be repeated. The 'film' is made to roll once again; the patient dreams the whole thing one more

62. Bernheim 1891/1892, 131/97*.

63. Ibid., 50/37*. On late-eighteenth- and early-nineteenth-century texts that describe the seeing of inner images in analogy to the magic lantern's phantasmagoria, see Andriopoulos, "Die Laterna magica der Philosophie: Gespenster bei Kant, Hegel und Schopenhauer" [The magic lantern of philosophy: specters of Kant, Hegel, and Schopenhauer] (2006).

64. Ibid., 34. Bernheim [1886a] 1888/1964, 210/149*. On the parallel between leaving the cinema and awakening from hypnosis, see also Roland Barthes, "En sortant du cinéma" (1975); and Noack ([1912] 1992), 74: "The people have paid their pennies and refuse to budge; they gaze and stare; completely *under the spell* of the 'sensational hit,' they forget everything around them. Drained, they leave their seats at 11 o'clock, *as though awakened from the deepest hypnosis*."

65. Münsterberg [1916] 2002, 90.

time."[66] In 1922 the physician Ernst Kretschmer likewise characterized the mental processes taking place in light hypnosis and free association as "picture strip thinking."[67] Kretschmer explicitly likened the reliving of past events under hypnosis to the viewing of a film: "What the hypnotized otherwise only thinks, he now experiences pictorially [bildhaft], episodes from his past are actually lived through in orderly, comprehensible scenes that correspond to memory. The mental experience unrolls like a picture strip, 'film-like' [filmartig], before him. The experience is passive, like in the dream; he maintains the sensations of a spectator."[68]

In the 1880s, Bernheim not only anticipated these later comparisons of hypnotic recall and film but also experimented with the hypnotic production of visual, film-like hallucinations. Similar to Pierre Janet in his healing of Achille (cf. 72), Bernheim conjured up "passive hallucinations," which his patients perceived like the spectators of a movie.[69] Although no material substrate corresponded to the suggested mental pictures, they were "as clear as reality." Bernheim even claimed that the hypnotized persons "*saw* the images with their own *eyes*."[70] The hallucinations engendered by suggestion took shape "as a passive dream." The hypnotized person experienced the "scene conjured up by his imagination . . . without any bodily participation." As "a second ego" he saw the suggested scenes while sitting "motionless in his chair."[71]

Bernheim's hypnotic production of visual hallucinations evoked the

66. Ernst Simmel, *Kriegsneurosen und "psychisches Trauma"* [War neuroses and "mental trauma"] (1918), quoted according to Kaes (2001), 124; see also Anton Kaes, *Shell Shock Cinema* (forthcoming).

67. "Bildstreifendenken": Kretschmer, *Medizinische Psychologie* (1922), 94. I owe this and the subsequent quotations from Kretschmer's book to Aaron Haddock's innovative analysis of the interrelation that links Robert Musil's theory of the "other condition" to Kretschmer's medical textbook; see Haddock, "Cinematic Trance: Robert Musil's 'Toward a New Aesthetic'" (2002).

68. Kretschmer 1922, 71. For a reformulation of Freud's "cathartic method" in explicitly cinematic terms, see 271. See also the following passage, which even alludes to Expressionist acting styles: "Thus the twilight state often is nothing else than the living photograph, a dramatic scene in which the original events are reenacted, so to speak, cinematographically, with extremely caricatured expression of affect" (ibid., 72).

69. Bernheim 1891/1892, 117/86.

70. Bernheim [1886a] 1888/1964, 57,40*; ibid., 249/176*.

71. Bernheim 1891/1892, 117/86*.

setting of a movie theater, where the viewer also sits motionless in his or her chair while being captivated by the moving images on the screen. It therefore seems almost inevitable that an equivalent hypnotic creation of hallucinatory cinematic visions is also enacted in the second part of Lang's *Dr. Mabuse, the Gambler,* which was first screened on May 26, 1922. There, Mabuse drives Count Told to suicide after eliminating "disturbing external influences." As the doctor demands from his patient before beginning his therapy: "For the duration of my treatment, you will not leave the house, nor receive anybody, nor speak to anybody. You must not see anyone who reminds you of your former life." Told obeys Mabuse's suggestions and thereby succumbs to "the compulsion of an overpowering, hostile will."[72] Yet in addition to Told's suicide, the film also shows "experiments with mass hypnosis, waking hypnosis, [and] trance," conducted by Mabuse under the pseudonym of Sandor Weltmann.[73]

By placing Weltmann on the very same stage where Dr. Mabuse has previously given his lecture titled "Psychoanalysis as a Factor in Modern Therapeutics," the scene undermines the boundary between scientific hypnotism and hypnotic stage shows, thereby recalling the double identity of Caligari as showman and doctor. At the same time, Lang's film exoticizes the magic of hypnosis. Weltmann creates mass suggestions in the audience gathered for his "experimental evening," performing a feat that he characterizes as "similar to the tricks of Indian fakirs."[74] The collective hallucinations produced in this manner are perceived by the members of the audience as if they were watching a movie. Standing on an empty stage (fig. 10), Weltmann suggests to his audience the image of a tropical landscape that fills the unoccupied space in front of

72. Lang's *Dr. Mabuse, der Spieler,* intertitle (see app. A).

73. In the twenties there was indeed a hypnotist called Weltmann who, according to Albert Moll, circumvented the prohibition against public hypnotic exhibitions by designating his experiments as waking suggestions: "The 'suggestors' Weltmann, Viebig, Ignot, and Krause used the pretext of waking suggestions to present ordinary hypnotic experiments, and it seems that the judgment of the authorities was affected by the word 'waking suggestion'" (Moll 1924, 559).

74. Lang's film may adapt here Harry Bondegger's book *Hindu-Hypnotismus: Theorie und Praxis der Fakir-Illusionen und hypnotischen Experimente* [Hindu-hypnotism: theory and practice of fakir illusions and hypnotic experiments] (1919). The alleged presentation of "Eastern" magic is clearly a Western construction, already signaled in the subtitle that claims to be both an "authorized translation" and a "free rendition" (*freie Wiedergabe*) of an Indian text.

FIGURES 10 AND 11. Meta-cinematic moment in Fritz Lang's *Dr. Mabuse, the Gambler* (1922): Sandor Weltmann's hypnotic production of visual hallucinations as cinema.

the seated spectators as a film screen (fig. 11). Mabuse, who stands to the right of the hypnotically generated screen, assumes the role of the film lecturer who in the first decades of cinema accompanied the projection of the moving images with an oral commentary and thereby exerted a decisive influence on the reception of the filmstrips.[75] The next images show Weltmann's spellbound audience as they begin to lose the ability to distinguish between reality and the suggested moving pictures. The boundary between screen and the realm of the viewers is erased by the

75. On the role of the film lecturer between 1895 and 1910, see also Gaudreault 1990.

caravan that intrudes on the space of the theater, proceeding through the aisle between the hallucinating spectators, until Weltmann brings them back to reality.

While Bernheim had characterized the relationship between hypnotic sleep and waking as a change of "nervous light," physicians like Kretschmer and Simmel explicitly compared the hypnotic suggestion of visual hallucinations to cinema. In representing the production of moving images by means of verbal suggestion, Lang's *Dr. Mabuse, the Gambler*, in turn, conceives of cinema as a form of hypnosis. The metacinematic commentary on the suggestive production of immaterial yet moving images that exert a fascinating spell simultaneously appropriated an extensive medical debate that described the cinematic apparatus as exerting an irresistible hypnotic influence.

Cinema's Hypnotic Influence

Literary authors such as Jean Cocteau, Walter Hasenclever, and Robert Musil invoked the "collective hypnosis into which the cinema audience is plunged by light and shade."[76] At the same time, numerous physicians and psychologists also emphasized the "photoplay's tremendous suggestive power."[77] Hugo Münsterberg explicitly employed the analogy of the "hypnotizer whose word awakens in the mind of the hypnotized person ideas which he cannot resist," in order to claim cinema's superiority over the theater (cf. 89, above).[78] In addition, Münsterberg described how susceptible viewers even developed sensory hallucinations of touch and smell when exposed to the suggestive influence of film: "The *intensity* with which the plays *take hold* of the audience cannot remain without strong social effects. It has even been reported that sensory hallucinations and illusions have crept in; neurasthenic persons are especially inclined to experience touch or smell or sound impressions from what they see on the screen. The associations become as vivid as realities,

76. Cocteau [1946] 1992, 25. See also Hasenclever [1913] 1992, 220: "Of all the technologies of our time, the photoplay is the most powerful. . . . In it, space and time serve to *hypnotize the audience*." Robert Musil's essay "Ansätze zu Neuer Ästhetik" [Toward a new aesthetics] (1925) similarly compares cinema's "concentration of consciousness" (*Einengung des Bewußtseins*) to a "light hypnosis" (1141)—on Musil's essay, see Haddock 2004.

77. Hellwig, *Die Reform des Lichtspielrechts* [Reforming cinema law] (1920), 7.

78. Münsterberg [1916] 2002, 97.

because the mind is so completely given up to the moving pictures. The applause into which the audience . . . break out at a happy turn of the melodramatic pictures is another symptom of the *strange fascination*."[79] In Germany, Robert Gaupp's essay "The Cinematograph from a Medical and Psychological Perspective" (1912) conceived of the enormously powerful impact of the new medium as "profoundly unsettling" the spectator's "nervous system."[80] According to Gaupp, cinema presented "everything to the eye as if it were real"—"under the psychologically most favorable conditions for a deep and often sustained *suggestive influence*": "The darkened room, the monotonous sound, the compelling nature of the exciting scenes that rapidly follow each other beat by beat—all of this *puts to sleep* any critical judgment in the receptive soul. . . . We know that all *suggestions* are more deeply imprinted when critical judgment *sleeps*."[81]

This comparison of cinema and hypnotic suggestion was also formulated by Konrad Lange, Albert Hellwig, and Georg Cohn, as well as by Hans Buchner, whose treatise *Under the Spell of Film* (1927) described "cinema man" as succumbing to "the hypnosis of cinema." Max Prel's book *Cinema* (1926) similarly warned against "cinema's mass hypnosis."[82]

79. Ibid., 154. On this point, see also Albert Hellwig, "Illusionen und Halluzinationen bei kinematographischen Vorführungen" [Illusions and hallucinations at cinematographic presentations] (1914b). In Hans Hyan's novel *Die Somnambule* [The somnambulist] (1929) these somatic effects of cinema are ascribed to Salvioli's manipulations. But the emphasis on the sensory hallucinations triggered in the spectators by the showing of a film as part of a spiritualist séance simultaneously functions as an oblique representation of film's suggestive power: "Something rained down in the dark on the spectators—rose petals fell from above, from the sides, from the front. . . . The rose petals strewn by that woman *from the screen* wafted down with their *lovely scent* on the people sitting in the room" (149). Compare also Polgar [1911–12] 1992, 163: "The lawn in the movie theater smells better than the one on the stage, because the cinematograph shows, after all, a real, genuine lawn, whose smell I am prepared to believe, being able to suggest it to my nose as perfectly as my totally undisturbed imagination dreams it into being."

80. Gaupp, "Der Kinematograph vom medizinischen und psychologischen Standpunkt" (1912), 9. A cinematic modification of the nervous system is also described in 1921 by Jean Epstein, who depicts the need to watch movies as a "hunger for a hypnosis far more intense than reading offers, because reading modifies the functioning of the nervous system much less" (240)

81. Gaupp 1912, 9. See also Gaupp [1911–12] 1992, 67.

82. Buchner, *Im Banne des Films* (1927), 41; Max Prels, *Kino* (1926), 67. The effect of the film on its audiences was described in numerous texts of the early twentieth

The concept of hypnotic suggestion thus came to figure as a central trope in early-twentieth-century medical, popular, and critical representations of cinema. Frequently invoked by Walter Benjamin and in recent film history, the notion of shock does aptly capture the interrelation of film and the change of sensory perception effected by World War I and the early-twentieth-century metropolis.[83] But already in 1916, an essay written by a forensic expert insisted on differentiating between shock and suggestion when describing cinema's gradual influence over its audience. As Albert Hellwig asserted in his "The Psychology of Cinematographic Displays" (1916): "One has to take into account, however, that the cinematographic display ... does not at all produce a shock in the nervous system as created by a sudden fright or by another strongly exciting impact; on the contrary, its *influence* affects the spectator, only gradually [*ganz allmählich*], before *growing to gigantic proportions*."[84] Fritz Lang's representation of Mabuse gradually entering into a hypnotic rapport with the disguised Wenk visualizes the exclusion of "disturbing external influences" that allows for the success of Mabuse's criminal suggestions. But in addition, the representation of Mabuse's head, slowly growing larger and larger before reaching gigantic proportions and dominating the entire screen, literalizes psychological accounts of how the photoplay gradually and almost surreptitiously subjects the spellbound audience to its growing and finally irresistible influence. In contrast to conservative critics like Hellwig, Lang's film, however, undermines the belief in the

century in terms of suggestion and hypnosis. Thus Georg Cohn speaks of the "suggestive influence of the cinematograph" (1909, 17). Hellwig stresses in numerous essays "the dangerous suggestive effect ... of photoplay presentations" (Hellwig 1920, 8; see also Hellwig 1911, 74; 1914a, 29; 1914c), while Konrad Lange warns "of the suggestive power of motion picture photography" (1920, 164). Compare also Sellmann 1912, 24; Warstat and Bergmann, *Kino und Gemeinde* [Cinema and community] (1913), 75; and Lange, *Das Kino in Gegenwart und Zukunft* [The cinema in present and future] (1920), 27–28 and 156. See also H. Duenschmann, "Kinematograph und Psychologie der Volksmenge" [The cinematograph and the psychology of the crowd] (1912), esp. 923–24; and Walther Pahl, "Die psychologischen Wirkungen des Films unter besonderer Berücksichtigung ihrer sozialpsychologischen Bedeutung" [The psychological effects of film, with specific consideration of its sociopsychological significance] (1926), 90, on the "fascinating spellbinding power of film."

83. See Anton Kaes, "The Cold Gaze" (1993), and Kaes, "Leaving Home: Film, Migration, and the Urban Experience" (1998).

84. Albert Hellwig, "Zur Psychologie kinematographischer Vorführungen" (1916a), 101–2.

complete surrender of the hypnotized viewer, since in the end Mabuse's suggestive powers fail in his battle with Wenk.

One particular fear expressed in many texts of the so-called cinema reform movement concerned the visuality of the medium. In comparing film to other established media such as theater and literature, Hellwig conceived of the motion picture as "immediately" (*unmittelbar*) address-ing and interpellating the human mind. Hellwig condemned the demor-alizing effect of "trash fiction" (*Schundliteratur*), but he considered the power of the moving image even more pernicious: "Pictures generally exert a more strongly inciting influence than mere descriptions of the same object by means of language."[85] Hellwig, Gaupp, and other con-servative critics thereby ignored the mediality of filmic representation, while simultaneously ascribing their own uncritical equation of image and reality to the ostensibly uneducated spectators (women, children, the working classes, and the "lower races"), who were allegedly unable to distinguish between cinematic representation and reality. Neglecting Bernheim's insight into the constitutive role of autosuggestion, the texts of the German cinema reform movement consequently characterized the spellbound viewer as exclusively passive, overwhelmed by the onslaught of life-like moving pictures. For authors such as Hellwig or Gaupp, the source of suggestive power resided exclusively in the cinematic appara-tus, not in the mind of the spectator.

In the late 1920s, however, after the motion picture's transition to synchronized sound, the alleged site of suggestion shifted from the purely visual to either the aural or a combination of sound and sight. Joseph Gregor's treatise *The Era of Film* (1932) contained a whole chapter on "optical-acoustical suggestion," describing how the "appropriate com-bination of optical and acoustical rhythm could enhance the capability of suggestion to the state of trance."[86] Fritz Lang's *The Testament of Dr. Mabuse* (1932–33), in turn, no longer focused on Mabuse's hypnotic gaze, displaying instead telephones and loudspeakers as the acoustic media that transmitted Mabuse's commands (fig. 12).[87] The rapid emergence

85. Ibid., 116.

86. See Gregor, *Das Zeitalter des Films* (1932), 153–77, esp. 159: "Die geeignete Verbindung des optischen und des akustischen Rhythmus kann also die Suggestions-fähigkeit bis an den Trancezustand bringen."

87. The transition from image to sound in Lang's *The Testament of Dr. Mabuse* is also emphasized in Jonathan Crary's essays "Spectacle, Attention, Counter-Memory"

FIGURE 12. The acoustic apparatus of loudspeaker and microphone transmits Dr. Mabuse's commands (from Fritz Lang's *The Testament of Dr. Mabuse* [1932–33]).

of radio as a mass medium after the first experimental broadcasts in 1923 simultaneously displaced the anxiety of an irresistible hypnotic influence on to another new medium capable of addressing a spatially dispersed but potentially infinite number of listeners at the very same time. In 1928 Theodor Mayer accordingly warned of the possibility that "certain persons . . . could impose their will via the radio on hundreds of thousands." Mayer invoked a terrifying scenario, testifying to both the changing political situation toward the end of the Weimar Republic and the conceptualization of new media as emanating a spellbinding influence: "One does not need a coup anymore, one simply seizes control of a large radio station during the hours of evening, when something is being broadcast that is of interest to as big a circle as possible. One suddenly interrupts the broadcast and transmits quite unexpectedly *the hypnotizing words* whose spell transforms hundreds of thousands into slaves of the one, slaves who are unable to liberate themselves from such control, unless the one grants it."[88]

(1989), 102, and "Dr. Mabuse and Mr. Edison" (1996), 272–73. On Lang's figuration of sound by means of the telephone, see Michel Chion, *The Voice in Cinema* ([1982] 1999), 31–44, 66–73.

88. Mayer, "Der Rundfunk—vom anderen Ufer betrachtet" [Radio—considered from a different perspective] (1928), 121. For an analysis of representations of early television as a hypnotic medium, see my "Psychic Television" (2005). Equivalent fears

In addition to such representations of radio's hypnotic power, the concept of suggestion also became central to theories of propaganda and the psychology of advertising. The German cinema reform movement of the 1910s and the early 1920s was most concerned, however, about the power of motion pictures to incite criminal actions. Münsterberg also replicated Bernheim's definition of hypnosis when he invoked the "high degree of suggestibility" of film spectators; but in accordance with the skeptical position of his essay "Hypnotism and Crime" (1908), he limited a direct connection between the suggestive power of "unwholesome photoplays" and "grave crimes" to "exceptional cases."[89] Writing in 1920, Konrad Lange, by contrast, found it "incomprehensible how in an earlier period one could assert that nobody had ever been able to give a certain proof for such cases of a direct incitement to crime." As Lange asserted, "Given the powerful effect of motion photography, . . . the young journeyman and apprentice" had "to succumb without a will of his own" to cinematic representations of crimes or suicides.[90] Before 1918, during the Wilhelmine Empire, the anxiety about this affinity between cinema and hypnotism had even led to repeated censorship of films showing, or inducing, hypnosis.[91]

While replicating the medical tales of hypnotic crime, the accounts of cinema's hypnotic power thus introduced a metacinematic dimension

---

led the American National Association of Broadcasters to ban the live broadcasting of hypnotists on radio and television—see Sconce, *Haunted Media* (2000), 108 and 77; see also Christina Bartz, "Telepathologien. Der Fernsehzuschauer unter medizinischer Beobachtung" [Telepathologies: the television viewer under medical observation] (2002), 377–80.

89. Compare Münsterberg [1916] 2002, 154–55: "Those may have been exceptional cases only when grave crimes have been traced directly back to impulses from unwholesome photoplays, but no psychologist can determine exactly how much the general spirit of righteousness, of honesty, of sexual cleanliness and modesty, may be weakened by the unbridled influence of plays of low moral standard. . . . The fact that millions are daily *under the spell* of the performances on the screen is established. The *high degree of suggestibility* during those hours in the dark house may be taken for granted."

90. Lange 1920, 39.

91. On the demand for censorship of cinematographic representations of hypnosis, see especially Albert Hellwig, "Hypnotismus und Kinematograph" (1916b); see also Moll 1924, 564: "The filmic exhibition of crimes committed under the influence of hypnosis therefore ought to caution the members of the Censorship Board in Berlin to exert the utmost vigilance."

into the filmic representations of criminal suggestion. For, similar to the plot of Wiene's *Caligari* or Lang's *Mabuse*, numerous medical researchers described the film spectator as the victim of a hypnotic suggestion that controlled his thoughts after leaving the movie theater. This anxiety seemed corroborated by a sensational child murder, frequently invoked as exemplary evidence for the pernicious influence of film. Albert Hellwig gave the first detailed account of the case in his essay "The Harmful Suggestive Power of Cinematographic Displays" (1914), published in the *Medical Expert Journal*. According to this article, the sixteen-year-old field hand of a farmer in Borbeck, a small village in the west of Germany, had murdered the four-year-old son of his employer in the fall of 1913 without any apparent motive. The perpetrator had always been kind to the child who later became his victim. Suspicions of any sadistic tendencies proved to be unfounded. The culprit was furthermore "very moderate in his drinking" and "equally restrained in his sexual practices." He did, however, frequent the local movie theater "once a week, and occasionally even several times a week." On the days preceding the crime, the delinquent had seen a Western and a cinematic adaptation of the fairy tale *Tom Thumb* (*Der kleine Däumling*)—films that "in certain telling details showed a striking resemblance to the circumstances of the crime."[92] The investigating judge consequently reached the astonishing conclusion that these two films had "exerted such a *suggestive influence* on the accused that, unwittingly subject to their influence and without any other motive, he had killed . . . his employer's small son, on whom he ordinarily looked with fondness, when on the afternoon in question he found himself alone with his victim in the hayloft."[93]

The case history seems to anticipate current anxieties about adolescents and the incitement to violence ostensibly emanating from new media such as video games or the Internet. But the medical notion of hypnotic suggestion, central to this account of the "Borbeck child murder," has lost its relevance today and has been replaced by a vague condemnation of the "corrupting" or "desensitizing" influence of modern media. To be sure, the forensic conceptualization of the Borbeck case certainly contained a moralizing subtext. But the representation of film's

92. Hellwig, "Ueber die schädliche Suggestivkraft kinematographischer Vorführungen" (1914c), 119.

93. Hellwig 1914c, 120–21; see also Hellwig, *Kind und Kino* [Child and cinema] (1914a), 37. The same account is also given in Buchner, *Im Banne des Films* (1927), 134.

hypnotic power invoked above all a then scientifically established notion of suggestion and hypnosis. For the judicial opinion that described the cinematic suggestion as controlling susceptible viewers even after leaving the theater, forcing them to commit criminal acts that they would abhor while awake, replicated Auguste Forel's warning against crimes committed after awakening from hypnosis. According to Forel, the particularly "insidious ruse" of such a criminal "posthypnotic suggestion" consisted in the perpetrator's belief that he was acting freely, of his own volition, while in reality under the control of a foreign hypnotic command (cf. above, 28).[94]

The sensationalist case history of the Borbeck child murder, often invoked in texts that warned against the danger of "trash movies" (*Schundfilme*), thus shows with unusual clarity why "crime and suggestion" came to be the "most popular subject" of cinema, as the avid moviegoer Victor Klemperer put it in his diary on April 18, 1921.[95] For the filmic representations of hypnotic crimes appropriated not only a lively scientific, medical, and legal debate about the unlimited power of hypnotism. In addition, contemporary representations of the new medium itself were predicated on a structural analogy between cinema and hypnosis, thereby giving rise to the fear that the spellbound audience might succumb to the irresistible influence emanating from the cinematic apparatus—just like Dr. Mabuse's hypnotized victims or Dr. Caligari's somnambulist medium Cesare.

Mabuse as a Criminal Corporation

The "cinema reformers," who advocated a rigorous censorship of dangerous "trash movies," regarded the "profit-oriented motion picture industry" as the actual author of crimes like the Borbeck child murder.[96] Nationalist critics turned in particular against American corporations, which after the end of the Great Inflation in 1923 intruded on the German film market. The foreign firms were represented as surreptitiously and ruthlessly subjecting the "German people" to their pernicious influ-

---

94. Forel, "Der Hypnotismus und seine strafrechtliche Bedeutung" (1889a), 184.

95. Klemperer, *Tagebücher* ([1918–24] 1996), 432.

96. Gaupp 1912, 9. Hermann Häfker, too, in *Das Kino und die Gebildeten* [Cinema and the educated] (1915), condemned the domination of the film market by corporations that in his view fed on German culture "like parasites" (71).

ence. Rudolph Stratz's novel *Storm of Film* (1926), for instance, described an American film company as a global actor that controlled the program of movie theaters in the entire world: "The 'Wide World Company' [sic] was one of the largest motion picture companies in the United States. It devoured the entire film program that was left after the other globe-encircling glasshouse octopuses of Los Angeles had eaten their fill. It controlled, together with those others, the cinematic screen from Patagonia to Korea, from the Sunda Islands to Capetown."[97]

Like Frank Norris's *Octopus* (1901), Stratz's novel resorts to the figure of a tentacled monster to represent an organization that exerts its agency—"with a hundred arms"—in numerous places at the same time.[98] Simultaneously, the text conceives of the "Americanization" clandestinely fostered by this company as a form of hypnosis that irresistibly emanates from the cinematic screen: "The wider public did not know the names of these Yankees, whose will . . . caused the customs and manners of the United States to creep slowly, *imperceptibly*, from the silver screen into the souls of all people, *hypnotizing* and Americanizing old Europe."[99] But the linkage between globalized, corporate control and the uncanny phenomenon of imperceptible hypnosis is to be found not only in anti-American and anti-Semitic texts such as Rudolph Stratz's *Storm of Film* (1926) or Hans Buchner's *Under the Spell of Film* (1927). Fritz Lang's *Dr. Mabuse, the Gambler* also connects the ominous power of suggestion to hidden economic forces.

In Norbert Jacques's novel and Lang's film, the figure of Dr. Mabuse functions as the personification or embodiment of an intangible corporate organism that eludes direct perception and manipulates the stock exchange. But while Lang's cinematic enactment of hypnosis relies on the close-up and the point-of-view shot, the ubiquity and opacity of a vast economic organization can be captured on film only through different modes of visualization. Tom Gunning has analyzed how the opening scenes of Lang's first *Mabuse* employ "one of [cinema's] specific means of representation, editing," to introduce a complex network of modernity that is based on the railway, the automobile, the telephone, and synchro-

97. Stratz, *Filmgewitter* (1926), 240.

98. "With a hundred arms": Regelsberger, *Pandekten* (1893), 328.

99. Stratz 1926, 241. For a more detailed analysis of the wider context from which Buchner's or Stratz's denunciations of the pernicious "Americanization" of Germany emerge, see Thomas Saunders, *Hollywood in Berlin* (1994), esp. 119 ff.

nization.[100] The omnipresence of an "invisible aggregate person" thus finds a cinematic equivalent in parallel editing, for Lang's juxtaposition of several interconnected story lines reveals an intricate organization responsible for the elaborately planned and synchronized attack on a messenger, the delivery of the stolen contract to Mabuse, and the manipulation of the "special editions" of the newspapers that "explode into the stock exchange at precisely the right moment."[101] The slump, in which panicking stockholders prematurely sell their shares, is followed by a rise in prices after the clandestine association passes the contract back to its owners. As if anticipating Lang's montage of the various machinations of Mabuse's organization, Münsterberg had affirmed already in 1916: "There is no limit to the number of threads which may be interwoven. A complex intrigue may demand cooperation at half a dozen spots, and we look now into one, now into another, and never have the impression that they come one after another."[102]

In addition to parallel editing, Lang's film also introduces the photographic device of double exposure, taken over from contemporary spirit photography, as a further, genuinely cinematic mode of representing an invisible corporate body that eludes direct perception. The opening scenes of *Dr. Mabuse, the Gambler* demonstrate the instability of Mabuse's identity, since he randomly picks the first disguise for "His Day" from a deck of photographs, which show ostensibly different persons.[103] Later, the camera shows the chaos at the stock exchange in a high-angle shot

100. Gunning, *The Films of Fritz Lang* (2000), 98.

101. "Invisible aggregate person": Gierke, *Das Wesen menschlicher Verbände* [The nature of human aggregates] ([1902] 1954) 30.

102. Münsterberg [1916] 2002, 95.

103. "His Day": Lang, Intertitles. The constant change of Mabuse's identities thus effects a proliferation and dissolution of this natural person, who almost seems to lack a stable body or gender. In Jacques's novel, Wenk keeps Dr. Mabuse's office under surveillance for several days and observes various persons enter and leave the building, without Wenk being able to identify them immediately: "So the one who had come out first, the soldier, and the lady were one and the same person. And yesterday and the day before, Wenk now understood, the chimney sweeper, the tabetic, the man with the parcel . . . all the same person and all of them—Mabuse!" (Jacques [1921-22] 1994, 198–99); see also 116: "He asked for a description of the man. And then something curious happened. People started arguing already when it came to his complexion. One man gave him blue eyes, another dark ones. He was tallish and thin and dressed like a sailor. He also looked a little bit like an athlete."

FIGURE 13. The double exposure of early-twentieth-century spirit photography renders even an "invisible aggregate person" visible (from Fritz Lang's *Dr. Mabuse, the Gambler*).

that contrasts the hectic, rapid movements of the brokers with the calm determination of the disguised Mabuse, who buys when the stocks are at their lowest in order to sell again later with huge profit. After the market's close, the camera lingers on the empty hall of the stock exchange, strewn with paper bills, before fading in, by means of a double exposure, the head of Mabuse, who stands behind the price fluctuations of the day (fig. 13).

The invisible machinations of Mabuse are thereby rendered visible to the spectator of the film. While double exposure and parallel editing constitute specifically filmic modes of representing the agency of an invisible "aggregate person," Norbert Jacques's novel similarly emphasizes in the statements of its protagonist Wenk that Mabuse can act ubiquitously, in different places at the very same time, through the bodies of his controlled "employees" or "organs."[104] But by ascribing nearly supernatural capabilities to the figure of Mabuse, Jacques's novel and

104. "Wenk stated that the task was not to capture any one person but to break up the entire living organization. . . . Without having one's hands on the director, it was quite meaningless to secure a dozen or so of these *employees*" (Jacques [1921–22] 1994, 119); "organs": Gierke (1887), 624. The novel also emphasizes the powers of a criminal organization when Wenk explicitly states: "Behind this attack there is an association, headed by a man [who] . . . has created a whole organization around his lawless life" ([1921–22] 1994, 107); see also 98: "What we are dealing with is not one crime but an organization of criminals."

Lang's film ultimately personify the "criminal gang that . . . has invisibly formed a *state* of its own, among the hustle and bustle of its fellow human beings."[105] In focusing on the conflict between Mabuse and Wenk, both novel and film rely on a model of heroic masculinity, representing the two antagonists as endowed with a special willpower. The intangibility and the autopoetic agency of an opaque complex organization are thus attributed to the extraordinary qualities of a single human being. This anthropomorphic reduction of complexity is avoided, however, in Hermann Broch's *The Sleepwalkers* as well as in Franz Kafka's *The Trial* and *The Castle*; for as the next chapter will show, these novels undertake a narrative representation of autopoetic "living" corporate organisms without lapsing into crude personalizations.

105. Jacques [1921–22] 1994, 177.

V HUMAN AND CORPORATE BODIES IN BROCH AND KAFKA

The institution and its members [are] actually one and the same. Franz Kafka,
Office Writings

In late-nineteenth-century fiction, it is above all the literature of the fantastic that links representations of invisible corporate bodies to tales of hypnotic crime. After 1900, however, modernist texts appropriate, on the level of figurative discourse, the scientific conceptions literalized by the story of Maupassant's *Horla* or Meyrink's *The White Dominican*.[1] In Hermann Broch's trilogy *The Sleepwalkers* (1928–32), the protagonists are repeatedly compared to somnambulists. At the same time, a demonic corporation—the "Middle Rhine Shipping Co."—plays a central role in the second part.[2] Broch's novel, which was translated into English upon its publication in 1932, sets out to represent three transitional histori-cal moments, and its epic ambitions have invited comparisons to the

1. For a literal enactment of the figurative demonic subtext inherent in the medi-cal debate about criminal suggestions, see also Somerset Maugham's novel *The Magi-cian* (1908), which on the one hand points to "the limits of hypnotism" (183), while on the other hand the metaphor of demonic possession assumes its literal meaning: "'If Margaret has broken her word to me . . . , it's because it's not the Margaret I know. Some *devil* must have taken possession of her body.' 'You use a *figure of speech*. I wonder if it can possibly be a reality'" (182).

2. "Middle Rhine Shipping Co.": Broch, *Die Schlafwandler* ([1928–32] 1994), 194. All in-text references are to the German original and its English translation.

work of Robert Musil, Thomas Mann, and James Joyce. The first part, *Pasenow or Romanticism (Pasenow oder die Romantik)*, takes place in 1888 Berlin, focusing on the pressures exerted on the Prussian landed gentry by an ascending capitalist economy through juxtaposing the aristocratic officer Pasenow and the capitalist entrepreneur Bertrand. *Esch or Anarchy (Esch oder die Anarchie)* is set in 1903 in Cologne and Mannheim. Its protagonist, the accountant Esch, seeks to gain access to Bertrand, the president of the company he used to work for. In the final part, *Huguenau or Objectivity (Huguenau oder die Sachlichkeit)*, the attitude of cool detached calculation, embodied in the figure of Huguenau, gains prevalence in the transitional period at the end of World War I. Juxtaposed to these multiple narrative threads is an essay entitled "The Disintegration of Values," giving a conceptual bend to the literary text that may have hindered its reception in the United States and England.[3] Our reading will focus on *Esch or Anarchy*, analyzing how the novel's depersonalized mode of narration represents corporate agency in the intangible figure of Bertrand. In contrast to previous interpretations of the trilogy that have isolated the title-giving figure of sleepwalking from any nonliterary, medical, or psychological meaning, we will also show how the novel appropriates medical notions of somnambulism.[4]

Somnambulism and Corporate Agency in Hermann Broch's *The Sleepwalkers*

Already in the first part of the trilogy, *Pasenow or Romanticism*, Eduard von Bertrand, the director of the Middle Rhine Company, is introduced as a businessman engaged in "worldwide transactions" (100/89*). The text initially invokes the figure of possession by focusing on the institution of the army, which "*takes hold* [of its members] far more strongly than any secular profession could," transforming Lieutenant Joachim von Pasenow into a "man *possessed* by the uniform."[5] Eduard von Bertrand, by contrast, has resigned from the military and is ruled by the "demon"

---

3. Theodore Ziolkowski's "In Search of the Absolute Novel" (1985) provides a good introduction to the novel and its American reception.

4. For one such alternate reading, see Steinecke 1972, 70.

5. Broch ([1928–32] 1994), 23/20*. On the function of the "uniform," see ibid., 23–28/20–24, esp. 24/21 on the uniform as boundary between "person" and "world" and 26/23 on the uniform as disciplining the body.

(33/29) of his enterprise. To Pasenow he appears as a man "*possessed* by the greed for profit" (33/29*).

Pasenow's imaginings anticipate Broch's description of the entrepreneur in his political writings from the 1940s. There, Broch conceived of both entrepreneur and worker as "*governed* by the economy." For Broch, the "unconditional surrender to an abstraction sometimes called 'the firm' or 'the enterprise'" transformed these economic organizations into an "invisible idol."[6] The "*demonic* inescapability" of the economic process thus turned the "rich man of past times" into a "semiconscious being [*Dämmerwesen*] who, *tied* to the enterprise, toils . . . for the 'firm' and its 'profit.'"[7]

While Broch's *Theory of Mass Delusion* gives a conceptual description of how the "capitalist economy" evolves from a "static to a dynamic-functional stage," *The Sleepwalkers* represents the same process with an increasingly depersonalized mode of narration.[8] Paralleling the economic transition to a dematerialized functionalism, the change of narrative strategies between the first and the second part of the work replaces the "*concretion* of the 'rich man'" by the *abstraction* of the 'enterprise.'"[9] In *Pasenow or Romanticism*, the figure of Bertrand already proliferates itself in the "soft bodies" of his "deputies," who "waddle" through the financial district of Berlin.[10] Bertrand himself even appears to change his own physical appearance, so that he is "concealed in all those shapes."[11] But he remains a real person, tangibly encountered by Pasenow. In *Esch*

6. Broch, "Die Demokratie im Zeitalter der Versklavung" [Democracy in the age of enslavement] ([1949] 1978), 127.

7. Broch [1939–48] 1979, 159. See also Broch [1949] 1978, 174: "Whether under the rule of capitalism or that of communism, man is prey to his institutions," and ibid., 124, on the "mythic self-regulation [*Eigengesetzlichkeit*] of the economy."

8. Broch, *Massenwahntheorie* ([1939–48] 1979), 159.

9. Ibid. See also Broch's play *Die Entsühnung* [Atonement] ([1932] 1979), in which the entrepreneur Filsmann kills himself because his family business is transformed into an anonymous stockholding company, so that the life of the legal person here literally presupposes the death of the natural person (see Broch [1932] 1979, esp. 204, 217–20).

10. Broch, *Die Schlafwandler* ([1928–32] 1994), 56/48 ("soft"); 58/50 ("waddling hastily into the Stock Exchange"); 64/54 ("deputies"); 141/126 ("waddled").

11. Ibid., 57/50; see also 55/48*: "He [Joachim] would not have been surprised if Bertrand himself, transformed like an actor, had waddled up to him, short and stocky, with a full beard: for why should Bertrand have preserved his former appearance after sliding into a different world?" In his letter to the Rhein-Verlag (Rhine Publish-

or Anarchy, however, Bertrand becomes the novel's absent center, which seems constantly present and yet can never be grasped. As Broch notes in his "Methodological Prospectus" (1929), Bertrand is the "actual hero" of the novel.[12] Yet in a metafictional passage of the literary text, he is characterized as "somebody . . . who does not even exist and who is nonetheless the main character"—an "*invisible* . . . puppeteer," acting through the characters of Lohberg, Ilona, or Erna as if "pulling them on strings" (311/277*). Bertrand thus functions less as a real character than as an incarnation of the "invisible idol[s]" that govern the economic process.[13] The "enormous phantasms . . . of cartels, syndicates, and trusts," which appear within the novel in the guise of the Middle Rhine Shipping Company, are thereby given a personal embodiment.[14] Marked by a ghostly omnipresence, Bertrand does "indeed control . . . the external events." His "apparition" (*Erscheinung*), however, manifests itself "only in a dreamlike manner."[15]

Accordingly, the accountant Esch fails in his repeated attempts to gain access to this "barely reachable figure" (295/262*). At the novel's beginning, the "clerk" (183/159) is let go by the firm of "Stemberg & Co." (187/165), whose stock lists have been forged by its executive secretary Nentwig.[16] Esch refuses to join the socialist "organization" (184/162*) represented by the union secretary Martin Geyring. He does, however, apply for and accept a position with the Middle Rhine Shipping Company, even though it seems to him "as if he had paid for the new position with his soul's salvation, or at least with his decency."[17]

---

ers) from June 24, 1930, Broch stated that he ought to avoid "further 'incarnating' [*verfleischlichen*]" Bertrand in *Pasenow* either (Broch [1913–38] 1981, 91–92).

12. "Der eigentliche Held": Broch, "Methodologischer Prospekt" ([1929] 1994), 720.

13. "Unsichtbare Götzen": Broch, "Die Demokratie im Zeitalter der Versklavung" ([1949] 1978), 127.

14. "Ungeheure Phantasiegebilde": A. Weber, "Der Beamte" [The official] ([1910] 1927), 85.

15. Broch, "Methodologischer Prospekt" ([1929] 1994), 721.

16. Compare Broch [1928–32] 1994, 188/166: "The fact that Nentwig had given in showed that he had a bad conscience. The inventories were forged then, and the man should be handed over to the police."

17. Ibid., 193/170*. See also Weber [1910] 1927, 87: "One seeks to chain civil servants and employees . . . to the apparatus. . . . In addition to the labor, one also demands the human being himself—his 'soul.'"

Like Conrad's *Heart of Darkness*, Broch's novel invokes a devil's pact to describe Esch's entry into an opaque organization whose global transactions remain inscrutable to its employees. Yet in contrast to Conrad's novel where the "ominous atmosphere" of the Company creates the impression of a "conspiracy" in Marlow from the very beginning, Esch is at first positively disposed toward the building in which the Middle Rhine Company has incarnated itself.[18] In his exploration of the firm, Esch does not get farther than the "president's anteroom." But the company's tangible embodiments—its building, the "doorman in grey livery," and the president's personal assistant—arouse sufficient "respect" in Esch that he is "glad to be a part of it" (195–96/172–73*). Just as in Alfred Weber's representation of the close tie between employees and employing institution, Esch is "sucked in," as it were, by the Middle Rhine Company.[19] The "various company signs" with the names of previously anonymous shipping firms now become to him "individuals and individualities."[20] And he considers his own position as an employee equivalent to that of a soldier or official in representing a higher authority: "And even though he [Esch] did not wear a uniform yet and was, so to speak, only a private employee, he told himself that by virtue of his associations with the customs and railway officials he had almost become an official figure himself" (196–97/174*).

Esch practices a form of "magical thinking" that, according to Broch's *Theory of Mass Delusion*, "concedes *magical* powers to the abstract units . . . of large corporate aggregates." In the same way that "civil law . . . ascribes to these *abstract unities* the rights and the dignity of *concrete persons*," Esch conceives of the Middle Rhine Company as a supernatural being.[21] It is only after the union secretary Martin Geyring has been arrested during a dockworker strike that Esch's positive attitude toward the joint-stock company abruptly changes. Attributing Geyring's arrest and conviction to the "insidious firm" (245/217), Esch holds the company responsible for the actions of the police and the courts. Bertrand's invisibility—"the

18. Conrad, *Heart of Darkness* ([1902] 1995), 25 (see also above, 61); Broch, *Die Schlaf-wandler* ([1928–32] 1994), 194/171.

19. "Eingesaugt": Weber ([1910] 1927), 82 and 85.

20. "Whereas in earlier days he [Esch] had been surprised, sometimes even annoyed, that there were so many shipping companies and that the uniform sheds along the docks were marked with such different company signs, now the separate firms all became individuals and individualities" (Broch [1928–32] 1994, 196/173*).

21. Broch, *Massenwahntheorie* ([1939–48] 1979), 88.

man was always hiding, just like Nentwig" (243/218*)—thus allows Esch
to assume a "diabolical intrigue of the Middle Rhine Shipping Company"
(257/228*), personified in the intangible figure of Bertrand. Similar to
Pasenow's imaginings in the first part of the trilogy, Bertrand becomes
to Esch the "demonic source of all misfortune" (128/114*).

After his departure from the company, Esch's brief "regret at no longer being a member of the fine organization" gives way to "rage against
a company that, behind its ostensible orderliness, its smooth corridors,
its smooth and flawless book-keeping, concealed all kinds of infamies"
(244/217*). But the accountant is forced to acknowledge that it is no longer possible to ascribe the responsibility for these "infamies" to natural
persons: "It simply was . . . no longer a question of individuals, they were
all the same, and it made no difference whether one *merged* into another
and one took the place of another—no, the world was no longer to be classified according to good and evil people but according to vague, good and
evil forces. . . . Disjoined from the acting person, that was how the wrong
persisted" (270/240*). Esch no longer blames individuals for their criminal actions, but "vague [anonymous] forces." Nonetheless he continues
to rely on anthropomorphic strategies, personifying the "unimaginable
figure" of the Middle Rhine Company in its "head"—the firm's president,
Eduard von Bertrand: "It was pointless to hand over a senior accountant
to justice, for what mattered was not to hack off an arm, even if that arm
held the threatening dagger; what mattered was to strike a blow against
the whole, or at least against a *head*" (274/243*).

In Esch's paranoid fantasies, Bertrand as the "head" of the Middle
Rhine Company thus comes to figure as the actual author of Geyring's
arrest. Just as in Gierke's representation of the corporate crime, the arrest and detention of the union secretary are not attributed to the acting
persons but to an invisible corporate organism that exerts its agency
through its controlled organs. Such an "indirect agent," eluding direct
observation, can only be represented in figures of the sublime: "The
source of the poison, however, was Nentwig, perhaps even something
hiding *behind* Nentwig, something *larger*—perhaps *as large and as hidden
as a company president in his inaccessibility*—something that one did not
know" (237/210*).[22] For Esch, Bertrand's "magnified and actually unimagi-

22. "The source of the poison": Broch [1928–32] 1994, 237/210*; "Mittelbarer Thäter":
Lilienthal, *Der Hypnotismus und das Strafrecht* (1887b), 110. Compare also Broch [1928–32]
1994, 325/289*, on the "largeness . . . of the inaccessible man."

nable figure" subsumes "all lesser murderers." In a somnambulist trance, the former clerk of the Middle Rhine Company therefore decides to kill this "overmurderer": "And as Esch strolled along the quai and the sign of the Middle Rhine Shipping Company once again stared him in the face, he said in a loud and clear voice: 'Either he or I'" (268/237–38*).

Whereas the trilogy earlier employed the trope of sleepwalking in representing protagonists who, like Pasenow, surrender to the "spell" of social conventions and move in the "twilight haze" (*Dämmerzustand*) of everyday routine, it is now the "heightened wakefulness of the sleeper" that is set apart from this somnolence as a different kind of somnambulism.[23] Lohberg lives his life "in peace and without torturing himself," but Esch's sleepwalking is described as a stepping out of the social order: "He [Esch], however, had awakened and taken on the task."[24]

It should be mentioned that the first part of the trilogy does hint at this contrast between a "lucid, clairvoyant" (329/293*) recognition of contingency and a "twilight haze" that renders it impossible to distinguish "culture" from "nature."[25] In *Pasenow*, Elisabeth recognizes "in a dream state" that her society's values are the "command of an unusual compulsion." But even though she resolves "to take . . . her fate into her own hands," she succumbs in the end to external "compulsion" and marries Pasenow without loving him (114–15/102*). Esch, however, overcomes "the threshold to sleepwalking" (328/292*, 333/296*), "dreaming in a heightened wakefulness" (337/300*) and leaving his social constraints. He thereby drifts into a "state [of] *irresponsibility*" (330/293*, 331/294*), in which he sets out to murder Bertrand. Contrary to previous interpretations of Broch's *Sleepwalkers*, the novel thus appropriates the juridical debate about the legal irresponsibility of somnambulists, whose "inno-

23. "Bann": Broch [1928–32] 1994, 125/111; "twilight haze . . . wakefulness": ibid., 351/313*. For a sociological theory from this period that traces the genesis and normative force of social conventions to the phenomenon of "suggestion," see Gabriel Tarde's *The Laws of Imitation* ([1890] 1903) (see also above, 7).

24. Broch ([1928–32] 1994), 323/287*; see also 351/313*: "Such ideas may seem illogical to the waking person, but he forgets that he himself lives for the most part in a kind of twilight haze [*Dämmerzustand*] and that only the sleeper in his heightened wakefulness thinks truly logically." Also 354/315*: "The waking in his twilight haze."

25. Compare Broch [1939–48] 1979, 70: "When living in a twilight haze [*Dämmerzustand*], one cannot distinguish between the conditions of nature and those of culture."

cence . . . exempts them from retribution."[26] Since Esch acts in a somnambulist trance, the intended murder eludes legal punishment: "And if this is murder, then it is a murder that the police are not allowed to judge" (291/259*).

The "epistemological" dimension of sleepwalking, which has been considered central to the novel, is therefore related not only to neo-Platonic and mystical traditions but also to early-twentieth-century spiritualist theories that ascribe a special clairvoyance or lucidity to somnambulists.[27] The "clairvoyant state" (333/296*) that Esch drifts into while traveling to Badenweiler accordingly facilitates his conversation with Bertrand—an encounter that, like a spiritualist séance, unfolds as the materialization of a ghostly being. When Esch, who had been planning to kill Bertrand, finally encounters the unreachable figure in his

26. Broch [1928–32] 1994, 331/294*. It is surprising that Broch's representation of sleepwalking has not been placed in a medical context before. In describing the figure of the veteran Gödicke, the novel expressly introduces a victim of shell shock, who was buried alive by a bursting grenade; according to Anton Kaes's study *Shell Shock Cinema*, this trauma frequently led to somnambulism: "Somnambulism was often the effect of so-called burial cases, in which soldiers were buried alive by shell explosions or left behind as if dead. 'The explosion lifted us up and dropped us again,' recounts one shell-shocked soldier under hypnosis. 'It seemed as if the ground underneath had been taken away.' The patient freed himself and was seen wandering in a somnambulistic state from the trench, past his own dressing station to that of another regiment" (n.p.). Within Broch's novel, the medical theory of a trauma without an organic substrate is also alluded to in the description of Pasenow's father, whose illness, according to the diagnosis of the consulted "nerve specialist," emerges from the "*shock* produced by the death of his son" (131/117*). The appropriation of medical discourse becomes even more pronounced in the description of Gödicke: "Chief Medical Officer Kuhlenbeck asserted that the *shock* was merely the result of being buried alive, thus *without organic cause*, and that the patient would in time get over it" (429/383*). In addition to war neuroses, *The Sleepwalkers* furthermore unfolds in Hanna Wendling's "nervousness" (421/376) the clinical nosography of hysteria, a neurosis frequently invoked in the *Theory of Mass Delusion* as an example for an illness without physiological cause (cf. Broch [1939–48] 1979, 249 and 259).

27. Broch's appropriation of occultist figures has hitherto been noted only by Osterle (1970, 236). For spirtualist texts on clairvoyance, see, for instance, Emil Felden, *Der Spiritismus* [Spiritualism] (1921), 84 ff., Albert Moll, *Prophezeien und Hellsehen* [Prophecy and clairvoyance] (1922), and Moll (1924), 660 ff. On early-twentieth-century theories of somnambulist clairvoyance, see also Andriopoulos, "Psychic Television" (2005). On the central importance of the epistemological dimension of sleepwalking to the novel, see Steinecke, "Das Schlafwandeln" (1972), 70.

dream state, he has to realize that Bertrand, too, "is only the symbol [*Sinnbild*] of another one" (335/298*). Bertrand is also merely the "mirror image of a more essential and perhaps larger figure who remains *hidden*" (335-36/298*).

Attributing the "infamies" of an "insidious firm" (245/217*) to a natural person thus fails even in the case of its president, since Bertrand's physical appearance functions only as a stand-in for an inaccessible corporate aggregate: "It seemed as if what Esch saw physically before him was only a symbolic representation [*sinnbildliche Stellvertretung*], created ... for *practical purposes*, a dream within a dream" (334/297*). In his correspondence, Broch pointed out how juridical discourse relied on "the fiction of the 'legal person'" for the practical purpose of representing intangible corporate bodies.[28] Similarly in Broch's literary text, Bertrand's apparition remains "a dream within a dream"—the materialization of an invisible organism that manifests itself in representative deputies. Esch cannot realize the goal of his trip to Badenweiler—murdering Bertrand—since the actual agent, the Middle Rhine Company, remains "hidden" (336/298*). Esch's "dream" does not turn into a "deed" but engenders "new insight" (340/303*).

Only in the last part of the trilogy, *Huguenau or Objectivity*, does Huguenau kill Esch in a somnambulist trance, which is characterized as an "illumination" (677/614). Broch's novel thereby appropriates the medical debate about crimes committed in spontaneous somnambulism, simultaneously integrating the representation of Huguenau's "deed" (689/625) into a teleological philosophy of history. The somnambulist crime is transformed into a synecdoche of World War I, in which the values of the Wilhelmine period lose their validity: "Huguenau would have conceded at most that in less warlike or less revolutionary times he would not have committed the deed" (689/625*).

The strategy of reinscribing the figure of hypnotic crime into a diagnostic account of historical and political developments is even more pronounced in Broch's *Die Verzauberung* (The spell) (1935).[29] As Thomas Mann did in "Mario and the Magician" (1930), Broch invokes the phenomenon

---

28. Broch, *Briefe* [Correspondence] ([1913–38] 1981), 77.

29. An English translation was published in 1987. Before turning to *Die Verzauberung*, Broch had worked on another business novel, entitled *Filsmann*, which he did not complete. On Broch's play *Die Entsühnung* [Atonement], which was based on the Filsmann material, see n. 9 above.

of suggestion in order to explain the suggestive power of fascism. *The Spell*, which in some passages quotes verbatim from Hanns Heinz Ewers's novel *The Sorcerer's Apprentice or the Devil Hunters* (1910), introduces the figure of Marius Ratti as a "hypnotist" who succeeds in casting a "spell" over an entire village.[30] Even the narrator cannot resist this hypnotic "fascination," which is so overwhelming that at the annual mountain festival a frenzied "crowd" kills Irmgard, the daughter of the farmer Miland—a murder carried out by the somnambulist Sabest, who functions as Ratti's hypnotized medium:

> And as this call rings out, Sabest appears from behind his counter *like a somnambulist*. He carries his butcher knife in front of him, holding it with both hands like a sword, and thus he approaches the "Cold Stone" with his eyes closed, approaches Marius's hand that is raised against him in a *conjuring* gesture, approaches the kneeling Irmgard who is looking upward *in ecstasy*, and when he has reached her, he thrusts the knife between her shoulder blades with all the deftness of the master butcher.
>
> The fairground has fallen completely silent. *Spellbound*, the crowd stares at Marius who remains standing as before, with his hand outstretched. . . . Then a voice rises over the silence . . . , giving the *spell* a different direction.[31]

Compared with *The Sleepwalkers*, a novel that only alludes to the figure of hypnotic crime, Broch's adaptation of the medical debate about somnambulist crimes is surprisingly explicit in *The Spell*. But contrasted with Ewers's *The Sorcerer's Apprentice*, which quoted in detail from Charcot's theory of "grand hypnotism," Broch's literary appropriation of medical discourse assumes a more mediated form: whereas Charcot's nosography of spontaneous somnambulism always emphasized the sleepwalkers' open eyes, Broch describes Sabest as walking "with his eyes closed."

30. Broch [1936a] 1969, 40. Compare also Broch [1935a] 1994, 310; [1936b] 1994, 377. On the relation between Broch's and Ewers's novels, see Fischer, "Brochs Nachlaßroman" [Broch's posthumous novel] (1972), 273 ff. On Ewers's novel, see also above, 36.

31. Broch, "Demeter oder die Verzauberung" [Demeter, or the enchantment] ([1936b] 1994), 378–79. "Verzauberung" (fascination): Broch [1935a] 1994, 252; see also ibid., 143, 233, 252, 262. "Crowd": Broch, *Bergroman* [Mountain novel], 2nd version ([1936a] 1969), 236.

A juxtaposition of *The Sleepwalkers* and *The Spell* shows how, under the pressure of National Socialism, the figure of sleepwalking lost its complexity within Broch's work. *The Spell* invokes hypnotism and somnambulism as simple explanations for the hypnotic influence of fascist dictators. *The Sleepwalkers*, in contrast, links somnambulism to the interpellation by intangible organizations that exert a "*suggestive* power" over their members to "seize hold" (23/20*) of them.[32] Representing the autopoetic agency of opaque organizations in Bertrand's hidden and unimaginable figure thus gives way to a simple personalization in Broch's later work. Like Norbert Jacques's *Mabuse*, *The Spell* explains complex social processes that elude immediate observation by appealing to the extraordinary abilities of an individual person.[33] Whereas in *Esch or Anarchy* the actual culprit remains "hidden" (336/298*), Ratti's indirect agency is unquestionable.[34] Broch's representation of the spell exerted by National Socialism attributes agency only to persons and not to organizations or corporate bodies. One notion developed in *The Sleepwalkers*—that the individual members of an organization "can no longer be distinguished and differentiated from each other" (271/240*)—is, however, also central to Franz Kafka's office and literary writings. By centering on "*living* institutions," these texts emphasize even more strongly the autopoetic agency of bureaucratic "organism[s]."[35]

The Merging of Human and Corporate Bodies in Kafka's *The Trial* and *The Castle*

In "Science as a Vocation" (1917–19), Max Weber described the "disenchantment of the world" as a process of demystification and rationalization that seemingly exorcizes all "mysterious, *incalculable* forces": "It is no longer necessary, as it was for the savage who believed in such forces, to resort to magic in order to control or supplicate the spirits. Instead, technical devices and calculation perform that function."[36] Ac-

32. "*Suggestive* power": Weber [1910] 1927, 93 and 92.

33. On Broch's typology of "leaders" in his *Theory of Mass Delusion*, see Broch [1939–48] 1979, 300–302.

34. "Yes, Sabest, the murderer—I had forgotten him, because after all to me Marius was the perpetrator" (Broch [1935a] 1994, 281).

35. Kafka, *Amtliche Schriften* (1907–21), CD-ROM, 643; Kafka, *Der Proceß* ([1914–15] 1990/1998), 126/120.

36. Weber, *Wissenschaft als Beruf* ([1917–19] 1992), 87.

cording to Weber, this transition from magic to science corresponds to the replacement of a charismatic form of government by a bureaucratic one. As the "most rational form of government," the latter is marked, in Weber's view, by "precision, consistency, discipline, rigor, and dependability, that is to say: *calculability* for the ruler as well as for the interested parties."[37]

However, while Weber's account of the modern, disenchanted world ostensibly presents magic as supplanted by science and technology, his peculiar wording hints at a curious equivalence or interchangeability of magic, on the one hand, and science and technology, on the other hand; for according to Weber, "technical devices and calculation" perform the very same function previously fulfilled by magic.[38] At the same time, Weber's definition of the exorcized "spirits" as "something assumed . . . to be material and yet invisible, impersonal and yet endowed with a sort of volition" coincides with Gierke's juridical description of occult corporate "organisms" with an invisible yet material body and a distinct corporate will.[39]

Franz Kafka, the "secretary" (*tajemník*) of the Workers' Accident Insurance in Prague, similarly emphasized the "uncanniness" (*tajemné*) of his "ghostly work at the office."[40] However, not only Kafka's office writings center on the "phantasmatic" entity of a "living institution."[41] His literary texts also present "large and intransparent organization[s]" that have a life, will, and agency of their own.[42] But in direct contrast to Weber's

37. Weber, *Wirtschaft und Gesellschaft* ([1910–20] 1985), 128. Compare also ibid., 562: "'Disinterested' settlement here means above all settlement . . . in accordance with *calculable* rules."

38. This functional equivalence is also suggested by the German original: "Nicht mehr, wie der Wilde, für den es solche Mächte gab, muß man zu magischen Mitteln greifen, um die Geister zu beherrschen oder zu erbitten. Sondern technische Mittel und Berechnung *leisten das*" (Weber [1917–19] 1992, 87). One could even argue for a reading of "das" or "that function" as referring to the conjuring of spirits.

39. Weber ([1910–20] 1985) 246; "Lebewesen": Gierke 1887, 121; cf. also: "Invisible beings that live in accordance with laws of their own" (Weber [1910–20] 1985, 247).

40. Kafka [1920–23] 1983/1990, 143/107; [1912–17] 1967/1973, 358/267*. Compare also Kafka [1912–17] 1967/1973, 356/265*: "This activity at my desk, in and of itself ghostly, overgrows me."

41. Kafka [1920–23] 1983, 168; [1907–21] 2004, CD-ROM 643.

42. "Ganz unübersichtlich große Organisation": Kafka [1914–15] 1990/1998, 253/254*. On the crucial role of Kafka's office writings for his literary work, see Benno

belief in the calculability of rational organizations, the "paths" of the court in *The Trial* are "incalculable," while the bureaucratic apparatus in *The Castle* arrives at its decisions "arbitrarily, . . . all by itself."[43] Instead of a "far-reaching congruence" between Max Weber's *Economy and Society* (1910–20) and Franz Kafka's *The Trial* (1914–15) and *The Castle* (1922), as has been postulated by Hans-Ulrich Derlien, one thus encounters fundamental differences between Weber's sociological theories and Kafka's novels.[44] We will first analyze *The Castle* (*Das Schloß*)—a text that centers on the figure of K., who arrives late one evening at a village claiming he has been hired as a land surveyor by the local authorities. A phone call to the castle that overlooks the village contradicts K.'s claims, but then a return call seems to confirm his assertions. The novel describes K.'s ensuing struggle to gain entrance to the castle, detailing his encounter with an inscrutable bureaucratic apparatus that manifests itself in a multitude of employees.

Max Weber characterized the "bureaucratic organization with . . . its division of responsibilities [*Kompetenzen*], its statutes and hierarchically differentiated chains of command" as a "*living* machine" that creates "an iron cage for the bondage of the future to which . . . human beings will . . . one day be helplessly forced to submit."[45] In *The Castle*, the inaccessible authorities also have a life of their own, while each of the employees has a specific "responsibility."[46] However, the boundaries between the responsibilities of different officials are not always clearly defined: "The secret lies in the regulations about responsibility. In fact, it is not true and in a *large living organization* cannot be true that there is only one specific secretary responsible for each case. It is just that one of them has the chief responsibility, while many others have a partial responsibility of lesser degree."[47]

The autopoetic agency of a "large living organization," emphasized

Wagner, "Poseidons Gehilfe: Kafka und die Statistik" (2002), "Überlieferung und Kommentar" (2004), and "Insuring Nietzsche: Kafka's Files" (2006).

43. Kafka's phrase "unberechenbar" ([1914–15] 1990/1998, 167/158*) can be translated as both "unpredictable" and "incalculable"; "arbitrarily": Kafka [1922] 1992/1998, 86/68.

44. Derlien, "Bureaucracy in Art and Analysis" (1991), 4.

45. Weber, *Wirtschaft und Gesellschaft* ([1910–20] 1985), 835.

46. "Zuständigkeit": Kafka, *Das Schloß* ([1922] 1992/1998), 322/267*.

47. Ibid.

here by its secretary Bürgel, precludes a single official from "keep[ing] together on his desk all of the ramifications of the smallest incident."[48] Simultaneously, it becomes impossible to attribute specific decisions of the "apparatus" to individual natural persons:

> When a matter has been deliberated for a very long time, it may happen, . . . that suddenly, like lightning, in some *unforeseeable* place, which cannot be located later on, a settlement emerges that usually very correctly but nonetheless *arbitrarily* brings the matter to a close. It is as if the bureaucratic apparatus . . . had made the decision *all by itself*, without help from the officials. Of course, *no miracle took place* and some official or other certainly wrote the settlement or reached an unwritten decision, at any rate one cannot determine from down here or indeed even from the administrative offices, which official reached the decision in this case and on what grounds.[49]

Just as Gierke described the corporate organism as "autopoetically [*selbsttätig*] intervening into the external world," the bureaucratic apparatus in the castle acts in a seemingly supernatural manner, "all by itself" (*aus sich selbst heraus*).[50] The site of any official decision therefore remains as inscrutable as the reasons for it. At the same time, Kafka's novel characterizes the transformation of contingency that takes place in the decision as in itself contingent: the settlement, which emerges, closes the matter "usually very correctly but nonetheless *arbitrarily*" (*meistens sehr richtig, so doch immerhin willkürlich*).

48. Ibid., 322/267. The blurring of an unambiguous division of responsibility within the bureaucracy of the castle thus clearly differs from the principles of the Workers' Accident Insurance, which in 1910 introduced the policy of delegating the entire administration and handling of a specific claim to one single employee: "The favorable results experienced by the institute in the uniform settlement of compensation claims by one and the same agent suggested the idea of also delegating to one and the same agent the collection of delinquent premiums, by both administrative and judicial means and through other legal methods" (Kafka, *Amtliche Schriften* [1907–21] 2004, CD-ROM 288–89).

49. Kafka, *Das Schloß* ([1922] 1992/1993), 86/68*.

50. Gierke, *Das Wesen der menschlichen Verbände* [The nature of human associations] ([1902] 1954), 30.

Max Weber described an efficient organization as oriented toward the rational "optimum" of an "accelerated, . . . precise, and unequivocal settlement of official matters."[51] The contingency of an arbitrary decision that could just as well have assumed a different form is thereby dissolved into the uniform, consistent treatment of cases whose (equally contingent) singularity makes no difference.[52] In *The Castle*, by contrast, one can observe a predominance of self-referential recursion, which re-opens the realm of contingency that was seemingly settled in a decision. Without solving or avoiding the problem of "arbitrariness," this recursion prevents an accelerated settlement of new cases by necessitating a constant scrutiny of old decisions.[53] The agencies in the novel function almost exclusively as "control agencies," which reach decisions about previously made decisions: "Only a total stranger can ask such a question. Are there control agencies? There are *only* control agencies." But these intervene "by definition *too late*," so that, instead of a rational settlement, "confusion" ensues.[54] The autopoetic agency of the apparatus is consequently no guarantee for its efficiency or rationality and serves in fact only to prevent the attribution of responsibility to specific individuals or natural persons.

Similar to the merging of distinct corporate members into the unity of an "aggregate person," the differences among the various officials in the castle are obliterated in the ostensible "homogeneity [*Einheitlichkeit*] of the service."[55] In his *Office Writings* Kafka emphasized: "The institution and its members [are] actually one and the same." Likewise, in Kafka's

51. Weber, *Wirtschaft und Gesellschaft* ([1910–20] 1985), 562.

52. On the irrelevance of the contingent, singular aspects of a specific case, see also Weber [1910–20] 1985, 562: "The fact that the bureaucratic apparatus can produce and indeed does produce certain obstacles to a settlement that *conforms* to the *individual* case is not the issue here."

53. The manner in which decisions are made by the authorities in the castle thus prevents a distinction between "continuity and discontinuity," since decisions here cannot be "used as premises of further decision-making" (Niklas Luhmann, *Organisation und Entscheidung* [Organization and decision] [1978], 16, 15).

54. Kafka [1922] 1992/1998, 82/65*, 76/60*.

55. Kafka [1922] 1992/1998, 72/57*; see also: "Yet what amazed him even more . . . was the homogeneity [*Einheitlichkeit*] of the official service there" (31/21*). On the merging of distinct corporate members into a single unity, see Gierke's theory of the aggregate corporate person described on 48, above.

novel, K. cannot perceive any difference between the assistants, who have been assigned to him by the castle: "I can only see with my eyes and *cannot distinguish between you with them*, ... I consider you *one single person*."[56] Furthermore, the officials and secretaries "fill in for one another," serving as organs of an intangible organization without any differences that would clearly distinguish them. In his function as village secretary, Momus is not "an independent individual" but "an instrument upon which Klamm's hand lies." Klamm, in turn, does not possess a stable, natural body but constantly changes his physical appearance: "They say he looks completely different when he comes into the village and different when he leaves it. ... And even within the village there are some rather significant differences in the reports, differences in size, posture, corpulence, beard."[57]

Klamm's mutability is given a natural explanation. Just as the autopoetic agency of the bureaucratic apparatus constitutes "no miracle," the instability of Klamm's body does not "come about by magic." Instead, as Olga remarks, "a man such as Klamm, who is so often the object of yearning and so rarely attained, easily takes on *a variety of shapes* in the imaginations of people."[58] Yet the ostensible lack of a stable, natural body simultaneously points to the intangible corporate body that underlies an "invisible aggregate person" such as the castle.[59]

In contrast to the embodiment of the Middle Rhine Company in Bertrand's "unimaginable figure" (268/237*), the living organization of the castle is personified neither in Klamm nor in the count, who is mentioned by K. only at the beginning of the novel. Whereas in *The Sleepwalkers* Bertrand figures as the "head" (274/243) of the joint-stock company, here "the apparatus in its inextricable largeness" appears as a polycentric

---

56. Kafka [1907–21] 2004, CD-ROM 643; Kafka, *Das Schloß* ([1922] 1992/1998), 28/18–19*. Compare also: "'There is *no difference* between the peasants and the Castle,' said the teacher" (19/9) and ibid., 78/61*: "Letting his eyes wander from the assistants to the chairman and back again to the assistants; he found the smiles of all three *indistinguishably alike*."

57. Kafka [1922] 1992/1998, 229/188, 124/115, 216/176.

58. Ibid., 86/68, 216/176, 222/181; see also ibid., 67/51*: "But ... I know nothing of Klamm, ... he is completely inaccessible [*unerreichbar*] to me."

59. "Unsichtbare Verbandsperson": Gierke ([1902] 1954), 30. Mark Anderson has emphasized the link between the Gothic novel and what he calls Kafka's "bureaucratic Gothic" (391) in his "The Shadow of the Modern" (2002).

unity, incarnating itself in a multitude of employees—Klamm, Erlanger, Bürgel, Sordini, Sortini—who act, like the villagers, under the "influence of the Castle."[60] In the course of the novel, K. also succumbs to this suggestive "influence" that increasingly paralyzes him.

As if insisting on a literal reading of the figurative dimension inherent in and constitutive of contemporary juridical theory, Kafka's novel invokes a merging of human and corporate bodies, highlighting the somatic effects caused by K.'s dealings with the living organization of the castle. The literary text thus describes in detail the physiological process of K.'s gradual descent into an ever-increasing "distraction" and "fatigue," which overtake him after his arrival in the village.[61] Checking in at the inn, K. "in his somnolence" does not notice the telephone that is installed above his sleeping place. His absentmindedness and exhaustion become more pronounced on the next day after he speaks with the village teacher, who dwells on the unity of village and castle: "But K. was *distracted*, the conversation had irritated him. For the first time since coming here, he felt truly *tired*. At first, the long journey hadn't seemed like much of a strain to him. . . . He felt an *irresistible* urge to seek out new acquaintances, but each new acquaintance only *increased* his *fatigue*. In his present state, if he could force himself to prolong his walk to the Castle entrance, that would be more than enough."[62]

It is this "power of scarcely perceptible influences" that K. rightly fears and to which he at last succumbs in his dealings with the authorities of the castle.[63] Drawing on early-twentieth-century medicine, the novel thereby appropriates clinical descriptions of a neurasthenic "weakness of the will that is caused mostly by external influences," simultaneously linking this medical conception to juridical and sociological representations of invisible corporate organisms that take possession of human bodies.[64] In the

---

60. "Die Behörde in ihrer unentwirrbaren Größe": Kafka [1922] 1992/1998, 226/184*; "Einfluß": ibid., 249/204 and 250/205.

61. "Zerstreutheit": Kafka [1922] 1992/1998, 62/48; "Müdigkeit": ibid., 147/118.

62. Ibid., 11/3*, 19/10*.

63. Ibid., 35/24.

64. The quoted material can be found in Karl Birnbaum, *Die krankhafte Willensschwäche und ihre Erscheinungsformen* [Pathological weakness of the will and its manifestations] (1911), 66. On the medical representation of abulia, see also F. C. R. Eschle, *Die krankhafte Willensschwäche* [Pathological weakness of the will] (1904); and John H. Smith, "Abulia: Sexuality and Diseases of the Will in the Late Nineteenth Century"

beginning, K. "still [seems] but slightly affected" by the power of the inaccessible organization and criticizes the "respect for the authorities" that is instilled in the villagers "in many different ways and from all sides." Yet in his "exchange [*Verkehr*] with [the] bureaucracies," K. himself is gradually overcome by a fatigue and distraction that prevent him from standing his ground in the "struggle" with the "remote and invisible gentlemen." It is not only Frieda who surrenders to "forces" for which she is "no match," when she allows herself to be "enchanted" by the assistants.[65] K.'s "fatigue," which corresponds to contemporary medical descriptions of a neurasthenic "abulia" or weakness of the will, similarly prevents him from taking advantage of the few opportunities that would allow him to break through the operative seclusion of the castle.

Already on the first day he hesitates, "no doubt out of *fatigue*" (*Müdigkeit*), to leave the road that encircles the castle at a never-changing distance. In his confrontation with Jeremias, it is "out of fatigue" (*Müdigkeit*) that K. fails to defend himself "as vigorously . . . as he ought to have done."[66] And this "truly great fatigue" also destroys the "almost never occurring opportunity" of K.'s nocturnal interview with secretary Bürgel in which the latter ceases "to be an official." K. has the chance to overcome the seemingly impenetrable "seamlessness [*Lückenlosigkeit*] of the official organization," since Bürgel's "vulnerability . . . literally tears apart the official organization." Yet just as the villagers "themselves contribute" to making the bureaucracy appear unassailable, the cause of K.'s failure lies—in Bürgel's words—in himself: "Get going now, . . . here everything is full of opportunities. Except that some opportunities are, as it were, too great to be acted upon; there are things that fail through nothing other than *themselves*."[67]

(1989). On the uncertain boundaries between neurasthenia and abulia, see Eschle (1904), 91. On "drowsiness" in neurasthenia, see also Beard 1880, 45–46; on the "feeling of profound exhaustion" in neurasthenia, see Beard 1880, 66.

65. Kafka, *Das Schloß* ([1922] 1992/1998), 137/110*, 223/182, 73/57*, 35/24, 73/58, 300/249, 306/253. Frieda even attempts to justify her disloyal behavior by suggesting a hypnotic influence of her environment: "Their [the assistants'] eyes, these naive but sparkling eyes, somehow remind me of the eyes of Klamm, yes, that's it, it is Klamm's gaze that sometimes leaps from their eyes and *cuts through* me" (171/139*).

66. Ibid., 19/10, 309/256*. Compare also Kafka 1922, 46/33*: "K. could have stated his wish more emphatically, but he was *distracted* by this particular response of the landlord."

67. Ibid., 309/256*, 320/265*, 324/269, 320/265, 324/269*, 223/182*, 327/271.

As K. continues to lose control over his own body, his "numb indiffer-
ence and drowsiness" prevent him from seizing the miraculous chance
that presents itself. While Bürgel points out that K. only needs to "somehow formulate his request, the fulfillment of which is ready and even
heading toward him," K. is caught in a somnambulist haze: "K. was asleep,
but it *wasn't really sleep*, he was still hearing what Bürgel was saying, perhaps better than earlier when he was still awake though dead tired, one
word after another accosted his ears, but that irritating *consciousness had
faded away*." K.'s trance thus approaches a state of light hypnosis: "He had
become so used to Bürgel's soft, complacent voice, which was obviously
trying in vain *to put itself to sleep*, that it *enhanced rather than disturbed his
own sleep*."[68] No longer able to pursue his own intention, K. seems caught
in a hypnotic rapport that links him with Bürgel in a "peculiar, entirely
inappropriate *exchange of persons*" (*ein sonderbarer, ganz und gar unpassender
Austausch der Personen*).[69]

In this "exchange of influences"—to borrow a phrase from Georg Simmel—neither Bürgel nor K. is clearly dominant.[70] Bürgel cannot resist

68. Ibid., 342/284*, 325/270, 318/264*, 322/267. K.'s distracted, somnolent state in
this situation is anticipated in various passages of the novel—see, for instance, his
first exchange with the landlady: "'What?' K. asked, *awakening* from a certain distraction [*Zerstreutheit*]" (Kafka [1922] 1992/1998, 62/48).

69. Ibid., 317/263*. The phrase "Austausch der Personen" used here by Kafka is
reminiscent of his short text "Persönlicher Verkehr mit den Unternehmern" [Per-
sonal communication with the entrepreneurs] (1911), where Kafka emphasizes the
positive effects of a "gegenseitige Aussprache" (mutual exchange) between the secretaries of the Accident Insurance and the directors of the insured companies (in
Amtliche Schriften [1907–21] 2004, 242–43).

70. Compare Simmel ([1908] 1992), 165:

A highly complex interaction . . . is thus concealed here under the semblance
of one element's clear superiority in contrast to the other's willingness to be
led. . . . Perhaps the most characteristic case of this type is offered by hypnotic
suggestion. An eminent hypnotist has pointed out that in every hypnosis an
influence, albeit one not easy to define, is exerted on the hypnotist by the
hypnotized subject; without it the effect could not be achieved. Whereas external appearance here presents an absolute exertion of influence on the one
side and an absolute yielding to that influence on the other, here too this
semblance covers an interaction, an *exchange of influences*, which transforms
the purely unilateral relation of dominance and subordination into a sociological form.

the "bewitching . . . invitation" of K.'s physical presence, so that it becomes "impossible [for him] to deny any request."[71] At the same time, the somnolent K. can no longer formulate this very request—as if K.'s body were now controlled by the "separate corporate will" of the intangible organization.[72] It is precisely K.'s inability to explain this process that foregrounds the "power of *scarcely perceptible* influences" to which he has been exposed since his arrival: "True, K. remained conscious of the fact that his *fatigue [Müdigkeit]* today had done him greater harm than all the unfavorable circumstances; why couldn't he, who had believed that he could *depend on his own body* and who, if it hadn't been for that belief, wouldn't have set out at all, why couldn't he put up with a few bad nights and one sleepless one, why did he become so *uncontrollably* tired, here of all places."[73] K. can no longer depend on "his own body," since his corporal system has become complicit with the intangible corporate organism—a process that has removed K.'s "own body" from his command, rendering it "uncontrollably tired." A similar possession by an intangible corporate aggregate takes place in Kafka's novel *The Trial* as well.

Like *The Castle*, *The Trial* (*Der Proceß*) centers on the somatic effects exerted on Joseph K. by his dealings with an intangible, "living" organiza-

71. "Berückende . . . Einladung": Kafka, *Das Schloß* ([1922] 1992/1998), 324/269*.

72. "Sonderwille": Hafter, *Die Delikts- und Straffähigkeit der Personenverbände* (1903), 43.

73. Kafka, *Das Schloß* ([1922] 1992/1998), 35/24*, 329–30/274. George M. Beard's *Practical Treatise on Nervous Exhaustion (Neurasthenia)* (1880) similarly emphasizes the "feeling of profound exhaustion" in neurasthenia, stressing a comparable unreliability of the neurasthenic's body:

> Neurasthenic patients *cannot depend upon themselves.* One day they can do with impunity what on the following day brings about distressing results. At one time they may be able to work hard, take long walks, and use the brain severely—but, under the same circumstances, in a few days they find themselves unequal to any of the kind. . . . When planning to go upon a journey or to undertake any responsibility of any kind, they cannot tell a day beforehand whether they will be equal to it—their strength is liable to drop away from them at any time when it is needed. (66)

The German translation from 1883, which Kafka might have read, contains this passage on page 55. On fatigue and neurasthenia, see also Anson Rabinbach, "Mental Fatigue, Neurasthenia, and Civilization" in his *The Human Motor* (1992), 146–78.

tion. But before examining this *Proceß*, which unfolds quite literally as a physiological "process" clandestinely "encroaching step by step on Joseph K.'s very body," it is first necessary to analyze Kafka's representation of the "large and intransparent organization" that gradually assumes possession of Joseph K.[74] The text opens famously with the description of "one morning" when Joseph K., without having done anything truly wrong, is unexpectedly arrested by two guards. One year later, two gentlemen come again for the young bank official, taking him outside of town where they kill the docile unresisting K. In chronicling the intervening year of K.'s case, his struggles and encounters with an invisible and intangible judicial system, the novel highlights the autopoetic agency of the "vast *organism*" whose "inaccessible courts" elude direct observation.[75]

As K.'s attorney emphasizes, even the court officials cannot gain a comprehensive overview of a single case: "Their involvement is limited to that part of the trial circumscribed for them by the law, and they generally know less about what follows, and thus about the results of their own efforts, than the defense." At the same time, K.'s lawyer describes the inner life of this "judicial organism" as "maintaining . . . a state of eternal equilibrium," which seems to imply a stable, calculable self-regulation. Yet according to the painter Titorelli, it remains unpredictable how the complex, inscrutable apparatus will react to individual changes such as an "ostensible acquittal":

> There is no further change in the files except for adding to them the certification of innocence, the acquittal, and the grounds for the acquittal. Otherwise the files remain in circulation; as required by the uninterrupted traffic of the court offices, they are passed on to the higher courts, come back to the lower ones, shuttling [*pendeln*] back and forth with larger or smaller oscillations, longer or shorter interruptions. These paths are *incalculable*. Viewed from the outside it may sometimes appear that everything has been long since forgotten, the file has been lost, and the acquittal is absolute. No initiate would ever believe that. No file is ever lost, there

74. "Wenn mir jetzt der Proceß förmlich im Geheimen *immer näher an den Leib rückt*": Kafka, *Der Proceß* ([1914–15] 1990/1998), 197/187*; "large and intransparent organization": ibid., 263/254*.

75. Ibid., 126/120, 128/121.

is no forgetting in the court. Someday—quite unexpectedly—some judge or other takes a closer look at the file, realizes that the case is still active, and orders an immediate arrest.[76]

The organism's self-regulation, particularly evident in the uninterrupted circulation of the files, does not proceed rationally but in an incalculable and seemingly arbitrary manner. Simultaneously, actions of the intangible organization cannot be attributed to its "organs" as natural persons or individuals. In his first interrogation, Joseph K. still accuses the "officials of corruption." But he soon realizes that "behind all the pronouncements of this court ... there exists an extensive organization"—an insight that renders a personal attribution of responsibility impossible. The indirect agency of the intangible organization that acts through its organs is emphasized even more strongly in K.'s attempt to prevent the punishment of the two guards who arrested him: "If I had suspected that they [the guards] would be punished, or even known they faced possible punishment, I would never have mentioned their names. Because I don't even consider them guilty; *it is the organization that is guilty.*" Yet even at this stage, K. underestimates the omnipresence of an intangible corporate organism that exerts its agency ubiquitously, "connected" to numerous natural persons.[77] The court's "peculiar *power of attraction*" thus eludes K.'s perception, even though it affects K. himself. In the course of the novel, it is accordingly Joseph K.'s body that succumbs to the judicial organism, despite K.'s increasingly desperate attempts to withstand the court's influence.[78]

Even upon his arrest, K. is so "*entranced [hingenommen]* by the inspector and the guards" that he does not notice the presence of Rabensteiner, Kulich, and Kaminer in Miss Bürstner's room. His exclusive concentration

76. Ibid., 124/118, 126/119. 164/154, 166-67/158-59*.

77. Ibid., 15/9*, 56/50*, 56/50, 90/83*: "connected,": ibid., 141/134; see also 158/150: "But [Titorelli] sat down in his chair again and said, half in jest and half in explanation: '*But everything is part of the court.*'" See also 172-73/164: "'Didn't you know that there were court offices here? There are court offices in practically every attic, why shouldn't they be here too? In fact my studio is part of the court offices too, but the court has placed it at my disposal.' K. wasn't so shocked at having found law offices here; he was more shocked at himself, at his ignorance in matters of the court."

78. Ibid., 35/29. Compare also: "The painter's work *attracted* K. more than he wished" (154/146).

on the bank officials, in turn, "diverts his attention" from the "inspector's and the guards' departure," leading him to question his "presence of mind." In a parallel manner, K. does not notice the chancellery director in the room of the attorney Huld, until Huld calls attention to him. Then again, after having left Huld's house, K. "in his distraction" (*Zerstreutheit*) fails to see the car in which his uncle is waiting for him.[79]

To what extent the success of the proceedings against Joseph K. rests on K.'s voluntary acceptance of the trial is shown with particular clarity in the famous cathedral chapter where K. willingly obeys the summons of a "priest." K., who had been instructed to show the cathedral to an Italian business traveler, is just about to return to his "office." But while he is leaving the cathedral, a priest calls out for him: "He [Joseph K.] had almost left the area of the pews and was approaching the *open space*, . . . when he heard the voice of the priest for the first time. . . . How it penetrated the willingly resonant cathedral! It was not the congregation that the priest addressed, however; it was quite clear, and *there was no escaping it*; he called: 'Joseph K.!'"[80]

Even though there is no escaping the fact that K. is addressed by his name, he still retains the ability to evade the interpellation of the court. Since he is not being subjected to any physical force or direct coercion, he could simply ignore the call: "K. hesitated and stared at the floor. For the time being he was *still free*; he could still keep walking and make his getaway through one of the three small dark wooden doors not far from him. That would mean that he had not understood or that he had indeed understood but could not be bothered to respond. But if he turned around, he was *caught [festgehalten]*, for then he had made the *confession [Geständnis]* that he had understood quite well, that he was indeed the person called, and *that he was willing to obey*." K. is quite aware that he could simply walk away, preserving his freedom by ignoring the court. But the cleric's silence prompts him to turn his head:

If the priest had called out again, K. would surely have walked away, but since all remained still, however long K. waited, he finally turned his head a bit, for he wanted to see what the priest was doing now. He was standing quietly in the pulpit as before, but he had clearly noticed the turning of K.'s head. It would have

79. Ibid., 24/18*, 25/19*, 109/102, 116/109*.
80. Ibid., 221/211, 220/210, 221/211*.

been a childish game of hide-and-seek for K. not to completely turn around now. He did so and he was summoned closer by a beckoning motion of the priest's finger. Now that everything could be done openly, he ran with long, rapid strides toward the pulpit.[81]

K. surrenders to the call of the court, even though he could choose to evade it. The voluntary acceptance of a seemingly superior authority, whose functioning depends on this recognition by the surrendering subject, is also described in Althusser's famous essay on "Ideology and Ideological State Apparatuses" (1970). There, Althusser formulated his famous concept of "interpellation" by developing a narrative scenario that is nearly identical to this episode in Kafka's novel:

> The ideology ... "functions" ... in consequence of a certain process that we shall name interpellation. One can conceive of this process after the model of the most common everyday police (or other) call: "Hey, you there!"
>
> Assuming that the theoretical scene we have imagined takes place in the street, the called [interpellé] individual turns around. By this simple physical turn of 180 degrees he becomes a subject. Why? Because he has acknowledged [reconnaît] that the call [interpellation] was "really" addressed to him and that it was "really" him who was called" (and not somebody else). .... Whether by a verbal shout or by a whistle, the one called always acknowledges [reconnaît] that it was really him who was called. That is a peculiar phenomenon, however, and—despite the great number of people who "have something on their conscience"—it cannot be explained solely by a "feeling of guilt."[82]

Althusser describes here the "peculiar phenomenon" of an interpellation that is not just recognized but voluntarily acknowledged by the subject, even though it could be easily ignored. In a parallel manner, Kafka's *The Trial* emphasizes that Joseph K. could simply ignore the call: "That would mean he hadn't understood or that he had indeed understood but couldn't be bothered to respond."[83] Both acts thereby correspond to the

81. Ibid., 221–22/211*.

82. Althusser [1970] 1976/2001, 126/118*. On Althusser's concept of interpellation, see now also Judith Butler's *The Psychic Life of Power* (1997), 106 ff.

83. Kafka, *Der Proceß* ([1914–15] 1990/1998), 221/210.

strange process of hypnotic suggestion, which relies on the autosuggestion of the hypnotized subject who chooses to believe in the hypnotist's
power. As Hippolyte Bernheim put it: "The induction of sleep does not
depend on the hypnotist but on the hypnotized subject; it is *his own belief*
that puts him to sleep."[84] The court's suggestive power over the paralyzed
Joseph K. likewise depends on K.'s voluntary recognition of the court's
authority.[85]

The court's paralyzing influence on Joseph K. becomes increasingly
pronounced in the second part of the novel as K. repeatedly falls into
"states of extreme fatigue" (*Müdigkeit*), in which "his thoughts are drift-
ing *without any exertion of his will*" (*willenlos*). At the beginning of the novel,
K. still feels "scarcely affected" (*wenig betroffen*) by the trial, but now he is
"completely numbed [*gänzlich benommen*] by the mere decision to defend
himself." As the text describes it: "His situation was no longer completely
independent of the course of the trial, *he himself* had been incautious
enough to mention the trial to a few acquaintances with a certain *inexplicable* feeling of gratification. . . . It was no longer a matter of accepting
or rejecting the trial, he was in the midst of it. . . . If he was *tired*, he was
in trouble."[86]

The trial not only consumes K.'s energy at the office, where "he
spends many an hour in merely the most superficial appearance of actual work."[87] Even in the court proceedings K.'s vigilance is lulled by the
intangible, omnipresent judicial organization: "And now of all times,

84. Bernheim [1886a] 1888/1964, 269/190*.

85. K.'s voluntary acknowledgment of the court thus constitutes the depressing
opposite to the Gnat's liberating proposal in Lewis Carroll's *Through the Looking-Glass*
([1871] 1971), where Alice is advised to lose her name: "The Gnat . . . remarked: 'I sup-
pose you don't want to lose your name?' 'No, indeed,' Alice said a little anxiously. 'And
yet I don't know,' the Gnat went on. . . . 'only think how convenient it would be if you
could manage to go home without it! For instance, if the governess wanted to call you
to your lessons, she would call out 'Come here—,' and there she would have to leave
off, because *there wouldn't be any name for her to call*, and of course *you wouldn't have to
go*'" (134–35). See also Kafka [1914–15] 1990/1998, 222/212: "'You're Joseph K.,' said the
priest. . . . 'Yes,' K. said; he recalled how openly he had always said *his name*; for some
time now it had been a burden."

86. Kafka [1914–15] 1990/1998, 131/124*, 138/131*, 139/132*, 131/125.

87. Ibid., 209/199; see also 175/166*: "The resolution [to dismiss the lawyer] had
drained K. of a great deal of energy the day he planned to visit the lawyer; he worked
even more slowly than usual."

when he should be gathering all his strength to act, previously unknown doubts about his own vigilance [*Wachsamkeit*] had to arise." Joseph K.'s "fatigue" (*Müdigkeit*) and 'distraction" (*Zerstreutheit*), which correspond to K.'s increasing exhaustion in *The Castle*, thus recall medical descriptions of neurasthenic "abulia"—a pathological weakness of the will that renders K. a defenseless victim of the court proceedings.[88] As in *The Castle*, K.'s control of his "own" body slips away from him. The intangible judicial organism gradually takes possession of K.'s body, turning it into an "organ" of the court. During a visit to the court offices, K. is thus caught by an unexpected attack of vertigo that renders him so weak that he has to be held up by two officers who escort him out of the chancelleries—a loss of control that K. can barely explain and that he himself comes to interpret as related to the court proceedings: "His normally sound constitution had never provided him with such surprises before. Was his *body* going to rebel and offer him *a new trial* [*einen neuen Proceß*], since he was handling the old one so easily?"[89]

The "new trial" offered by K.'s body implies a complicity between K.'s own body and the living organization of the court, a merging of human and corporate body that occurs first surreptitiously and then becomes progressively pronounced. By introducing this new trial, the novel emphasizes the somatic effects emanating from a judicial organism that gradually seizes control of K.'s body—as if K.'s corporal system were being "possessed" by the corporate unity of an "aggregate person" whose "homogenous life . . . passes through its very part[s]."[90] This absorption of K.'s body by the unity of an intangible "aggregate person" is literalized at

---

88. Ibid., 144/137*, 213/203. See also Beard 1880, 22–23: "Deficient Mental Control.—Inability to concentrate the intellect on any task, as in writing or thinking, is a notable symptom [of neurasthenia]. The mind wanders away in every direction, and when brought back by an effort of the will, is liable to be soon lost again in reverie. In some cases, the exercise of concentration, or even slight attention, is exceedingly irksome and painful. . . . Such a person often finds himself absorbed in *a kind of dream*, perhaps sitting quite still and forgetful of the work to which he has directed himself." The equivalent in the German translation of 1883 is on 18. On the indistinct boundaries between abulia and neurasthenia, see also Eschle 1904, 91: "The latter [abulic] form of nervousness or neurasthenia constitutes, as it were, the paradigm of that weakness of will that I have termed 'perseverative insufficiency.'" On "absent-mindedness" in abulia, see Eschle 1904, 85.

89. Kafka [1914–15] 1990/1998, 85/79.

90. Gierke 1887, 625.

the end of the novel, when "two gentlemen" come for K., picking him up at his home: "Just beyond the entrance . . . they took his arms in a manner K. had never before experienced in walking with anyone. They held their shoulders right behind his, did not bend their arms, but instead wrapped them around the entire length of his, seizing K.'s hands below with a well-trained, practiced and *irresistible* grip. K. walked along stiffly between them; . . . now the three of them formed such a close *unity* that had one of them been smashed they would all have been smashed. It was a *unity* as it can be formed almost only by lifeless matter" (*eine Einheit, wie sie fast nur Lebloses bilden kann*).[91]

In representing the "unity" formed by K. and the guards, Kafka appropriates a dream of his, in which he and his fiancée Felice Bauer were walking along a street in Prague. Kafka reported the dream in detail to Felice in a letter dated February 11, 1913: "Although not walking arm in arm, we were *even closer* to each other than one is when walking arm in arm. Alas, it is difficult to describe on paper the invention I had made. . . . How am I to describe the way we walked in the dream? When walking arm in arm, the arms touch in only two places, and each person preserves his *independence*; but as we walked our shoulders also touched and we were joined *along the entire length* of our arms."[92]

In his letter, Kafka seemed favorably disposed toward this dissolution of his "independence" (*Selbständigkeit*), but the bachelor ultimately avoided a permanent merging with Felice Bauer by breaking off the engagement. In *The Trial*, however, Joseph K. is thoroughly assimilated by the institution of the court. Gierke's *Theory of Associations* describes how the "plurality" of distinct corporate members are coupled into the aggregate "unity" of a corporate body where "the subjects that form parts of it are no longer *separate, self-contained* persons."[93] In a corresponding manner, Joseph K.'s body and the guards' bodies merge to form a corporate and corporal unity. At the novel's beginning, the arrested K. still makes "a movement as if he were *tearing himself loose from the two men*, who were, however, standing at some distance from him."[94] But by now the trial has "encroached" so closely "on his very body" that the life of the emerging

---

91. Kafka [1914–15] 1990/1998, 237/226*.
92. Kafka, *Briefe an Felice* ([1912–17] 1967/1973), 294/213–14*.
93. "Getrennte, in sich geschlossene Personen": Gierke 1887, 182.
94. Kafka [1914–15] 1990/1998, 10/5.

"unity" can no longer be separated from that of its parts.[95] Like Mark Twain's representation of the Siamese twins Luigi and Angelo in *Those Extraordinary Twins* (cf. 62, above), Kafka's novel literalizes the juridical and sociological descriptions of aggregate corporate bodies. Whereas Albert Schäffle emphasized that "the individual persons who grow together into one social body do not *corporally grow together*," *The Trial* describes a bodily aggregate whose parts appear as literally merged: "Had one of them been smashed they would all have been smashed."[96]

K.'s body is absorbed by a unity beyond the control of his will: the two gentlemen seize K.'s hands "with an . . . *irresistible* grip." The separate will of this corporate unity is, however, not completely identical with the intentions of the two guards either: "Now all three of them, *in complete accord* [*in vollem Einverständnis*], crossed a bridge in the moonlight, the men *yielding willingly* to K.'s slightest move."[97] Appropriating and transforming contemporary representations of invisible corporate bodies, Kafka's novel describes how K.'s body gradually succumbs to the large living organization—a "new trial" that comes to coincide with the actual court proceedings. At the end of a prolonged juridical and physiological process, Joseph K. becomes part of a "vast judicial organism" that "sucks in" the bodies of natural persons.[98] But the juridical "particularity of ascribing a *certain* life to lifeless matter" not only allows for the legal conceptualization of an invisible aggregate person.[99] It also leads to a "certain" lifelessness of the animate, since K. is dissolved into a "unity as it can be formed *almost* only by lifeless matter" (*eine Einheit, wie sie fast nur Lebloses bilden kann*). In Kafka's *The Trial*, the animation of the inanimate thus produces a mortification that is not limited to a merely figurative depersonalization but is literalized in K.'s execution.

95. Ibid., 197/187.

96. Schäffle, *Bau und Leben des socialen Körpers* ([1875a] 1996), 18; Kafka [1914–15] 1990/1998, 237/226.

97. Kafka [1914–15] 1990/1998, 239/228*.

98. "New trial": ibid., 85/79; "vast judicial organism": ibid., 126/119; "sucks in": Weber [1910] 1927, 82.

99. "Besonderheit, dem Leblosen ein *gewisses* Leben zuzuschreiben": Gierke, *Der Humor im deutschen Recht* (1871), 14.

Novels such as Broch's *The Sleepwalkers* and Kafka's *The Trial* and *The Castle* adapted medical and legal representations of hypnotic and corporate agency. In addition, the scientific notions analyzed in this book also played a crucial role for the poetological strategies and manifestos of modernism and the avant-garde in the early twentieth century. The loss of control over one's "own" body constitutes the center of Alfred Döblin's early narratives "The Dancer and Her Body" (1910) and "The Somnambulist" (1914).[1] But Döblin's "Berlin Program" (1914) similarly invoked the medical notion of "dépersonnalisation," calling for a "depersonation" of the author in order to facilitate a new "cinema style."[2] What Döblin celebrated as "breaking the hegemony of the author"—thereby throwing off the restrictions of nineteenth-century realism—had been described by Pierre Janet as a clinical symptom of "psychasthenia," a neurosis marked by phenomena of "possession" and "depersonation."[3]

At the same time, Döblin's turn against traditional notions of authorship corresponds to the analysis of "automatic writing" in Janet's *L'automatisme psychologique* (1889).[4] Both authors, Döblin and Janet, thus anticipated a crucial aspect of André Breton's famous "Surrealist Manifesto" (1924), in which Breton described surrealism as emerging from a

1. Alfred Döblin,"Die Tänzerin und ihr Leib" (1910); and Döblin, "Die Nachtwandlerin' (1914).

2. Alfred Döblin,"An Romanautoren und ihre Kritiker Berliner Programm" ([1914] 1989); "depersonation": ibid., 123; 'Kinostil": ibid., 121; see also ibid., 122: "The hegemony of the author must be broken."

3. See Janet and Raymond, "Dépersonnalisation et possession chez un psychasthénique' (1904). Janet introduced the notion of "psychasthenia" in order to replace the vague concept of "neurasthenia."

4. See Janet 1889, esp. 376–404.

"psychic automatism" (*automatisme psychique*).[5] For Breton, the surrealist production of art occurred "under the dictation of pure thought, without any control by reason, beyond any aesthetic or moral consideration."[6]

Breton's programmatic definition of surrealism cited verbatim from Janet's medical study of *Psychological Automatism* (1889). Furthermore, in a footnote to his "Manifesto," Breton alluded to the "forensic" debate about the "irresponsibility" of somnambulist mediums.[7] He thereby drew on representations of possession that emerged from a mutual exchange among law, literature, and medicine to produce the popular tales of hypnotic crime along with its theatrical and cinematic enactments (chapters 1, 3, and 4). The legal discussion about the irresistible power of hypnotic suggestion coincided with juridical representations of invisible corporate bodies that assumed control of their possessed members or "organs" (chapter 2). Breton, however, appropriated the forensic debate about suggestion and automatism by applying it to future "criminal acts of unquestionably surrealistic character."[8]

Hoping that a court of law would determine the legal status of such criminal acts, Breton expressly lamented that "press crimes" were hardly prosecuted anymore. But if, against all expectations, a member of the surrealist movement were to be indicted for publishing an illegal text or for committing a crime, then—as Breton claimed—the defendant's innocence would be strikingly obvious. For just as a hypnotized subject acting under a criminal suggestion could not be considered the actual author of his or her deed, the person writing down a surrealist text or committing a criminal act in a state of psychic automatism could not be held legally responsible for that surrealist action: "In his defense, he [the surrealist artist] need only assert that he does not consider himself the author of his book insofar as the latter can only be regarded as a surrealist production, therefore excluding any question of merit or fault on the part of the person whose name it bears."[9]

5. Breton, "Manifeste du surréalisme" ([1924] 1988), 328. For a comparison of automatic writing with mediumship, see Rosalind Morris, "Modernity's Media and the End of Mediumship?" (2000), 465.

6. "Dictée de la pensée, en l'absence de tout contrôle exercé par la raison, en dehors de toute préoccupation esthétique ou morale": Breton [1924] 1988, 328.

7. Ibid., 344n1.

8. "Actes delictueux dont le caractère surréaliste ne pourra faire aucun doute": ibid.

9. Ibid.

In this manner, the surrealist poetics of *écriture automatique* invoked medical conceptions of automatic writing, while simultaneously borrowing from the late-nineteenth-century juridical debate about the irresponsibility of somnambulist mediums. The literary adaptation of legal theory and medicine was accordingly not limited to the textual levels of story and discourse in fictional narratives. Instead, the exchange of rhetorical figures and scientific concepts among law, literature, and medicine also encompassed the "depersonal poetics" and aesthetic programs that engendered the actual production of these literary texts.[10] The "marked tendency to repetition," observed by Gertrude Stein and Leon Solomons in their experiments on automatic writing and second personality at the *Harvard Psychological Laboratory*, reemerged as an aesthetic strategy in sentences such as "A rose is a rose is a rose."[11]

While avant-garde texts like Gertrude Stein's *Sacred Emily* transformed medical representations of automatism and possession into a strategy of literary writing, one can also find an unexpected equivalent to such a poetics in Rainer Maria Rilke's *The Notebooks of Malte Laurids Brigge* (1910). There the narrator, whose diary entries constitute the novel, remarks at one point: "For a while I can still write down all of this and say it. But there will be a day, when my hand will be far away from me and when I order it to write, it will write words that I do not mean. . . . I remember that it was often similar inside me before I started writing. But this time *I will be written*."[12]

Rilke here appropriates theories of psychical mediumship such as Carl du Prel's conception of "Automatic Writing" (1891), which—in contrast to Pierre Janet's *Psychological Automatism* (1889)—described such phenomena not as "inferior" or pathological but as enabling a communication with the spiritual realm.[13] The novel, in which the narrator is subsequently

10. "Depersonal poetics": Kleinschmidt, "Depersonale Poetik" (1982).

11. Solomons and Stein, "Normal Motor Automatism" (1896), 506. See also Gertude Stein, "Cultivated Motor Automatism: A Study of Character and Its Relation to Attention" (1898). The crucial role of automatism and mediumship for English modernism has been analyzed in Helen Sword's *Ghostwriting Modernism* (2001). On Gertrude Stein, see also Steven Meyer, *Irresistible Dictation* (2001).

12. Rilke, *Die Aufzeichnungen des Malte Laurids Brigge* ([1910] 1997), 47–48.

13. See Carl du Prel, "Automatisches Schreiben" (1891). The interrelation between Rilke's literary texts and spiritualist theories has been analyzed in detail by Priska Pytlik in her study *Okkultismus und Moderne* [Occultism and modernity] (2005), 167–194. On Carl du Prel's texts about hypnotic crimes, see above, 32. On du Prel's theories of

sent to the Salpêtrière by a doctor who does not understand his patient, thereby introduces a mystical dimension into the representation of "being written."[14] In this respect Rilke's valorization of spiritual communication offers a stark contrast to Guy de Maupassant's narrative, which served as the starting point for our analysis of scientific, literary, and cinematic representations of hypnotism and invisible corporate bodies; for *Le Horla* (1887) formulates a decidedly demonic account of automatic textual production under external command. In Maupassant's tale, the act of writing in his diary seems to provide the narrator with a realm of independence, allowing him to oppose the otherwise complete control and possession by an invisible organism. The closing diary entry that also constitutes the last lines of the text displays, however, the same tendency to repetition that Solomons and Stein described in 1896 as characteristic of automatic writing: "No . . . no . . . without doubt, without doubt . . . he is not dead. . . . Then . . . then . . . I will have to kill—myself."[15] The final sentence thus appears to be written under the influence of the occult invisible being that has seized control of the narrator's last refuge.

Maupassant's anticipation of automatic writing was alleged to go beyond his literary tales. According to medical pathographers who crudely equated narrator and author, Maupassant's own mental life prefigured a poetics of *écriture automatique* under a foreign will as well. In his neurological study *Maupassant's Illness* (1908), Gaston Vorberg described a psychic pathology that resembles the fatal hallucinations of the shoemaker Mollinier. In the spring of 1887, Jean Mollinier participated as a medium in several hypnotic experiments and consequently obeyed the command of an invisible spirit that demanded his death. In addition to publishing a narrative with a surprisingly similar plot, Maupassant is said to have lived through a comparable episode two years later. As reported by Vorberg and others, Maupassant himself then underwent a "depersonation" that in its loss of authorial agency comes close to the "death of the author."[16] On an afternoon in the fall of 1889—two years after conceiving

clairvoyance and psychic "television in time and space," see Andriopoulos, "Psychic Television" (2005).

14. Rilke [1910] 1997, 49.

15. "Non . . . non . . . sans aucun doute, sans aucun doute . . . il n'est pas mort. . . . Alors . . . alors . . . il va donc falloir que je me tue, moi!": Maupassant, *Le Horla* ([1887] 1979/1990), 938/302*.

16. Döblin [1914] 1989, 123; Barthes, "The Death of the Author" ([1968] 1977). On Maupassant's "depersonation," see Paul Sollier, *Les phénomènes d'autoscopie* (1903),

Le Horla and concurrent to the publication of Pierre Janet's *L'automatisme psychologique*—Maupassant withdrew to his study. The author asked his servant not to admit anyone who might disturb him in his writing. Yet two hours later, the door of his study opened. Maupassant looked up and saw himself enter the room. The apparition approached his desk and sat down in a chair, opposite the author. Everything he now wrote down followed the phantom's irresistible dictation. It was only after the work was completed that the hallucination disappeared.

10–11; Gaston Vorberg, *Guy de Maupassants Krankheit* (1908), 16; and Otto Rank, *Der Doppelgänger* ([1914–15] 1925), 55.

Der Andere (The other one)
Germany, 1912/1913
DIRECTOR: Max Mack
SCRIPT: Paul Lidau, based on his play
PRODUCTION: Vitascope GmbH Berlin
LENGTH: 5 acts, 1,766 meters
FIRST PERFORMANCE: January 21, 1913 (only for members of the press
    [Berlin])
CINEMATOGRAPHY: Hermann Böttger
CAST: Albert Bassermann, Emmerich Hanus, Nelly Ridon, Hanni Weisse,
    Léon Reseman, Otto Collot, Willi Lengling, Paul Passarge.
ARCHIVE HOLDINGS: Deutsche Kinemathek, Berlin; Deutsches Filminstitut,
    Frankfurt am Main

Die Augen der Mumie (The eyes of the mummy)
Germany, 1918
DIRECTOR: Ernst Lubitsch
SCRIPT: Hanns Kräly, Emil Rameau
SET: Kurt Richter
PRODUCTION: Projektions-AG ' Union" (PAGU) (Berlin)
LENGTH: 1,221 meters, 43 minutes
FIRST PERFORMANCE: October 3, 1918 (Berlin)
CINEMATOGRAPHY: Theodor Sparkuhl, Alfred Hansen
CAST: Pola Negri, Emil Jannings, Harry Liedtke, Max Laurence, Margarete
    Kupfer
ARCHIVE HOLDINGS: Deutsches Filminstitut, Frankfurt am Main

Augen. Im Banne der Hypnose (Eyes: under the spell of hypnosis)
Germany, 1919
DIRECTOR: Arthur Brenken, Georg Schubert
SCRIPT: Aage Holgers

PRODUCTION: Citograph-Film GmbH (Berlin)
CINEMATOGRAPHY: Paul Holzki, Karl Freund
CAST: Fritz Achterberg, Max Wilmsen, Bobby Flip, Ethel Orff, Boris Michailow, Theo Radoslawoff, P. van der Burk, Margrit Edion, Emil Stammer

Das Cabinet des Dr. Caligari (The cabinet of Dr. Caligari)
Germany, 1919/1920
DIRECTOR: Robert Wiene
SCRIPT: Carl Mayer and Hans Janowitz
SET: Hermann Warm, Walter Reimann, Walter Röhrig
PRODUCTION: Decia-Film-Ges. Holz & Co. (Berlin)
LENGTH: 6 acts, 1,780 meters
FIRST PERFORMANCE: February 26, 1920
CINEMATOGRAPHY: Willy Hameister
CAST: Werner Krauß, Conrad Veidt, Friedrich Fehér, Lil Dagover, Hans Heinrich von Twardowski, Rudolf Lettinger, Ludwig Rex, Elsa Wagner, Henri Peters-Arnolds, Hans Lanser-Rudolff
ARCHIVE HOLDINGS: restored film copy, Filmmuseum Munich

The Criminal Hypnotist
United States, 1909
DIRECTOR: D. W. Griffith
SCRIPT: D. W. Griffith
PRODUCTION: American Mutoscope & Biograph
LENGTH: 7 minutes, 191 meters
RELEASE DATE: January 18, 1909
CINEMATOGRAPHY: G. W. Bitzer
CAST: Owen Moore, Marion Leonard, Arthur V. Johnson, David Miles, Charles Inslee, George Gebhardt, Harry Solter, Florence Lawrence
ARCHIVE HOLDINGS: LC Paper Print Collection

Der Einäugige (The one-eyed man)
Germany, 1920
DIRECTOR: Josef Coenen
SET: Kurt Dürnhöfer
PRODUCTION: Eduard Herminghaus
FIRST PERFORMANCE: March 4, 1921
CINEMATOGRAPHY: Willy Großstück
CAST: Fritz Greiner, Carl Auen, Lisa Kresse, Mely Lagarst

Geheimnisse einer Seele (Secrets of a soul)
Germany, 1925/1926
DIRECTOR: G. W. Pabst
SCRIPT: Colin Ross and Hans Neumann
PSYCHOANALYTIC ADVICE: Dr. Karl Abraham and Dr. Hanns Sachs
SET: Ernö Metzner
PRODUCTION: Neumann-Film Produktion GmbH (Berlin)
LENGTH: 6 acts, 2,214 meters
FIRST PERFORMANCE: March 24, 1926
CINEMATOGRAPHY: Guido Seeber, Curt Oertel, Walter Robert Lach
CAST: Werner Krauß, Ruth Weyher, Ilka Grüning, Jack Trevor, Pawel Pawlow,
    Hertha von Walther, Renate Brausewetter, Colin Ross
ARCHIVE HOLDINGS: Deutsches Filminstitut, Frankfurt am Main

Hypnose. Hanussens erstes Abenteuer (Hypnosis: Hanussen's first adventure)
Germany, 1919
PRODUCTION COMPANY: Neue Berliner Film-GmbH (Georg Alexander) (Berlin)
CAST: Erik Jan Hanussen, Grete Jacobsen, Bogia Horska, Walter Illig,
    A. Latinowitz

Im Banne der Suggestion: Der Chiromant (Under the spell of suggestion: the
    chiromancer)
Germany, 1920
DIRECTOR: Siegfried Philippi
SCRIPT: Robert Groß, Siegfried Philippi
PRODUCTION COMPANY: Turma-Film GmbH (Berlin)
CAST: Lissy Lind, Theodor Loos, Victor Janson

Im Banne fremden Willens (Under the spell of foreign will)
Germany, 1915
DIRECTOR: Siegfried Dessauer
PRODUCTION: Imperator-Film-Co. GmbH (Berlin)

Dr. Mabuse, der Spieler (Dr. Mabuse, the gambler)
Germany, 1922
DIRECTOR: Fritz Lang
SCRIPT: Thea von Harbou and Fritz Lang, based on the novel by Norbert
    Jacques
SET: Otto Hunte, Carl Stahl-Urach, Erich Kettelhut
PRODUCTION: Uco-Film GmbH (Berlin)

LENGTH: Pt. 1 – *Der grosse Spieler: Ein Bild der Zeit*, 3,496 meters; Pt. 2 – *Inferno, ein Spiel von Menschen unserer Zeit*, 2,560 meters

FIRST PERFORMANCE: April 27, 1922 (pt. 1), May 26, 1922 (pt. 2)

CINEMATOGRAPHY: Carl Hoffmann

CAST: Rudolf Klein-Rogge, Bernhard Goetzke, Alfred Abel, Aud Egede Nissen, Gertrud Welcker, Paul Richter, Hans Adalbert Schlettow, Georg John, Grete Berger, Julius Falkenstein, Robert Forster-Larrinaga

COSTUMES: Vally Reinecke

ARCHIVE HOLDINGS: Bundesarchiv/Filmarchiv Berlin

The Magician
United States, 1926

DIRECTOR: Rex Ingram

SCRIPT: Somerset Maugham (novel), Rex Ingram (adaptation)

PRODUCTION: Metro-Goldwyn-Mayer Pictures

LENGTH: 7 reels; 6,960 feet

RELEASE DATE: October 24, 1926

CINEMATOGRAPHY: John F. Seitz

CAST: Alice Terry, Paul Wegener, Ivan Petrovich, Firmin Burdon, Gladys Hamer

ARCHIVE HOLDINGS: Em Gee Film Library

Le Magnétiseur
France, 1897

DIRECTOR: George Méliès

Der Mann im Hintergrund (The man in the background)
Netherlands/Germany, 1922

DIRECTOR: Ernst Winar

CAST: Adolphe Engers, Eduard Ijdo, Paula de Waart, Coba Kinsberger

ARCHIVE HOLDINGS: Deutsches Filminstitut, Frankfurt am Main

Orlacs Hände (Hands of Orlac)
Austria, 1924

DIRECTOR: Robert Wiene

SCRIPT: Louis Nerz, based on the story by Maurice Renard

SET: Stefan Wessely, Hans Rouc, and Karl Exner

PRODUCTION: Berolina-Film GmbH (Berlin); Pan Fil AG (Vienna)

LENGTH: 7 acts, 2,507 meters

CINEMATOGRAPHY: Günther Krampf, Hans Androschin
CAST: Conrad Veidt, Alexandra Sorina, Carmen Cartellieri, Fritz Kortner, Paul Askonas, Fritz Strassny
ARCHIVE HOLDINGS: Deutsches Filminstitut (restored copy)

Schatten: Eine nächtliche Halluzination (Shadows: a nocturnal hallucination; commercial release under: Warning shadows)
Germany, 1923
DIRECTOR: Arthur Robison
SCRIPT: Arthur Robison and Rudolf Schneider
SET: Albin Grau
PRODUCTION: Pan-Film GmbH (Berlin)
LENGTH: 1,710 meters, 90 minutes
FIRST PERFORMANCE: October 16, 1923
CINEMATOGRAPHY: Fritz Arno Wagner
CAST: Fritz Kortner, Ruth Weyher, Gustav von Wangenheim, Alexander Granach, Eugen Rex, Max Gülstorff, Ferdinand von Alten, Fritz Rasp, Karl Platen, Lilly Harder
ARCHIVE HOLDINGS: Deutsches Filminstitut, Frankfurt am Main

Sklaven fremden Willens (Slaves of a foreign will; commercial release as: Hypnosis)
Germany, 1919
DIRECTOR: Richard Eichberg
SCRIPT: Carl Schneider
SET: Willi A. Hermann
PRODUCTION: Eichberg-Film GmbH (Central-Film-Vertriebs GmbH) (Berlin)
CINEMATOGRAPHY: Joe Rive
CAST: Gertrud de Lalsky, Karl Halden, Bela Lugosi, Marga Köhler, Violette Napierska, Rudolf Klein-Rohden, Emil Rameau, Jenny Höhne, Gustav Birkholz

Somnambul (Somnambulist)
Germany, 1928
DIRECTOR: Adolf Trotz
CAST: Erna Morena, Fritz Kortner, Veit Harlan, Jaro Fürth
PRODUCTION: Essem-Film GmbH, Berlin
ARCHIVE HOLDINGS: Deutsches Filminstitut, Frankfurt am Main

Spellbound
United States, 1916
DIRECTOR: Harry Harvey
SCRIPT: Bess Meredyth
PRODUCTION: Balboa Amusement Producing Co.
LENGTH: 5 reels
RELEASE DATE: May 17, 1916
CAST: Lois Meredith, William Conklin, Bruce Smith, Edward J. Brady, Frank
    Erlanger, Edward Peters, R. Henry Grey

Die Spinnen (Spiders)
Germany, 1919/1920
DIRECTOR: Fritz Lang
SCRIPT: Fritz Lang
SET: Hermann Warm, Otto Hunte, Carl Ludwig Kirmse, Heinrich Umlauff
PRODUCTION: Decia-Film-Ges. Holz & Co. (Berlin)
LENGTH: Pt. 1—*Der goldene See*, five acts, 1,951 meters; Pt. 2—*Das Brillanten-
    schiff*, 6 acts, 2,815 meters
FIRST PERFORMANCE: October 3, 1919 (pt. 1), February 6, 1920 (pt. 2)
CINEMATOGRAPHY: Carl Hoffmann, Emil Schünemann, Karl Freund (pt. 2)
CAST: Carl de Vogt, Ressel Orla, Georg John, Lil Dagover, Rudolf Lettinger,
    Edgar Pauly, Paul Morgan, Meinhardt Maur, Reiner Steiner
ARCHIVE HOLDINGS: Deutsches Filminstitut, Frankfurt am Main

Spione (Spies)
Germany, 1927/1928
DIRECTOR: Fritz Lang
SCRIPT: Fritz Lang and Thea von Harbou (based on her novel)
SET: Otto Hunte, Karl Vollbrecht
PRODUCTION: Universum-Film AG (UFA) (Berlin)
LENGTH: 10 acts, 4,358 meters
CINEMATOGRAPHY: Fritz Arno Wagner
CAST: Rudolf Klein-Rogge, Gerda Maurus, Lien Deyers, Louis Ralph, Craighall
    Sherry, Willy Fritsch, Paul Hörbiger, Hertha von Walther, Lupu Pick,
    Fritz Rasp, Julius Falkenstein, Georg John, Paul Rehkopf
ARCHIVE HOLDINGS: Deutsches Institut für Filmkunde, Wiesbaden
MUSIC: Werner R. Heymann

Svengali
Austria, 1914
DIRECTOR: Jacob Fleck
PRODUCTION: Wiener Kunstfilm
CAST: Ferdinand Bonn, Fräulein Nording

Das Testament des Dr. Mabuse (The testament of Dr. Mabuse)
Germany, 1932
DIRECTOR: Fritz Lang
SCRIPT: Thea von Harbou, based on the novel by Norbert Jacques
SET: Karl Vollbrecht, Emil Hasler
PRODUCTION: Nero-Film AG (Berlin)
LENGTH: 12 acts, 3,334 meters, 122 minutes
FIRST PERFORMANCE: May 12, 1933 (Vienna)
CINEMATOGRAPHY: Karl Vass, Fritz Arno Wagner
CAST: Rudolf Klein-Rogge, Oskar Beregi, Theodor Loos, Otto Wernicke,
    Wera Liessem, Gustav Diessl
ARCHIVE HOLDINGS: Bundesarchiv/Filmarchiv Koblenz
MUSIC: Hans Erdmann

Trilby
France, 1915
DIRECTOR: Maurice Tourneur
ASSISTANT DIRECTOR: Clarence L. Brown
SCRIPT: George Du Maurier (novel), E. Magnus Ingleton (scenario)
ART DIRECTOR: Ben Carré
CINEMATOGRAPHY: John van den Broek
PRODUCTION: Equitable Motion Pictures Corp.
LENGTH: 5 reels
RELEASE DATE: September 20, 1915
CAST: Clara Kimball Young, Wilton Lackaye, Chester Barnett, Paul McAllister
ARCHIVE HOLDINGS: The George Eastman House

Les yeux qui fascinent
France, 1916
DIRECTOR: Louis Feuillade
SCRIPT: Louis Feuillade
NOTES: Sixth sequel of the serial *Les Vampires* (1915–16)
PRODUCTION: Société des Etablissements L. Gaumont

CINEMATOGRAPHY: Manichoux

CAST: Edoudard Mathé, Delphine Renot, Louise Lagrange, Jeanne-Marie
Laurent, Marcel Levesque, Musidora, Jean Aymé, Stacia Naperkowska,
Renée Carl, Fernand Hermann, Bout de Zaan

ARCHIVE HOLDINGS: Cinemathèque Française

BIBLIOGRAPHY

III. Strafsenat. 1888. "Urteil des III. Strafsenats vom 26. Mai 1888." *Entscheidungen des Reichsgerichts in Strafsachen* 16:121–26.

Althusser, Louis. [1970] 1976. "Idéologie et appareils idéologiques d'État (Notes pour une recherche)." In *Positions*, 79–137. Paris: Editions Sociales. Originally published in *La pensée*, vol. 151.

———. [1970–71] 2001. "Ideology and Ideological State Apparatuses." In *Lenin and Philosophy*, 85–126. Translated by Ben Brewster. New York: Monthly Press.

Anderson, Mark. 2002. "The Shadow of the Modern: Gothic Ghosts in Stoker's Dracula and Kafka's Amerika." In *Literary Paternity, Literary Friendship*, ed. Gerhard Richter, 382–98. Chapel Hill: University of North Carolina Press.

Andriopoulos, Stefan. 1996a "Die Zirkulation von Figuren und Begriffen in kriminologischen, juristischen und literarischen Darstellungen von 'Unfall' und 'Verbrechen.'" *Internationales Archiv für Sozialgeschichte der deutschen Literatur* 21, no. 2:113–42.

———. 1996b. *Unfall und Verbrechen: Konfigurationen zwischen juristischem und literarischem Diskurs um 1900.* With a preface by Sebastian Scheerer. Hamburger Studien zur Kriminologie 21. Pfaffenweiler: Centaurus.

———. 1998. "Die Unzurechnungsfähigkeit somnambuler Medien: Der 'Roman' und das 'Schauspiel' des 'hypnotischen Verbrechens' (1885–1900)." In *Unzurechnungsfähigkeiten: Diskursivierungen unfreier Bewußtseinszustände seit dem 18. Jahrhundert*, ed. Michael Niehaus and Hans-Walter Schmidt-Hannisa, 133–54. Frankfurt am Main and Bern: Lang.

———. 1999. "The Invisible Hand: Supernatural Agency in Political Economy and the Gothic Novel." *English Literary History* 66, no. 3:739–58.

———. 2004. "Ungeheuer, Vampire, Werwölfe: Fiktionale Strategien der Horrorliteratur in kriminologischen Darstellungen von Serienmördern." In *Serienmord: Kriminologische und kulturwissenschaftliche Darstellungen eines ungeheuren Phänomens*, 314–29. Munich: belleville.

———. 2005. "Psychic Television." *Critical Inquiry* 31, no. 3 (Spring): 618–37.

———. 2006a. "The Terror of Reproduction: Early Cinema's Ghostly Doubles and the Right to One's Own Image." *New German Critique*, no. 99, 151–70.

————. 2006b. "Die Laterna magica der Philosophie: Gespenster bei Kant, Hegel und Schopenhauer." *Deutsche Vierteljahrsschrift für Literaturwissenschaft und Geistesgeschichte* 80, no. 2:173–211.

Aragon, Louis, and André Breton. [1928] 1988. "Le cinquantenaire de l´hystérie, 1878–1928." In André Breton, *Œuvres completes*, edited by Marguerite Bonnet, 948–50. Paris: Gallimard.

Arnheim, Rudolf. [1932] 1979. *Film als Kunst*. With a new preface. Frankfurt am Main: Fischer.

Artaud, Antonin. [1932–38] 1964. *Le théâtre et son double*. Vol. 4 of *Œuvres complètes*. Paris: Gallimard.

Babinski, Jean. 1891. *Hypnotisme et hystérie: Du rôle de l'hypnotisme en thérapeutique*. Paris: G. Masson.

Bachem-Tonger, Cätty. 1922. *Im Banne der Hypnose*. Munich: Universal-Verlag.

Bacmeister, Ferdinand. 1922. "Der Hypnotismus und seine Beziehungen zum Strafrecht." J.D. diss., Universität Göttingen.

Bahr, Hermann. 1904. *Dialog vom Tragischen*. Berlin: Fischer.

Bamberg, Hugo. 1896. "Zur Lehre von der Deliktsfähigkeit der juristischen Personen." J.D. diss., Universität Greifswald.

Barthes, Roland. [1968] 1977. "The Death of the Author." In *Image, Music, Text*, 142–48. Translated by Stephen Heath. New York: Hill & Wang.

————. 1975. "En sortant du cinéma." *Communications* 23:104–7.

Bartz, Christina. 2002. "Telepathologien: Der Fernsehzuschauer unter medizinischer Beobachtung." In *Medienkultur der 50er Jahre: Diskursgeschichte der Medien nach 1945*, ed. Irmela Schneider and Peter Spangenberg, 1:373–86. Wiesbaden: Westdeutscher Verlag.

Baxmann, Inge. 1991. "Traumtanzen oder die Entdeckungsreise unserer Kultur." In *Paradoxien, Dissonanzen, Zusammenbrüche. Situationen offener Epistemologie*, ed. Hans-Ulrich Gumbrecht and Karl Ludwig Pfeiffer, 316–40. Frankfurt am Main: Suhrkamp.

Beard, George M. 1880. *A Practical Treatise on Nervous Exhaustion (Neurasthenia), Its Symptoms, Nature, Sequences, Treatment*. New York: William Wood & Co.

————.1883. *Die Nervenschwäche (Neurasthenia), ihre Symptome, Natur, Folgezustände und Behandlung*. Translated by M. Neisser. 2d ed. Leipzig: F. C. W. Vogel.

Beaunis, Henri E. 1886. *Le somnambulisme provoqué*. Études physiologiques et psychologiques. Paris: Baillière.

Beer-Hofmann, Richard. [1892] 1984. *Pierrot Hypnotiseur: Regiebuch einer Pantomime*. In Rainer Hank, *Mortifikation und Beschwörung: Zur Veränderung ästhetischer Wahrnehmung in der Moderne am Beispiel des Frühwerkes Richard Beer-Hofmanns*, 261–310. Frankfurt am Main: Lang.

Beizer, Janet L. 1994. *Ventriloquized Bodies: Narratives of Hysteria in Nineteenth-Century France*. Cornell, NY: Cornell University Press.

Bell, Charles. 1889. "Hypnotism." *Medico-Legal Journal* 7:363–71.

Bellour, Raymond. 1979. "Alternation, Segmentation, Hypnosis: Interview with Raymond Bellour." *Camera Obscura* 3–4:97–106.

———. [1986] 1990. "Believing in the Cinema." In *Psychoanalysis and Cinema*, ed. E. Ann Kaplan, 98–109. New York and London: Routledge.

Bellour, Raymond, and Jacques Kermabon. 1988. "La 'machine à hypnose,' entretien avec Raymond Bellour." *CinémAction* 47 (April): 67–72.

Belot, Adolphe. 1887. *Alphonsine*. Paris E. Dentu.

Bentivegni, Adolf von. 1890. *Die Hypnose und ihre civilrechtliche Bedeutung*. Schriften der Gesellschaft für Experimental-Psychologie 5. Leipzig: E. Günther.

Berger, Alfred Freiherr von. 1897. "Wahrheit und Irrtum in der Katharsistheorie des Aristoteles." In *Aristoteles' Poetik*, 69–98. Translated and edited by Theodor Gomperz. Leipzig: Veit.

Bernays, Jacob. 1880. *Zwei Abhandlungen ueber die aristotelische Theorie des Dramas*. Berlin: Hertz.

Bernheim, Hippolyte. 1884. *De la suggestion dans l'état hypnotique et dans l'état de veille*. Paris: Doin.

———. [1886a] 1888. *De la suggestion et ses applications à la thérapeutique*. 2d ed., rev. and enlarged. Paris: Doin.

———. [1886b] 1888. *Die Suggestion und ihre Heilwirkung*. Translated by Sigmund Freud and Otto von Springer. Leipzig and Vienna: Franz Deuticke.

———. [1886] 1964. *Hypnosis and Suggestion*. Translated by Christian A. Herter. New York: University Books.

———. 1891. *Hypnotisme, suggestion, psychothérapie: Études nouvelles*. Paris: Doin.

———. [1891] 1980. *New Studies in Hypnotism*. Translated by Richard S. Sandor. New York: International Universities Press.

———. 1892. *Neue Studien ueber Hypnotismus, Suggestion und Psychotherapie*. Translated by Sigmund Freud. Leipzig: Franz Deuticke.

———. 1897. *L'hypnotisme et la suggestion dans leurs rapports avec la médecine légale*. Nancy: A. Crépin-Leblond.

Bibliographie de la France. 1887. Vol. 87, 349.

Bierce, Ambrose G. [1891] 1966. "An Adventure at Brownville." In *The Collected Works of Ambrose Bierce*, 2:247–65. New York: Gordian Press.Originally published in.

———. [1897] 1966. "The Hypnotist." In *The Collected Works of Ambrose Bierce*, 8:177–84. New York: Gordian Press.

———. [1903] 1966. "Hypnotism." In *The Collected Works of Ambrose Bierce*, 11:349–52. New York: Gordian Press.

Binder, Julius. 1907a. "Der Gegenstand." *Zeitschrift für Handelsrecht* 59:1–78.

———. 1907b. *Das Problem der juristischen Persönlichkeit*. Leipzig: Deichert.

Binswanger, Otto. 1892. "Gutachten über Hypnose und Suggestion." In *Die Suggestion und die Dichtung. Gutachten über Hypnose und Suggestion von Otto Binswanger, Emil du Boys-Reymond et al.*, ed. Karl Emil Franzos, 3–11. Berlin: F. Fontane und Co.

Birnbaum, Karl. 1911. *Die krankhafte Willensschwäche und ihre Erscheinungsformen: Eine psychopathologische Studie für Ärzte, Pädagogen und gebildete Laien*. Wiesbaden: Bergmann.

Bluntschli, Johann Caspar. 1853. *Deutsches Privatrecht*. Vol. 1. Munich: Verlag der litterarisch-artistischen Anstalt.

Böhlau, Hugo. 1871. *Rechtssubject und Personenrolle*. Rostock: Universitäts-Buchdruckerei.

Bölsche, Wilhelm. 1891. *Die Mittagsgöttin: Ein Roman aus dem Geisteskampfe der Gegenwart*. Stuttgart: Deutsche Verlags-Anstalt.

Bondegger, Harry W., trans. 1919. *Hindu-Hypnotismus: Theorie und Praxis der Fakir-Illusionen und hypnotischen Experimente*, by Vairagyananda. Berlin: C. Georgi.

Borchert, Theodor. 1888. *Die strafrechtliche Verantwortlichkeit für Handlungen Dritter, insbesondere die Theilnahme am Verbrechen und die mittelbare Thäterschaft*. Berlin: Müller.

Borch-Jacobsen, Mikkel. 1989. "Hypnosis in Psychoanalysis." *Representations* 27 (Summer): 92–110.

———. 2006. "The Bernheim Effect: Fragments of a Theory of Generalized Artifact." *Qui Parle* 16, no. 1:47–70.

Bouvier, Émile. 1887. *De la responsabilité civile et pénale des personnes morales*. Lyon: Faculté de Droit.

Brandstetter, Gabriele. 1992. "Psychologie des Ausdrucks und Ausdruckstanz: Aspekte der Wechselwirkung am Beispiel der 'Traumtänzerin' Madeleine." In *Ausdruckstanz: Eine mitteleuropäische Bewegung der ersten Hälfte des 20. Jahrhunderts*, ed. Gunhild Oberzaucher-Schüller, 199–211. Wilhelmshaven: Florian Noetzel.

———. 1995. *Tanz-Lektüren: Körperbilder und Raumfiguren der Avantgarde*. Frankfurt am Main: Fischer.

Breton, André. [1924] 1988. "Manifeste du surréalisme." In *Œuvres complètes*. Edited by Marguerite Bonnet, 1:309–46. Paris: Gallimard.

Breuer, Josef, and Sigmund Freud. [1895] 1987. *Studien über Hysterie*. Frankfurt am Main: Fischer.

Broch, Hermann. [1913–38] 1981. *Briefe 1 (1913–1938)*. Edited by Paul M. Lützeler. Frankfurt am Main: Suhrkamp.

———. [1928–32] 1994. *Die Schlafwandler: Eine Romantrilogie*. Edited by Paul Lützeler. Frankfurt am Main: Suhrkamp.

———. [1928–32] 1964. *The Sleepwalkers: A Trilogy*. Translated by Willa Muir and Edwin Muir. New York: Pantheon Books.

———. [1929] 1994. "Methodologischer Prospekt: Der Roman *Die Schlafwandler*." In *Die Schlafwandler: Eine Romantrilogie*, 719–22. Edited by Paul Lützeler. Frankfurt am Main: Suhrkamp.

———. [1932] 1979. "Die Entsühnung" (stage version). In *Dramen*, 133–234. Vol. 7 of *Kommentierte Werkausgabe*. Edited by Paul Michel Lützeler. Frankfurt am Main: Suhrkamp.

———. [1935a] 1994. *Die Verzauberung* [First version 1935]. Vol. 3 of *Kommentierte Werkausgabe*. Edited by P. M. Lützeler. Frankfurt am Main: Suhrkamp.

———. [1935b] 1969. *Bergroman: Erste Fassung*. Edited by Frank Kress and Hans Albert Maier. Frankfurt am Main: Suhrkamp.

———. [1935–51] 1969. *Bergroman: Entstehungsvarianten und Anmerkungen*. Edited by Frank Kress and Hans Albert Maier. Frankfurt am Main: Suhrkamp.

———. [1936a] 1969. *Bergroman*. 2d version. Edited by Frank Kress and Hans Albert Maier. Frankfurt am Main: Suhrkamp.

———. [1936b] 1994. "Demeter oder die Verzauberung (Inhalt)." In *Die Verzauberung* [First version 1935], 373–82. Vol. 3 of *Kommentierte Werkausgabe*. Edited by P. M. Lützeler, vol. 3. Frankfurt am Main: Suhrkamp.

———. [1939–48] 1979. *Massenwahntheorie: Beiträge zu einer Psychologie der Politik*. Vol. 12 of *Kommentierte Werkausgabe*. Edited by Paul Michael Lützeler. Frankfurt am Main: Suhrkamp.

———. [1949] 1978. "Die Demokratie im Zeitalter der Versklavung." In *Politische Schriften*, 110–92. Vol. 11 of *Kommentierte Werkausgabe*. Edited by P. M. Lützeler. Frankfurt am Main: Suhrkamp.

———. [1950–51] 1969. *Bergroman: Dritte Fassung*. Edited by Frank Kress and Hans Albert Maier. Frankfurt am Main: Suhrkamp.

Brody, Jane E. 1996. "When Can Killers Claim Sleepwalking as a Legal Defense?" *New York Times*, January 16, Science B7, B11.

Brooks, Peter. 2002. "Narrativity of the Law." *Law and Literature* 14, no. 1:1–10.

Brown, Charles Brockden. [1805] 1987. "Somnambulism." In *Somnambulism and Other Stories*, ed. Alfred Weber, 5–24. Studien und Texte zur Amerikanistik Texte 4. Frankfurt am Main: Peter Lang. Originally published in *Literary Magazine and American Register* 1805.

Brown, Ruth Rae. 2001. "From Charcot to Charlot: Unconscious Imitation and

Spectatorship in French Cabaret and Early Cinema." *Critical Inquiry*, 27, no. 3 (Spring): 515–49.

Bruns, Karin. 1995. *Kinomythen, 1920–1945: Die Filmentwürfe der Thea von Harbou*. Stuttgart and Weimar: Metzler.

Buchner, Hans. 1927. *Im Banne des Films: Die Weltherrschaft des Kinos*. Munich: Deutscher Volksverlag E. Boepple.

Burgl, Georg. 1912. *Die Hysterie und die strafrechtliche Verantwortlichkeit der Hysterischen: Ein praktisches Handbuch für Ärzte und Juristen; Mit 20 ausgewählten Fällen krimineller Hysterie mit Aktenauszug und gerichtlichen Gutachten*. Stuttgart: Enke.

Busch, Richard. 1933. *Grundfragen der strafrechtlichen Verantwortlichkeit der Verbände*. Leipzig: Weicher.

Butler, Judith. 1997. *The Psychic Life of Power: Theories in Subjection*. Stanford, CA: Stanford University Press.

Campili, Giulio. 1886. *Il grande Ipnotismo e la Suggestione ipnotica nei Rapporti col Diretto penale e civile*. Turin: Bocca.

Carroll, Lewis. [1871] 1971. "Through the Looking-Glass and What Alice Found There." In *Alice in Wonderland*, 101–209. Edited by Donald J. Gray. New York and London: Norton.

Castle, Terry. 1995. "Spectral Politics: Apparition Belief and the Romantic Imagination." In *The Female Thermometer*, 168–89. Oxford and New York: Oxford University Press.

Charcot, Jean-Martin. [1877] 1892. *Leçons sur les maladies du système nerveux, faites à la Salpêtrière: Recueillies et publiées par Bourneville*. Vol. 1 of *Oeuvres complètes*. Paris: Bureaux du Progrès Médical.

———. 1877. *Lectures on Diseases of the Nervous System: Delivered at La Salpêtrière*. Vol. 1. Translated by George Sigerson. London: New Sydenham Society.

———. 1878. *Lectures on Localization in Diseases of the Brain*. Translated by Edward P. Fowler. New York: W. Wood.

———. [1886] 1890. *Leçons sur les maladies du système nerveux, faites à la Salpêtrière: Recueillies et publiées par MM. Babinski, Bernard, Féré, Guinon, Marie et Gilles de la Tourette*. Vol. 3 of *Oeuvres complètes*. Paris: Bureaux du Progrès Médical.

———. 1886. *Neue Vorlesungen über die Krankheiten des Nervensystems insbesondere über Hysterie*. Translated by Sigmund Freud. Leipzig and Vienna: Toeplitz & Deuticke.

———. [1886] 1889. *Clinical Lectures on the Diseases of the Nervous System, Delivered at the Infirmary of La Salpêtrière*. Vol. 3. Translated by Thomas Savill. London: Sydenham Society.

———. [1887] 1987. *The Tuesday Lessons: Excerpts from Nine Case Presentations on*

General Neurology Delivered at the Salpêtrière Hospital in 1887–88. Edited and translated by Christopher G. Goetz. New York: Raven Press.

———. [1887] 1892. *Schuljahr, 1887–1888* Vol. 1 of *Poliklinische Vorträge*. Translated by Sigmund Freud. Leipzig and Vienna: Franz Deuticke.

———. [1888] 1895. *Schuljahr, 1888–1889* Vol. 2 of *Poliklinische Vorträge*. Translated by Max Kahane. Leipzig and Vienna: Franz Deuticke.

———. 1889. Preface to *Der Hypnotismus und die verwandten Zustände vom Standpunkte der gerichtlichen Medizin*, by Georges Gilles de la Tourette, iii–iv. Hamburg: Verlagsanstalt und Druckerei.

———. 1890. "Hypnotism and Crime." *Forum* 9:159–68.

Charcot, Jean-Martin, and Paul Richer. 1887. *Les démoniaques dans l'art*. Paris: Adrien Delahaye et Émile Lecrosnier.

Chéroux, Clement, et al., eds. 2005. *The Perfect Medium: Photography and the Occult*. New Haven, CT, and London: Yale University Press.

Chion, Michel. [1982] 1999. *The Voice in Cinema*. Edited and translated Claudia Gorbman. New York: Columbia University Press.

Claretie, Jules. 1881. *Les amours d'un interne*. Paris: E. Dentu.

———. 1885. *Jean Mornas*. Paris: E. Dentu.

———. [1885] 1889. *Jean Mornas*. Translated by Auguste Scheibe. Stuttgart: Engelhorn.

———. [1885] 1892. *Hypnotism*. Chicago: Neeley.

Coates, James. [1911] 1973. *Photographing the Invisible*. New York: Arno.

Cocteau, Jean. [1946] 1992. "Speech at the *Institut des hautes études cinématographiques*." In *The Art of Cinema*, trans. Robin Buss, 25. New York: Marion Boyars.

Cohn, Georg. 1909. *Kinematographenrecht: Vortrag, gehalten in der juristischen Gesellschaft zu Berlin am 12. Juni 1909*. Berlin: Decker.

Coleman, James. 1974. *Power and the Structure of Society*. New York: Norton.

Collins, Mabel. 1892. *Suggestion*. New York: Lovell, Gestefeld & Co.

Condon, Richard. [1959] 2003. *The Manchurian Candidate*. New York: Thunder's Mouth Press.

Conrad, Joseph. [1902] 1995. *Heart of Darkness*. Edited by Robert Hampson. London: Penguin.

Coryell, John R. 1892. *The Hypnotist's Victim*. New York: Street & Smith.

Coxey, Willard Douglas. 1896. *A Hypnotic Crime, and Other Like True Tales: Being a Free Adaptation from the Minutes of the Society for Psychical Research*. Maywood, IL: Wright.

Crary, Jonathan. 1989. "Spectacle, Attention, Counter-Memory." *October* 50 (Fall): 97–107.

———. 1996. "Dr. Mabuse and Mr. Edison." In *Art and Film since 1945: Hall of Mirrors*, ed. Russell Ferguson, 262–79. Los Angeles: Museum of Contemporary Art.

———. 1999. *Suspensions of Perception: Attention, Spectacle, and Modern Culture*. Cambridge, MA: MIT Press.

Crocq, Jean. 1894. *L'hypnotisme et le crime*. Brussels: H. Lamertin.

Cuninghame, Caroline M. 1891. *The Slave of His Will*. London: Spencer Blackett.

Cushing, Paul. 1887. *Doctor Caesar Crowl: Mind-Curer*. 3 vols. London: John & Robert Maxwell.

Daudet, Léon. [1894] 1984. *Les Morticoles*. Paris: Grasset.

Delboeuf, Joseph. 1886. "De l'influence de l'imitation et de l'éducation dans le somnambulisme provoqué." *Revue Philosophique* 22:146–71,

———. 1888. *L'hypnotisme et la liberté des représentations publiques*. Liège: Desoer.

———. 1893–94. "Die verbrecherischen Suggestionen." *Zeitschrift für Hypnotismus* 2:177–98, 221–40, 247–68.

———. 1897. "Les suggestions criminelles." In *Dritter internationaler Congress für Psychologie in München vom 4. bis 7. August 1896*, 335–37. Munich: Lehmann.

de Lorde, André. 1908. *Une Leçon à la Salpêtrière, tableau dramatique en deux actes*. Paris: Fasquelle.

———. [1913] 1924. "L'acquittée." In *Théâtre de la peur*, 153–82. Paris: Librairie théâtrale.

de Man, Paul. [1978] 1996. "The Epistemology of Metaphor." In *Aesthetic Ideology*, ed. Andrzej Warminski, 34–50. Theory and History of Literature 65. Minneapolis and London: University of Minnesota Press.

———. [1982] 1996. "Sign and Symbol in Hegel's *Aesthetics*." In *Aesthetic Ideology*, 91–104. Minneapolis: University of Minnesota Press.

Demelius, Gustav. 1858. *Die Rechtsfiktion in ihrer geschichtlichen und dogmatischen Bedeutung: Eine juristische Untersuchung*. Weimar: Böhlau.

———. 1861. "Ueber fingirte Persönlichkeit." *Jahrbücher für die Dogmatik des heutigen römischen und deutschen Privatrechts* 4:113–58.

Derlien, Hans-Ulrich. 1991. "Bureaucracy in Art and Analysis." *Journal of the Kafka Society of America* 15:4–20.

Derrida, Jacques. 1979. *Éperons: Les styles de Nietzsche/Spurs: Nietzsche's Styles*. Bilingual ed. Chicago and London: University of Chicago Press.

Didi-Huberman, Georges. [1982] 2003. *Invention of Hysteria: Charcot and the Photographic Iconography of the Salpêtrière*. Translated by Alisa Hartz. Cambridge, MA: MIT Press.

———.1984. "Postface: Charcot, l'histoire et l'art." In Jean Martin Charcot and Paul Richer, *Les démoniaques dans l'art*, 125–88. Paris: Macula.

Döblin, Alfred. 1910. "Die Tänzerin und der Leib." In *Erzählungen aus fünf Jahrzehnten*, 18–21. Freiburg i.Br.: Walter.

———. [1914] 1989. "An Romanautoren und ihre Kritiker: Berliner Programm." In *Schriften zu Ästhetik, Poetik und Literatur*, ed. E. Kleinschmidt, 119–23. Olten and Freiburg i.Br.: Walter. Originally published in *Der Sturm* (May).

———. 1914. "Die Nachtwandlerin." In *Erzählungen aus fünf Jahrzehnten*, 148–61. Freiburg i.Br.: Walter.

"Dr. Mabuse, der Spieler." [1922a] 1994. *Berliner Fremden-Zeitung* 1, no. 5. Reprinted in Norbert Jacques, *Dr. Mabuse, der Spieler*. Edited by Michael Farin and Günter Scholdt, 313–14. Hamburg: Rogner & Bernhard.

———. [1922b] 1994. *Die Neue Zeit*, May 4. Reprinted in Norbert Jacques, *Dr. Mabuse, der Spieler*. Edited by Michael Farin and Günter Scholdt, 316–17. Hamburg: Rogner & Bernhard.

Dominik, Hans. [1922] 1954. *Die Macht der Drei*. Berlin and Schöneberg: Weiss.

———. 1925. *Atlantis*. Berlin: Scherl.

Dormer, Daniel. 1888. *The Mesmerist's Secret*. London: John & Robert Maxwell.

Doyle, Arthur Conan. 1885. "The Great Keinplatz Experiment." In *The Great Keinplatz Experiment and Other Stories*, 7–30. Chicago and New York: Rand, McNally & Co.

———. 1895. *The Parasite*. New York: Harper.

Drucker, Leopold. 1893. *Die Suggestion und ihre forensische Bedeutung*. Vienna: Manz.

du Bois-Reymond, Emil. 1892. "Gutachten über Hypnose und Suggestion." In *Die Suggestion und die Dichtung: Gutachten über Hypnose und Suggestion von Otto Binswanger, Emil du Boys-Reymond et al.*, ed. Karl Emil Franzos, 12–13. Berlin: F. Fontane und Co.

Duenschmann, H. 1912. "Kinematograph und Psychologie der Volksmenge." *Konservative Monatsschrift* 69, no. 9:920–30.

Du Maurier, George. 1895. *Trilby*. London: Osgood, McIlvaine & Co.

du Prel, Carl. 1889. *Das hypnotische Verbrechen und seine Entdeckung*. Munich: Verlag der Akademischen Monatshefte.

———. [1890] 1928. *Das Kreuz am Ferner: Ein hypnotisch-spiritistischer Roman*. Stuttgart and Berlin: Cotta.

———. 1891. "Das automatische Schreiben." *Sphinx* 6, no. 11:65–70, 152–60, 201–7.

Durkheim, Emile. [1912] 1995. *Elementary Forms of Religious Life*. Translated by Karen E. Fields. New York: Free Press.

Ebner-Eschenbach, Moritz von. 1897. *Hypnosis perennis und Ein Wunder des heiligen Sebastian: Zwei Wiener Geschichten*. Stuttgart: Cotta.

Eisner, Lotte H. [1952] 1969. *The Haunted Screen: Expressionism in the German Cin-*

ema and the Influence of Max Reinhardt. Translated by Roger Greaves. Berkeley: University of California Press.

Elsaesser, Thomas. 2000. *Weimar Cinema and After: Germany's Historical Imaginary.* New York: Routledge.

Epstein, Jean. 1921. "Magnification." In *French Film Theory and Criticism.* Vol. 1, *1907–1929*, ed. Richard Abel, 235–41. Princeton, NJ: Princeton University Press.

Esch, Josef. 1910. "Die kriminalistische Deliktsfähigkeit der Körperschaften." J.D. diss., Universität Rostock.

Eschle, F. C. R. 1904. *Die krankhafte Willensschwäche und die Aufgaben der erziehlichen Therapie.* Berlin: Fischer's Medicinische Buchhandlung.

Esser, Josef. 1940. *Wert und Bedeutung der Rechtsfiktionen: Kritisches zur Technik der Gesetzgebung und zur bisherigen Dogmatik des Privatrechts.* Frankfurt am Main: Klostermann.

Eulenburg, Albert. 1892. "Gutachten über Hypnose und Suggestion." In *Die Suggestion und die Dichtung: Gutachten über Hypnose und Suggestion von Otto Binswanger, Emil du Boys-Reymond et al.,* ed. Karl Emil Franzos, 14–30. Berlin: F. Fontane und Co.

Ewers, Hanns Heinz. 1910. *Der Zauberlehrling oder Die Teufelsjäger.* Munich and Leipzig: Georg Müller.

———. 1911a. *Alraune: Geschichte eines lebenden Wesens.* Munich: G. Müller.

———, ed. 1911b. *Memoiren einer Besessenen, von Soeur Jeanne des Anges.* Stuttgart: Lutz.

———. 1922. *Der Geisterseher: Aus den Papieren des Grafen O**.* Munich: Georg Müller.

"Faits du jour, Les." 1887. *Gil Blas,* May 23.

Felden, Emil. 1921. *Der Spiritismus und die anderen okkulten Systeme unserer Zeit.* Leipzig: Oldenburg & Co.

Fischer, Jens Malte. 1972. "Hermann Brochs Nachlaßroman und eine Vorlage von Hanns Heinz Ewers." In *Hermann Broch: Perspektiven der Forschung,* ed. Manfred Durzak, 271–76. Munich: Fink.

Fischer-Homberger, Esther. 1975. *Die traumatische Neurose: Vom somatischen zum sozialen Leiden.* Bern: Hans Huber.

Flüggen, Christian. 1920. "Münchener Erstaufführungen." *Deutsche Lichtspielzeitung,* March 3. Reprinted in *Das Cabinet des Dr. Caligari: Drehbuch von Carl Mayer und Hans Janowitz mit einem einführenden Essay und Materialien zum Film,* ed. Uli Jung and Walter Schatzberg, 147. Munich: text + kritik, 1995.

Fodéré, François. 1813. *Traité de médecine légale et d'hygiène publique.* Paris: Mame.

Ford, James L. 1891. *Hypnotic Tales.* New York: Kepler & Schwarzmann.

Forel, Auguste. 1864–1924. *Briefe: Correspondance, 1864–1927.* Edited by M. Bleuler. Bern and Stuttgart: Huber.

——. 1889a. "Der Hypnotismus und seine strafrechtliche Bedeutung." *Zeitschrift für die gesamte Strafrechtswissenschaft* 9:131–93.

——. 1889b. *Der Hypnotismus, seine Bedeutung und seine Handhabung.* Stuttgart: Enke. [88 pages]

——. 1891. *Der Hypnotismus, seine psychophysiologische, medicinische, strafrechtliche Bedeutung und seine Handhabung.* 2d rev. ed. Stuttgart: Enke. [172 pages]

——. 1892. "Gutachten über Hypnose und Suggestion." In *Die Suggestion und die Dichtung: Gutachten über Hypnose und Suggestion von Otto Binswanger, Emil du Bois-Reymond, August Forel, Richard v. Krafft-Ebing et al.*, ed. Karl Emil Franzos, 38–58. Berlin: Fontane.

——. 1895. *Der Hypnotismus, seine psycho-physiologische, medicinische, strafrechtliche Bedeutung und seine Handhabung.* 3d ed. with annotation by Oskar Vogt. Stuttgart: Enke. [233 pages]

——. 1902. *Der Hypnotismus und die suggestive Psychotherapie.* 4th rev. ed. Stuttgart: Enke. [256 pages]

——. 1907. *Der Hypnotismus oder Die Suggestion und Psychotherapie: Seine psychologische, psychophysiologische und therapeutische Bedeutung.* 5th rev. ed. Stuttgart: Enke. [287 pages]

——. 1907–8. *Hypnotism or Suggestion and Psychotherapy: A Study of the Psychological, Psycho-Physiological and Therapeutic Aspects of Hypnotism.* Translated by H.W. Armit. New York: Rebman Co.

——. 1911. *Der Hypnotismus oder die Suggestion und die Psychotherapie: Ihre psychologische, psychophysiologische und medizinische Bedeutung.* 6th rev. ed. Stuttgart: Enke. [306 pages]

——. 1918. *Der Hypnotismus oder die Suggestion und die Psychotherapie: Ihre psychologische, psychophysiologische und medizinische Bedeutung mit Einschluss der Psychoanalyse, sowie der Telepathiefrage.* 7th rev. ed. Stuttgart: Enke. [355 pages]

——. 1919. *Der Hypnotismus oder die Suggestion und die Psychotherapie: Ihre psychologische, psychophysiologische und medizinische Bedeutung mit Einschluss der Psychoanalyse, sowie der Telepathiefrage.* 8th and 9th ed. Stuttgart: Enke. [355 pages]

——. 1921. *Der Hypnotismus oder die Suggestion und die Psychotherapie: Ihre psychologische, psychophysiologische und medizinische Bedeutung mit Einschluss der Psychoanalyse, sowie der Telepathiefrage.* 10th and 11th ed. Stuttgart: Enke. [377 pages]

——. 1923. *Der Hypnotismus oder die Suggestion und die Psychotherapie: Ihre psychologische, psychophysiologische und medizinische Bedeutung mit Einschluss der Psychoanalyse, sowie der Telepathiefrage.* 12th ed. Stuttgart: Enke. [386 pages]

Foucault, Michel. [1969] 1972. *Archaeology of Knowledge*. Translated by A. M. Sheridan Smith. New York: Pantheon.

——. 1975a. *Surveiller et punir: Naissance de la prison*. Paris: Gallimard.

——. [1975b] 1994. "Pouvoir et corps." In *Dits et écrits*. Vol. 2, *1970–1975*, 754–60. Edited by Daniel Denfert and François Ewald. Paris: Gallimard.

——. [1977] 1994. "Les rapports de pouvoir passent à l'intérieur des corps." In *Dits et écrits*. Vol. 3, *1976–1979*, 228–36. Edited by Daniel Denfert and François Ewald: Gallimard.

Franzos, Karl Emil. 1892. Preface to *Die Suggestion und die Dichtung: Gutachten über Hypnose und Suggestion von Otto Binswanger, Emil du Bois-Reymond, August Forel, Richard v. Krafft-Ebing et al.*, ed. Karl Emil Franzos, vi–xxx. Berlin: Fontane. Originally published in *Deutsche Dichtung*, vol. 9, no. 7 (1890).

Freud, Margit. [1922] 1994. "Ein Film und die Psychoanalyse." In Norbert Jacques, *Dr. Mabuse, der Spieler: Roman*, 343–44. Edited by Michael Farin and Günter Scholdt. Hamburg: Rogner & Bernhard. Originally published in *Das blaue Heft* 3, no. 38 (June 24): 870–71.

Freud, Sigmund. 1888. Translator's preface to *Die Suggestion und ihre Heilwirkung*, by Hippolyte Bernheim, iii–xii. Leipzig and Vienna: Franz Deuticke. Reprinted in *Standard Edition of the Complete Psychological Works of Sigmund Freud*, edited and translated by James Strachey, 24 vols. (London: Hogarth, 1953–74).

——. [1889] 1987. "Rezension von August Forel *Der Hypnotismus*." In *Gesammelte Werke: Nachtragsband: Texte aus den Jahren 1885 bis 1938*, 123–39. Frankfurt am Main: Fischer. Originally published in *Wiener medizinische Wochenschrift* 39 (1889): 1097–1100, 1892–96.

——. [1890] 1942. "Psychische Behandlung (Seelenbehandlung)." In *Gesammelte Werke: Chronologisch Geordnet*, 5:287–315. London: Imago.

——. 1892. "Ein Fall von hypnotischer Heilung nebst Bemerkungen über die Entstehung hysterischer Phänomene durch den 'Gegenwillen.'" *Zeitschrift für Hypnotismus* 1:102–7, 123–29.

——. [1893] 1952. "Charcot." In *Gesammelte Werke: Chronologisch Geordnet*, 1:19–35. London: Imago.

——. [1905] 1971. "Bruchstück einer Hysterie-Analyse." In *Studienausgabe*. Vol. 6, *Hysterie und Angst*, 83–186. Frankfurt am Main: Fischer.

——. [1914a] 1946. "Erinnern, Wiederholen, Durcharbeiten." In *Gesammelte Werke: Chronologisch Geordnet*, 10:125–36. London: Imago.

——. [1914b] 1946. "Zur Geschichte der psychoanalytischen Bewegung." In *Gesammelte Werke: Chronologisch Geordnet*. 10:43–113. London: Imago.

——. [1915] 1946. "Das Unbewußte." In *Gesammelte Werke: Chronologisch Geordnet*. 10:263–303 London: Imago.

———. [1917] 1948. *Vorlesungen zur Einführung in die Psychoanalyse.* Vol. 11 of *Gesammelte Werke: Chronologisch Geordnet.* London: Imago.

———. [1919] 1982. "Das Unheimliche." In *Psychologische Schriften.* Vol. 4 of *Studienausgabe,* 241–74. Frankfurt am Main: Fischer.

———. [1921] 1974. "Massenpsychologie und Ich-Analyse." In *Gesellschaft/Religion.* Vol. 9 of *Studienausgabe,* 63–134. Frankfurt am Main: Fischer.

———. [1923] 1940. "Eine Teufelsneurose im siebzehnten Jahrhundert." In *Gesammelte Werke: Chronologisch Geordnet.* 13:315–53. London: Imago.

———. [1926] 1948. "Die Frage der Laienanalyse. Unterredungen mit einem Unparteiischen." In *Gesammelte Werke: Chronologisch Geordnet.* 14:207–96. London: Imago.

———. [1927] 1948. "Fetischismus." In *Gesammelte Werke.* 14:309–17. London: Imago.

———. [1938] 1950. "Abriss der Psychoanalyse." In *Gesammelte Werke.* Vol. 17, *Schriften aus dem Nachlass,* 63–138. London: Imago.

———. 1953–74. *Standard Edition of the Complete Psychological Works of Sigmund Freud.* Edited and translated by James Strachey. 24 vols. London: Hogarth.

Freund, Ernst. 1897. *The Legal Nature of Corporations.* Chicago: University of Chicago Press.

Freytag, Gustav. [1856] 1896. *Soll und Haben: Roman in sechs Büchern.* Vols. 4 and 5 of *Gesammelte Werke von Gustav Freytag.* Leipzig: Hirzel.

Fuchs, Friedrich. [1890] 1895. "Die Komödie der Hypnose." In *Ueber die Bedeutung der Hypnose in forensischer Hinsicht: Ein in dem Prozess Czynski abgegebenes Gutachten Nebst einigen anderen Schriftstücken verwandten Inhalts,* 7–22. Bonn: Friedrich Cohen. Originally published in *Berliner Klinische Wochenschrift* (1890).

———. 1895. "Gutachten in dem Processe Czynski." In *Ueber die Bedeutung der Hypnose in forensischer Hinsicht,* 26–36. Bonn: Friedrich Cohen.

Fuhrmann, Manfred. 1983. "Die Fiktion im römischen Recht." In *Funktionen des Fiktiven,* ed. Dieter Henrich and Wolfgang Iser, 413–15. Poetik und Hermeneutik 10. Munich: Fink.

Garnier, Paul. 1888. *L'automatisme sommambulique devant les tribunaux.* Paris: Baillière et fils.

Gaudreault, Andre. 1990. "Showing and Telling: Image and Word in Early Cinema." In *Early Cinema: Space, Frame, Narrative,* ed. Thomas Elsaesser, 274–81. London: British Film Institute.

Gauld, Alan. 1992. *A History of Hypnotism.* Cambridge: Cambridge University Press.

Gaupp, Robert. [1911–12] 1992. "Die Gefahren des Kino." In *Prolog vor dem Kino,* ed. Jörg Schweinitz, 64–69. Leipzig: Reclam. Originally published in *Süddeutsche Monatshefte* 2, no. 9:363–66.

———. 1912. "Der Kinematograph vom medizinischen und psychologischen Standpunkt." In Robert Gaupp and Konrad Lange, *Der Kinematograph als Volksunterhaltungsmittel*, 1–12. Vorträge gehalten am 21. Mai 1912 in Tübingen. Flugschriften zur Ausdruckskultur 100. Munich: Dürerbund.

Gelfand, Toby. 1989. "Charcot's Response to Freud's Rebellion." *Journal of the History of Ideas* 50:293–307.

Genter, Robert. 2006. "'Hypnotizzy' in the Cold War: The American Fascination with Hypnotism in the 1950s." *Journal of American Culture* 29, no. 2:154–69

Gierke, Otto v. 1871. *Der Humor im deutschen Recht*. Berlin: Weidmann.

———. 1883. "Labands Staatsrecht und die deutsche Rechtswissenschaft." *Jahrbuch für Gesetzgebung, Verwaltung und Volkswirthschaft im Deutschen Reich*, n.s. 7:1097–1195.

———. 1887. *Die Genossenschaftstheorie und die deutsche Rechtssprechung*. Berlin: Weidmann.

———. 1889. *Die soziale Aufgabe des Privatrechts*. Berlin: Julius Springer.

———. 1895. *Deutsches Privatrecht*. Vol. 1, *Allgemeiner Teil und Personenrecht*. Leipzig: Duncker & Humblot.

———. [1902] 1954. *Das Wesen der menschlichen Verbände*. Darmstadt: Wissenschaftliche Buchgesellschaft.

Gilles de la Tourette, Georges. 1887. *L'hypnotisme et les états analogues au point de vue médico-légale*. Paris: E. Plon.

———. 1887–89. *Der Hypnotismus und die verwandten Zustände vom Standpunkte der gerichtlichen Medizin*. With a preface by Jean-Martin Charcot. Hamburg: Verlagsanstalt und Druckerei .

———. 1894. *Traité clinique et thérapeutique de l'hystérie d'après l'enseignement de la Salpêtrière*. 3 vols. Paris: E. Plon.

Goldstein, Jan. 1982. "The Hysteria Diagnosis and the Politics of Anticlericalism in Late Nineteenth-Century France." *Journal of Modern History* 54:209–39.

———. 1991. "The Uses of Male Hysteria: Medical and Literary Discourse in Nineteenth-Century France." *Representations* 34 (Spring): 134–66.

Greenblatt, Stephen. 1988. *Shakespearean Negotiations: The Circulation of Social Energy in Renaissance England*. The New Historicism: Studies in Cultural Poetics 4. Berkeley and Los Angeles: University of California Press.

———. 1990. *Learning to Curse: Essays in Early Modern Culture*. New York and London: Routledge.

Gregor, Joseph. 1932. *Das Zeitalter des Films*. Vienna: Reinhold-Verlag.

Grimm, Jacob. 1816. "Von der Poesie im Recht." *Zeitschrift für geschichtliche Rechtswissenschaft* 2:25–99.

Guillain, Georges. [1955] 1959. *Jean-Martin Charcot: His Life and Work*. Translated by P. Bailey. London: Pitman.

Gumbrecht, Hans Ulrich, and Karl-Ludwig Pfeiffer, eds. [1988] 1994. *Materialities of Communication*. Translated by William Whobrey. Stanford, CA: Stanford University Press.

Gunning, Tom. [1986] 1990. "The Cinema of Attractions: Early Film, Its Spectator and the Avant-Garde." In *Early Cinema: Space, Frame, Narrative*, ed. Thomas Elsaesser, 56–62. London: British Film Institute. Originally published in *Wide Angle*, vol. 8.

———. 1990. "'Primitive' Cinema: A Frame-up? Or, The Trick's on Us." In *Early Cinema: Space, Frame, Narrative*, ed. Thomas Elsaesser, 95–103. London: British Film Institute.

———. 1994. "The Horror of Opacity: The Melodrama of Sensation in the Plays of André de Lorde." In *Melodrama: Stage, Picture, Screen*, ed. Jacky Bratton et al., 50–61. London: British Film Institute.

———. 1995a. "Phantom Images and Modern Manifestations: Spirit Photography, Magic Theater, Trick Films, and Photography's Uncanny." In *Fugitive Images: From Photography to Video*, ed. Patrice Petro, 42–71. Bloomington: Indiana University Press.

———. 1995b. "'Animated Pictures': Tales of Cinema's Forgotten Future." *Michigan Quarterly Review* 34, no. 4 (Fall): 465–85.

———. 1995c. "An Aesthetics of Astonishment: Early Film and the (In)Credulous Spectator." In *Viewing Positions: Ways of Seeing Film*, ed. Linda Williams, 114–33. New Brunswick, NJ: Rutgers University Press.

———. 2000. *The Films of Fritz Lang: Allegories of Vision and Modernity*. London: British Film Institute.

Hacking, Ian. 1995. *Rewriting the Soul: Multiple Personality and the Sciences of Memory*. Princeton, NJ: Princeton University Press.

Haddock, Aaron D. 2004. "Cinematic Trance: Robert Musil's 'Toward a New Aesthetic.'" Master's Thesis, Columbia University.

Häfker, Hermann. 1915. *Der Kino und die Gebildeten*. Mönchengladbach: Volksvereins-Verlag.

Hafter, Ernst. 1903. *Die Delikts- und Straffähigkeit der Personenverbände*. Berlin: Julius Springer.

Hammerschlag, Heinz E. 1954. *Hypnose und Verbrechen: Ein Beitrag zur Phänomenologie der Suggestion und der Hypnose*. Munich and Basel: Ernst Reinhardt.

———. 1956. *Hypnotism and Crime*. Translated by John Cohen. London: Rider.

Harms, Rudolf. 1926. *Philosophie des Films: Seine ästhetischen und metaphysischen Grundlagen*. Leipzig: Felix Meiner.

Harris, Ruth. 1985. "Murder under Hypnosis in the Case of Gabrielle Bompard: Psychiatry in the Courtroom in Belle Epoque Paris." In *The Anatomy of Mad-*

ness: Essays in the History of Psychiatry. Vol. 2, *Institutions and Society*, ed. William F. Bynum et al., 197–241. London: Tavistock.

———. 1989. *Murders and Madness: Medicine, Law, and Society in the Fin de Siècle*. Oxford: Oxford University Press.

Hasenclever, Walter. [1913] 1992. "Der Kintopp als Erzieher: Eine Apologie." In *Prolog vor dem Film: Nachdenken über ein neues Medium, 1909–1914*, ed. Jörg Schweinitz, 219–22. Leipzig: Reclam. Originally published in *Revolution*, vol. 1, no. 4 (December 1913).

Heberle, Max. 1893. *Hypnose und Suggestion im deutschen Strafrecht: Eine Studie*. Munich: Schweitzer.

Hellpach, Willy. 1904. *Die geistigen Epidemien*. Die Gesellschaft. Sammlung sozialpsychologischer Monographien 11. Frankfurt am Main: Literarische Anstalt Rütten & Loening.

Hellwig, Albert. 1911. *Schundfilms. Ihr Wesen, ihre Gefahren und ihre Bekämpfung*. Halle a.d.S.: Verlag der Buchhandlung des Waisenhauses.

———. 1914a. *Kind und Kino*. Beiträge zur Kinderforschung und Heilerziehung 119. Langensalza: Beyer.

———. 1914b. "Illusionen und Halluzinationen bei kinematographischen Vorführungen." *Zeitschrift für pädagogische Psychologie* 15, no. 1:37–40.

———. 1914c. "Über die schädliche Suggestivkraft kinematographischer Vorführungen." *Ärztliche Sachverständigen-Zeitung* 20, no. 6:119–24.

———. 1916a. "Zur Psychologie kinematographischer Vorführungen." *Zeitschrift für Psychotherapie und medizinische Psychologie* 6:88–120.

———. 1916b. "Hypnotismus und Kinematograph." *Zeitschrift für Psychotherapie und medizinische Psychologie* 6:310–15.

———. 1920. *Die Reform des Lichtspielrechts*. Pädagogisches Magazin, Heft 763. Langensalza: Beyer & Mann.

Hirsch, William. 1896. *Die menschliche Verantwortlichkeit und die moderne Suggestionslehre*. Berlin: Karger.

Höfelt, I. A. 1889. *Het hypnotisme in verband met het strafrecht. Academisch proefschrift*. Leiden: Gebr. Belinfante.

Hofer, G. 1920. "Berichte aus den wissenschaftlichen Vereinen: Gesellschaft der Aerzte in Wien: Sitzung vom November 1920." In *Wiener Medizinische Wochenschrift*, no. 49, 2077–78.

Hoffmann, Volker. 1991. "Strukturwandel in den 'Teufelspaktgeschichten' des 19. Jahrhunderts." In *Modelle des literarischen Strukturwandels*, ed. Michael Titzmann, 117–27. Studien und Texte zur Sozialgeschichte der Literatur 33. Tübingen: Niemeyer.

Hofmannsthal, Hugo von. [1889–1929] 1980. *Aufzeichnungen aus dem Nachlaß*. In *Reden und Aufsätze III: Aufzeichnungen*, 311–627. Frankfurt am Main: Fischer.

———. [Loris, pseud.]. [1892] 1993. "Einleitung." In Arthur Schnitzler, *Anatol*, 33–35. Frankfurt am Main: Fischer.

———. [1901] 1979. *Der Schüler*. In *Dramen*. Vol. 4, *Ballette, Pantomimen, Bearbeitungen, Übersetzungen*, 53–66. Edited by B. Schoeller. Frankfurt am Main: Fischer. Originally published in *Neue Deutsche Rundschau*, vol. 12.

———. [1903] 1979. *Elektra*. In *Dramen*. Vol. 2, *1892–1905*, 185–242. Edited by B. Schoeller. Frankfurt am Main: Fischer.

———. [1904] 1979. *Das Leben ein Traum: Ein Bruchstück*. In *Dramen*. Vol. 3, *1893–1927*, 177–254. Edited by B. Schoeller. Frankfurt am Main: Fischer.

———. [1900–1909] 1937. *Briefe, 1900–1909*, Vienna: Bermann-Fischer-Verlag.

———. [1921] 1979. "Der Ersatz für die Träume." In *Reden und Aufsätze*. Vol. 2, *1914–1924*, edited by B. Schoeller, 141–45. Frankfurt am Main: Fischer.

Hölder, Eduard. 1886. *Ueber das Wesen der juristischen Personen*. Erlangen: Metzer.

———. 1905. *Natürliche und juristische Personen*. Leipzig: Duncker & Humblot.

Holitscher, Arthur. 1919. *Schlafwandler: Erzählung*. Berlin: Fischer.

Höpfner. 1902. "Zur Lehre von der mittelbaren Täterschaft." *Zeitschrift für die gesamte Strafrechtswissenschaft* 22:205–17.

Hörisch, Jochen. 1990. "Die Armee, die Kirche und die Alma mater: Eine Grille über Körperschaften." *Merkur* 44:546–53.

Hubert, Henri, and Marcel Mauss. [1904] 1972. *A General Theory of Magic*. Translated by Robert Brain. London: Routledge.

Hückel, Armand. 1888. *Die Rolle der Suggestion bei gewissen Erscheinungen der Hysterie und des Hypnotismus*. Jena: Gustav Fischer.

Hyan, Hans. 1929. *Die Somnambule: Kriminalroman*. Bücherei moderner Autoren 5. Berlin: Sieben Stäbe Verlag.

Ivers, Hellmut. 1927. *Die Hypnose im deutschen Strafrecht*. Kriminalistische Abhandlungen 3. Leipzig: Wiegardt.

Jacques, Norbert. [1921–22] 1994. *Dr. Mabuse, der Spieler: Mit einem Dossier zum Film von Fritz Lang*. Hamburg: Rogner & Bernhard (Zweitausendeins). Originally published in *Berliner Illustrirte Zeitung* (September 25, 1921–January 29, 1922).

Janet, Pierre. 1889. *L'automatisme psychologique: Essai de psychologie expérimentale sur les formes inférieures de l'activité humaine*. Paris: Felix Alcan.

———. 1893. *État mental des hystériques: Les stigmates mentaux*. Paris: Rueff.

———. [1894] 1904. "Un cas de possession et l'exorcisme moderne." In *Névroses et idées fixes*, 1:375–406. 2d ed. Paris: Alcan.

Janet, Pierre, and F. Raymond. 1904. "Dépersonnalisation et possession chez un psychasthénique." *Journal de psychologie normale et pathologique* 1:28–63.

Janowitz, Hans. [1939] 1990. "Caligari—the Story of a Famous Story (Excerpts)."

In *The Cabinet of Dr. Caligari: Texts, Contexts, Histories*, ed. Mike Budd, 221–40. New Brunswick, NJ: Rutgers University Press.

Jhering, Rudolph von. 1865. *Der Geist des römischen Rechts auf den verschiedenen Stufen seiner Entwicklung.* Pt. 3, sec. 1. Leipzig: Breitkopf und Härtel.

———. [1884] 1992. *Scherz und Ernst in der Jurisprudenz.* Darmstadt: Wissenschaftliche Buchgesellschaft.

Kaes, Anton. 1993. "The Cold Gaze: Notes on Mobilization and Modernity." *New German Critique* 59 (Spring–Summer): 105–17.

———. 1995. "German Cultural History and the Study of Film: Ten Theses and a Postscript." *New German Critique* 65 (Spring–Summer): 47–58.

———. 1998. "Leaving Home: Film, Migration, and the Urban Experience." *New German Critique* 74 (Spring–Summer): 179–92.

———. 2001. "War–Film–Trauma." In *Modernität und Trauma: Beiträge zum Zeitenbruch des Ersten Weltkrieges*, ed. Inka Mülder-Bach, 121–30. Vienna: Universitätsverlag Wien.

———. Forthcoming. *Shell Shock: Film and Trauma in Weimar Germany.* Princeton, NJ: Princeton University Press.

Kafka, Franz. [1907–21] 2004. *Amtliche Schriften: Kritische Ausgabe.* Edited by Klaus Hermsdorf and Benno Wagner. Frankfurt am Main: S. Fischer. Contains a CD-ROM with additional texts.

———. [1912–17] 1967. *Briefe an Felice und andere Korrespondenz aus der Verlobungszeit.* Edited by Erich Heller and Jürgen Born. Frankfurt am Main: Fischer.

———. [1912–17] 1973. *Letters to Felice.* Translated by James Stern and Elisabeth Duckworth. New York: Schocken.

———. [1914–15] 1990. *Der Proceß: In der Fassung der Handschrift.* Edited by Malcolm Pasley. Frankfurt am Main: Fischer.

———. [1914–15] 1998. *The Trial.* Translated by Breon Mitchell. New York: Schocken Books.

———. [1920–23] 1983. *Briefe an Milena.* Edited by Jürgen Born and Michael Müller. Frankfurt am Main: Fischer.

———. [1920–23] 1990. *Letters to Milena.* Translated by Philip Boehm. New York: Schocken.

———. [1922] 1992. *Das Schloß: In der Fassung der Handschrift.* Edited by Malcolm Pasley. Frankfurt am Main: Fischer.

———. [1922] 1998. *The Castle.* A new translation, based on the restored text. Translated by Mark Harman. New York: Schocken.

Kapferer, Bruce. [1983] 1991. *A Celebration of Demons: Exorcism and the Aesthetics of Healing in Sri Lanka.* Washington, DC: Smithsonian Press.

Kasten, Jürgen. 1990. *Der expressionistische Film: Abgefilmtes Theater oder avantgard-*

istisches Erzählkino? Eine stil-, produktions- und rezeptionsgeschichtliche Untersuchung. Münster: MAkS Publikationen, 1990.

Keller, Gottfried. [1877] 1945. "Ursula." In *Züricher Novellen*. Vol. 10 of *Sämtliche Werke*, 91–182. Edited by Jonas Fränkel and Carl Helbling. Bern: Benteli.

———. [1886] 1943. *Martin Salander: Roman*. Vol. 12 of *Sämtliche Werke*. Edited by Jonas Fränkel and Carl Helbling. Bern and Leipzig: Benteli.

Kittler, Friedrich. [1985] 1990. *Discourse Networks, 1800–1900*. Translated by Michael Metteer. Stanford, CA: Stanford University Press.

———. [1986] 1999. *Gramophone, Film, Typewriter*. Translated by Geoffrey Winthrop-Young and Michael Wutz. Stanford, CA: Stanford University Press.

———. 1997. *Literature, Media, Information Systems: Essays*. Edited by John Johnston. Amsterdam: G+B Arts International.

Klaar, Alfred. [1913] 1992. "Paul Lindau als Filmdramatiker." In *Prolog vor dem Film*, ed. Jörg Schweinitz, 343–47. Leipzig: Reclam.

Kleinschmidt, Erich. 1982. "Depersonale Poetik: Dispositionen des Erzählens bei Alfred Döblin." *Jahrbuch der deutschen Schillergesellschaft* 26:383–401.

Klemperer, Victor. [1918–24] 1996. *Leben sammeln, nicht fragen wozu und warum: Tagebücher 1918–1924*. Edited by W. Nowojski. Berlin: Aufbau-Verlag.

Klingmüller, Fritz. 1900. *Die Haftung für die Vereinsorgane*. Studien zur Erläuterung des bürgerlichen Rechts 3. Breslau: Marcus.

Kohler, Josef. 1917. "Straffähigkeit der juristischen Person." *Goltdammer's Archiv für Strafrecht und Strafprozess* 64:500–506.

Kollak, Ingrid. 1997. *Literatur und Hypnose: Der Mesmerismus und sein Einfluß auf die Literatur des 19. Jahrhunderts*. Frankfurt and New York: Campus.

Kracauer, Siegfried. 1947. *From Caligari to Hitler: A Psychological History of the German Film*. Princeton, NJ: Princeton University Press.

Krafft-Ebing, Richard von. 1892. "Gutachten über Hypnose und Suggestion." In *Die Suggestion und die Dichtung. Gutachten über Hypnose und Suggestion von Otto Binswanger, Emil du Bois-Reymond, August Forel, Richard v. Krafft-Ebing et al.*, ed. Karl Emil Franzos, 90–96. Berlin: Fontane.

Kretschmer, Ernst. 1922. *Medizinische Psychologie: Ein Leitfaden für Studium und Praxis*. 2d ed. Leipzig: Georg Thieme Verlag.

Krüger, Gottfried. 1901. *Die Haftung der juristischen Personen aus unerlaubten Handlungen*. Berlin: Struppe & Winkler.

Kubin, Alfred. [1909] 1994. *Die andere Seite: Ein phantastischer Roman*. Reinbek: Rowohlt.

Kuh, Sydney. 1898. "The Medico-Legal Aspects of Hypnotism." *American Journal of the Medical Sciences* (December).

Kürnberger, Ferdinand. [1873] 1967. "Die Verkannte." In *Feuilletons*, ed. Karl Riha, 85–91. Frankfurt am Main: Insel.

Ladame, Paul L. 1888. *L'hypnotisme et la médecine légale*. Lyon: Storck.

Lange, Konrad. 1920. *Das Kino in Gegenwart und Zukunft*. Stuttgart: Enke.

Langholf, Volker. 1990. "Die kathartische Methode: Klassische Philologie, literarische Tradition und Wissenschaftstheorie in der Frühgeschichte der Psychoanalyse." *Medizinhistorisches Journal* 25:5–39.

Laurence, Jean-Roch, and Charles Perry 1988. *Hypnosis, Will, and Memory: A Psycho-Legal History*. New York and London: Guilford.

le Bon, Gustave. 1895. *Psychologie des foules*. Paris: Alcan.

———. [1895] 1896. *The Crowd: A Study of the Popular Mind*. London: Ernest Benn.

Legue, Gabriel, ed. 1886. *Soeur Jeanne des Anges, supérieure des Ursulines de Loudon: Autobiographie d'une hystérique possédée*. Notes by Gabriel Legue and Georges Gilles de la Tourette. Preface by Jean-Martin Charcot. Paris: Charpentier.

Leiris, Michel. [1958] 1996. "La possession et ses aspects théâtraux chez les Éthiopiens de Gondar." In *Miroir de l'Afrique*, ed. Jean Jamin, 947–1067. Paris: Gallimard.

Lepenies, Wolf. 1978. "Der Wissenschaftler als Autor." *Akzente* 25:129–47.

Leys, Ruth. 2000. *Trauma: A Genelaogy*. Chicago: University of Chicago Press.

Liébeault, Ambroise Auguste. 1866. *Du somneil et des états analogues au point de vue de l'action du moral sur le physique*. Paris: Masson.

———. [1866] 1892. *Der künstliche Schlaf und die ihm ähnlichen Zustände*. Translated by Otto Dornblüth. Leipzig and Vienna: Deuticke.

———. 1889. *Le somneil provoqué et les états analogues*. Paris: O. Doin.

———. 1891. *Thérapeutique suggestive: son mécanisme. Propriétés diverses du somneil provoqué et des états analogues*. Paris: O. Doin.

———. 1894–95. "Criminelle hypnotische Suggestionen: Gründe und Thatsachen, welche für dieselben sprechen." *Zeitschrift für Hypnotismus* 3:193–206, 225–29.

Liégeois, Jules. 1884. *De la suggestion hypnotique dans ses rapports avec le droit civil et le droit criminel*. Paris: Alphonse Picard.

———. 1889. *De la suggestion et du somnambulisme dans leurs rapports avec la jurisprudence et la médecine légale*. Paris: Doin.

Lilienthal, Karl von. 1887a. "Der Hypnotismus und seine strafrechtliche Bedeutung." *Zeitschrift für die gesamte Strafrechtswissenschaft* 7:281–394.

———. 1887b. *Der Hypnotismus und das Strafrecht*. Berlin: Guttentag.

Lindau, Paul. 1893. *Der Andere: Schauspiel in vier Aufzügen*. Dresden: Teubner.

Liszt, Franz von. 1888. *Lehrbuch des deutschen Strafrechts*. 3d ed. Berlin and Leipzig: Guttentag.

———. 1889. *Die Grenzgebiete zwischen Privatrecht und Strafrecht: Kriminalistische Be-*

denken gegen den Entwurf eines Bürgerlichen Gesetzbuches für das Deutsche Reich. Berlin and Leipzig: Guttentag.

———. 1898. *Lehrbuch des deutschen Strafrechts.* 9th ed. Berlin: J. Guttentag.

Littré, Émile. 1869. "Un fragment de médecine rétrospective (Miracles de Saint Denis)." *Revue de philosophie positive* 5:103–36.

Lloyd, Henry D. 1894. *Wealth against Commonwealth.* New York: Harper.

Loers, Veit, Carl Aigner, and Urs Stahel, eds. 1997. *Im Reich der Phantome: Fotografie des Unsichtbaren.* Mönchengladbach: Cantz.

Loewenfeld, Leopold. 1901. *Der Hypnotismus: Handbuch der Lehre von der Hypnose und der Suggestion, Mit besonderer Berücksichtigung ihrer Bedeutung für Medicin und Rechtspflege.* Wiesbaden: Bergmann.

Lombroso, Cesare 1909. *Hypnotische und spiritistische Forschungen.* Translated by Carl Grundig. Stuttgart: Julius Hoffmann.

Loos, Otto. 1894. *Der Hypnotismus und die Suggestion in gerichtlich-medicinischer Bedeutung.* Berlin: Vogts.

Lucas, Werner. 1930. *Der Hypnotismus in seinen Beziehungen zum deutschen Strafrecht und Strafprozess.* Berlin: Dümmler.

Luhmann, Niklas. 1978. *Organisation und Entscheidung.* Opladen: Westdeutscher Verlag.

———. [1984] 1987. *Soziale Systeme: Grundriß einer allgemeinen Theorie.* Frankfurt am Main: Suhrkamp.

———. [1984] 1995. *Social Systems.* Translated by John Bednarz with Dirk Baecker. Stanford, CA: Stanford University Press.

Maartens, Maarten. 1906. *The Healers.* Leipzig: Tauchnitz.

Machen, Arthur. 1911. "Corporate Personality." *Harvard Law Review* 24:253–67, 347–65.

Maitland, Frederic W. 1900. Translator's introduction to *Political Theories of the Middle Age,* by Otto von Gierke, v–xlv. Cambridge: Cambridge University Press.

Mann, Thomas. [1894] 1986. "Gefallen." In *Die Erzählungen,* 8–43. Frankfurt am Main: Fischer.

———. [1924] 1989. *Der Zauberberg: Roman* Frankfurt am Main: Fischer.

———. [1930] 1986. "Mario und der Zauberer: Ein tragisches Reiseerlebnis." In *Die Erzählungen,* 793–853. Frankfurt am Main: Fischer.

Mannoni, Octave. 1980. *Un commencement qui n'en finit pas: Transfert, interprétation, théorie.* Paris: Éditions du Seuil.

Marcus, Steven. 1985. "Freud and Dora: Story, History, Case History." In *In Dora's Case: Freud—Hysteria—Feminism,* ed. Charles Bernheimer and Claire Kahane, 56–91. New York: Columbia University Press.

Marcuse, H. 1917. "Die Verbrechensfähigkeit der juristischen Person." *Goltdammer's Archiv für Strafrecht und Strafprozess* 64:478–99.

Maugham, William Somerset. 1908. *The Magician*. London: William Heinemann.

Maupassant, Guy de. [1882] 1974. "Magnétisme." In *Contes et nouvelles*, 1:406–10. Edited and annotated by Louis Forestier. Paris: Gallimard. Originally published in *Gil Blas* (April 5).

———. [1886] 1979. "Le Horla" [version 1]. In *Contes et nouvelles*, 2:822–30 Edited and annotated by Louis Forestier. Paris: Gallimard. Originally published in *Gil Blas*, October 26, 1886.

———. [1887] 1979. "Le Horla" [version 2]. In *Contes et nouvelles*, 2:913–43. Edited and annotated by Louis Forestier. Paris: Gallimard. Originally published as *Le Horla* (Paris: Ollendorff).

———. [1887] 1990. "Le Horla." In *A Day in the Country and Other Stories*, 275–302. Translated by David Coward. Oxford: Oxford University Press.

Mayer, Carl, and Hans Janowitz. [1919] 1995. "Das Cabinett des Dr. Calligaris [*sic*]: Phantastischer Filmroman in 6 Akten." In *Das Cabinet des Dr. Caligari: Drehbuch von Carl Mayer und Hans Janowitz zu Robert Wienes Film von 1919–20*, 47–111. Munich: edition text + kritik.

Mayer, Ludwig. 1937. *Das Verbrechen in Hypnose und seine Aufklärungsmethoden*. Munich: J. F. Lehmanns.

Mayer, Theodor Heinrich. 1928. "Der Rundfunk—vom anderen Ufer betrachtet." *Funk: Die Wochenschrift des Funkwesens* 16:119–24.

McCarren, Felicia. 1998. *Dance Pathologies: Performance, Poetics, Medicine*. Stanford, CA: Stanford University Press.

Méric, Elie. 1888. *Le merveilleux et la science: Étude sur l'hypnotisme*. Paris: Alcan.

Mestre, Achille 1899. *Les personnes morales et leur responsabilité pénale*. Paris: Rousseau.

Metz, Christian. [1977] 1982. *The Imaginary Signifier: Psychoanalysis and the Cinema*. Translated by Celia Britton, Annwyl Williams, Ben Brewster, and Alfred Guzzetti. Bloomington: Indiana University Press. Originally published as *Le signifiant imaginaire: Psychanalyse et cinéma* (Paris: Union Générale d'Editions).

Meurer, Christian. 1885. *Der Begriff und Eigenthümer der heiligen Sachen, zugleich eine Revision der Lehre von den juristischen Personen*. Düsseldorf: Bagel.

———. 1901. *Die juristischen Personen nach deutschem Reichsrecht*. Stuttgart: Enke.

Meyer, Steven. 2001. *Irresistible Dictation: Gertrude Stein and the Correlations of Writing and Science*. Stanford, CA: Stanford University Press.

Meyrink, Gustav. 1908. *Das Wachsfigurenkabinett*. Munich: Langen, 1908.

———. [1916] 1998. *Das grüne Gesicht. Roman*. Berlin: Ullstein.

———. 1917. *Walpurgisnacht: Fantastischer Roman*. Leipzig: Wolff.

———. 1921. *Der weiße Dominikaner: Aus dem Tagebuch eines Unsichtbaren*. Vienna and Berlin: Rikola.

———. [1927] 1975. *Der Engel vom westlichen Fenster*. Munich: Langen-Müller.

Mezger, Eugen. 1912. "Die Suggestion in kriminalpsychologisch-juristischer Beziehung." *Zeitschrift für die gesamte Strafrechtswissenschaft* 33:847–910.

Micale, Mark. 1990. "Charcot and the Idea of Hysteria in the Male: Gender, Medical Science, and Medical Diagnosis in Late Nineteenth-Century France." *Medical History* 34:363–411.

Michaels, Walter Benn. 1987. "Corporate Fiction." In *The Gold Standard and the Logic of Naturalism: American Literature at the Turn of the Century*, 181–213. The New Historicism: Studies in Cultural Poetics 2. Berkeley: University of California Press.

Mishra, Vijay. 1994. *The Gothic Sublime*. Albany: SUNY Press.

"Mittheilung vermischten Inhalts." 1893–94. *Zeitschrift für Hypnotismus* 2:176.

Mößmer, Franz. 1892. *Die mittelbare Thäterschaft in gleichzeitiger Berücksichtigung des Hypnotismus im Strafrecht*. Munich: Schweitzer.

Moll, Albert. 1889. *Der Hypnotismus*. Berlin: Fischer's Medicinische Buchhandlung.

———. 1892–93. "Die Bewusstseinsspaltung in Paul Lindaus neuem Schauspiel." *Zeitschrift für Hypnotismus* 1: 306–10.

———. 1895. *Der Hypnotismus*. 3d ed. Berlin: Fischer's Medicinische Buchhandlung. [308 pages]

———. 1907. *Der Hypnotismus: Mit Einschluss der Hauptpunkte der Psychotherapie und des Okkultismus*. 4th ed. Berlin: Fischer's Medicinische Buchhandlung. [642 pages]

———. 1907–9. *Hypnotism, Including a Study of the Chief Points of Psycho-Therapeutics and Occultism*. Translated by Arthur F. Hopkirk. London: W. Scott.

———. 1922. *Prophezeien und Hellsehen*. Stuttgart: Franckh.

———. 1924. *Der Hypnotismus: Mit Einschluß der Psychotherapie und der Hauptpunkte des Okkultismus*. 5th ed. Berlin: Fischers medizinische Buchhandlung. [744 pages]

———. 1928. "Hypnose und Verbrechen." *Kriminalistische Probleme: Sonderbeilage der Kriminalistischen Monatshefte* 8:17–35.

Moore, Rachel. 2000. *Savage Theory: Cinema as Modern Magic*. Durham, NC: Duke University Press.

Morris, Rosalind C. 2000. "Modernity's Media and the End of Mediumship?

On the Aesthetic Economy of Transparency in Thailand." *Public Culture* 12, no. 2:457–75.

Münsterberg, Hugo. 1908. "Hypnotism and Crime." In *On the Witness Stand: Essays on Psychology and Crime*, 203–28. Garden City, NY: Doubleday.

———. [1916] 2002. *The Photoplay: A Psychological Study.* Edited by Allan Langdale. New York: Routledge.

Murray, Bruce. 1990. *Film and the German Left in the Weimar Republic. From Caligari to Kuhle Wampe.* Austin: University of Texas Press.

Musil, Robert. [1925] 1978. "Ansätze zu Neuer Ästhetik: Bemerkungen über eine Dramaturgie des Films" (March 1925). In *Gesammelte Werke*, 8:1137–54. Edited Adolf Frisé. Reinbek: Rowohlt.

———. [1930–42] 1978. *Der Mann ohne Eigenschaften.* In *Gesammelte Werke.* Edited by Adolf Frisé. Vols. 1–5. Reinbek: Rowohlt.

Myers, Frederic W. H. [1903] 1975. *Human Personality and Its Survival of Bodily Death.* New York: Arno Press.

Neumeister, Georg. 1900. *Mittelbare Thäterschaft und Hypnotismus.* Greifswald: Kunike.

Niemann, Hans Werner. 1982. *Das Bild des industriellen Unternehmers in deutschen Romanen der Jahre 1890–1945.* With a foreword by Wilhelm Treue. Berlin: Colloquium.

Nietzsche, Friedrich. [1882–87] 1979. "Die fröhliche Wissenschaft." In *Nietzsches Werke: Kritische Gesamtausgabe.* Edited by Giorgo Colli und Mazzino Montinari, 11–335. Vol. 2, sec. 5. Berlin and New York: de Gruyter.

Noack, Victor. [1912] 1992. "Der Kientopp." In *Prolog vor dem Film*, ed. Jörg Schweinitz, 70–75. Leipzig: Reclam. Originally published in *Die Aktion* 2, no. 29 (July 17): 905–9.

Norris, Frank. [1901] 1986. *The Octopus: A Story of California.* With an introduction by Kevin Starr. New York and London: Penguin.

Obersteiner, Heinrich. 1887. *Der Hypnotismus mit Berücksichtigung seiner klinischen und forensischen Bedeutung.* Klinische Zeit- und Streitfragen 2. Vienna: Breitenstein.

———. 1893. *Die Lehre vom Hypnotismus.* Leipzig: F. Deuticke.

Oesterreich, Konstantin Traugott. 1907. *Die Entfremdung der Wahrnehmungswelt und die Depersonnalisation in der Psychasthenie: Ein Beitrag zur Gefühlspsychologie.* Leipzig: Barth, 1907. Originally published in *Journal für Psychologie und Neurologie* 7:255–76, 8:61–97, 141–74, 220–37, 9:15–53.

———. [1921] 1930. *Possession: Demoniacal and Other among Primitive Races, in Antiquity, the Middle Ages, and Modern Times.* Translated by D. Ibberson. New York: Richard Smith.

Ong, Aihwa. 1988. "The Production of Possession: Spirits and the Multinational Corporation in Malaysia." *American Ethnologist* 15:28–42.

Osterle, Heinz. 1970. "Hermann Broch: Die Schlafwandler. Kritik der zentralen Metapher." *Deutsche Vierteljahrsschrift für Literaturwissenschaft und Geistesgeschichte* 44:229–68.

Ouerd, Michèle. 1984. Introduction to *Leçons sur l'hystérie virile* by Jean-Martin Charcot, 11–31. Paris: Sycomore.

Pahl, Walther. 1926. "Die psychologischen Wirkungen des Films unter besonderer Berücksichtigung ihrer sozialpsychologischen Bedeutung." Ph.D. diss., Universität Leipzig.

Peter, Josef. 1921. *Die Photographie des Unsichtbaren.* Pfullingen: Baum.

Petersen, Klaus. 1988. *Literatur und Justiz in der Weimarer Republik.* Stuttgart: Metzler.

Pohl, Hans. 1982. "Die Entwicklung der Formen der Betriebs- und Unternehmensorganisation, insbesondere der Großorganisation im Verhältnis zum persönlich geführten Geschäft." In *Wissenschaft und Kodifikation des Privatrechts im 19. Jahrhundert.* Vol. 6, *Zur Verselbständigung des Vermögens gegenüber der Person im Privatrecht,* ed. Helmut Coing and Walter Wilhelm, 93–125. Frankfurt am Main: Klostermann.

Polgar, Alfred. [1911–12] 1992. "Das Drama im Kinematographen." In *Prolog vor dem Kino,* ed. Jörg Schweinitz, 159–64. Leipzig: Reclam. Originally published in *Der Strom* 1, no. 2.

Prels, Max. 1926. *Kino.* 2d ed. Bielefeld and Leipzig: Velhagen & Klasing.

Preyer, William. 1895. *Ein merkwürdiger Fall von Fascination.* Stuttgart: Enke.

Pytlik, Priska. 2005. *Okkultismus und Moderne: Ein kulturhistorisches Phänomen und seine Bedeutung für die Literatur um 1900.* Paderborn: Schöningh.

Rabinbach, Anson. 1992. *The Human Motor: Energy, Fatigue, and the Origins of Modernity.* Berkeley: University of California Press.

Rank, Otto. [1914] 1925. *Der Doppelgänger: Eine psychoanalytische Studie.* Leipzig: Internationaler Psychoanalytischer Verlag.

Reeve, Clara. [1778] 1967. *The Old English Baron: A Gothic Story.* Edited with an introduction by James Trainer. London: Oxford University Press.

Regelsberger, Ferdinand. 1893. *Pandekten.* Vol. 1. Leipzig: Duncker & Humblot.

Reiter, Paul J. 1958. *Antisocial or Criminal Acts and Hypnosis.* Springfield, IL: Thomas.

Rhomberg, Eduard. 1899. *Körperschaftliches Verschulden.* Munich: Schweitzer.

Richer, Paul. 1881. "Épidémies de possession démoniaque." In *Études cliniques sur l'hystero-épilepsie ou grande hystérie,* 623–77. With a preface by M. le professeur Charcot. Paris: Adrien Delahaye et Émile Lecrosnier.

Richet, Charles. 1875. "Du somnambulisme provoqué." *Journal d'anatomie et physiologie* 11:348–78.

———. 1880. "Les démoniaques d'aujourd'hui." *Revue des deux mondes* 37: 340–72.

———. [Charles Epheyre, pseudo.]. 1887. *Possession*. Paris: Ollendorff.

Rieger, Conrad. 1888. "Einige irrenärztliche Bemerkungen über die strafrechtliche Bedeutung des sogenannten Hypnotismus." *Zeitschrift für die gesamte Strafrechtswissenschaft* 8:315–24.

Rilke, Rainer Maria. [1910] 1997. *Die Aufzeichnungen des Malte Laurids Brigge*. Edited by Manfred Engel. Stuttgart: Reclam.

"Robert Wiene's *Das Cabinet des Dr. Caligari*." [1920] 1995. *Lichtbildbühne*, February 28. Reprinted in *Das Cabinet des Dr. Caligari: Drehbuch von Carl Mayer und Hans Janowitz mit einem einführenden Essay und Materialien zum Film*, ed. Uli Jung and Walter Schatzberg, 140–41. Munich: text + kritik.

Robinson, David. 1997. *Das Cabinet des Dr. Caligari*. London: British Film Institute.

Roux, Hughes le 1887. "La vie à Paris: Les dangers de l'hypnotisme." *Le temps,* June 1, 2.

Sadger, Isidor. 1914. *Über Nachtwandeln und Mondsucht: Eine medizinisch-literarische Studie*. Schriften zur angewandten Seelenkunde 16. Leipzig and Vienna: Deuticke.

Salten, Felix. [1932–33] 1984. "Über Schnitzlers hypnotische Versuche." In *Arthur Schnitzler, Aspekte und Akzente: Materialien zu Leben und Werk*, ed. Hans-Ulrich Lindken, 55. Frankfurt am Main and Bern: Peter Lang. Originally published in *Jahrbuch deutscher Bibliophilen und Literaturfreunde* 18–19:33.

Samarow, Gregor [Oskar Meding]. 1888. *Unter fremdem Willen*. Stuttgart: Deutsche Verlagsanstalt.

Sanders, Hans-Theodor. 1921. *Hypnose und Suggestion: Ein Überblick über den modernen Hypnotismus und die Suggestion und ihre praktische Bedeutung*. Stuttgart: Franckh.

Sardou, Victorien. 1904. *La sorcière: Drame en cinq actes*. Paris: C. Lévy.

Saunders, Thomas J. 1994. *Hollywood in Berlin: American Cinema and Weimar Germany*. Weimar and Now: German Cultural Criticism 6. Berkeley and Los Angeles: University of California Press.

Savigny, Friedrich Carl von. 1840. *System des heutigen Römischen Rechts*. Vol. 2. Berlin: Veit.

———. [1840] 1884. *Jural Relations; or, The Roman Law of Persons as Subjects of Jural Relations: Being a Translation of the Second Book of Savigny's System of Modern Roman Law*. Translated by W. H. Rattigan. London: Wildy & Sons.

Schäffle, Albert. [1875a] 1895. *Bau und Leben des socialen Körpers*. 2d ed. Vol. 1, *Allgemeine Sociologie*. Tübingen: H. Laupp.

———. [1875b] 1896. *Bau und Leben des socialen Körpers*. 2d ed. Vol. 2, *Specielle Sociologie*. Tübingen: H. Laupp.

Schapira, David. 1893. *Der Hypnotismus in seiner psychologischen und forensischen Bedeutung*. Berlin: Steinitz.

Schenkel, Daniel. 1859. *Die christliche Dogmatik vom Standpunkte des Gewissens aus dargestellt*. Vol. 2. Wiesbaden: Kreitel & Niedner.

Schikorski, Felix. 1978. *Die Auseinandersetzung um den Körperschaftsbegriff in der Rechtslehre des 19. Jahrhunderts*. Berlin: Duncker & Humblot.

Schlossmann, Siegmund 1905. *Persona und prosopon im Recht und im christlichen Dogma*. Kiel: Lipsius & Tischler.

Schmidt-Hannisa, Hans-Walter. 1998. "Das eiserne Szepter des Schlafes: Über die Unzurechnungsfähigkeit von Schlaftrunkenen, Nachtwandlern und Träumern im 18. Jahrhundert." In *Unzurechnungsfähigkeiten: Diskursivierungen unfreier Bewußtseinszustände seit dem 18. Jahrhundert*, ed. Michael Niehaus and Hans-Walter Schmidt-Hannisa, 57–83. Frankfurt am Main and Bern: Peter Lang.

Schneider, Manfred. 1985. "Hysterie als Gesamtkunstwerk." In *Ornament und Askese im Zeitgeist des Wien der Jahrhundertwende*, ed. Alfred Pfabigan, 212–29. Vienna: Brandstätter.

Schnitzler, Arthur. [1889a] 1984. "Krankenprotokoll Flora Trebitsch 1889." In *Arthur Schnitzler, Aspekte und Akzente: Materialien zu Leben und Werk*, ed. Hans-Ulrich Lindken, 45–54. Frankfurt am Main and Bern: Peter Lang.

———. [1889b] 1984. "Krankenprotokoll Anna Kletter 1889." In *Arthur Schnitzler, Aspekte und Akzente: Materialien zu Leben und Werk*, ed. Hans-Ulrich Lindken, 56–60. Frankfurt am Main and Bern Peter Lang.

———. [1889c] 1991. "Rezension von H. Bernheim, *Die Suggestion und ihre Heilwirkung*." In *Medizinische Schriften*, ed. Horst Thomé, 210–15. Frankfurt am Main: Fischer. Originally published in *Internationale Klinische Rundschau* 3:891–93.

———. [1889d] 1993. "Die Frage an das Schicksal." In *Anatol: Das dramatische Werk in chronologischer Ordnung*. Vol. 1, *Dramen, 1889–1891*, 36–48. Frankfurt am Main: Fischer.

———. 1889e. *Über funktionelle Aphonie und deren Behandlung durch Hypnose und Suggestion*. Vienna: Wilhelm Braumüller. Originally published in *Internationale Klinische Rundschau* (March 10–April 7, 1889).

———. [1893] 1991. "Rezension von Heinrich Obersteiner, *Die Lehre vom Hypnotismus*." In *Medizinische Schriften*, ed. Horst Thomé, 316–17. Frankfurt am

Main: Fischer. Originally published in *Internationale Klinische Rundschau* 7:1292–93.

———. [1898] 1994. "Paracelsus: Versspiel in einem Akt." In *Das Vermächtnis: Dramen 1897–1898*, 177–216. Frankfurt am Main: Fischer.

———. [1902] 1989. "Die Weissagung" In *Der blinde Geronimo und sein Bruder: Erzählungen, 1900–1907*. Vol. 4 of *Das erzählerische Werk in chronologischer Ordnung*, 128–52. Frankfurt am Main: Fischer.

———. [1920] 1981. *Jugend in Wien: Eine Autobiographie*. Edited by Therese Nickl and Heinrich Schnitzler. Frankfurt am Main: Fischer.

Scholdt, Günter. 1994. "Mabuse, ein deutscher Mythos." In Norbert Jacques, *Dr. Mabuse, der Spieler*, ed. Michael Farin and Günter Scholdt, 359–82. Hamburg: Rogner & Bernhard.

Schönert, Jörg, ed. 1991. *Erzählte Kriminalität: Zur Typologie und Funktion von narrativen Darstellungen in Strafrechtspflege, Publizistik und Literatur zwischen 1770 und 1920*. Tübingen: Niemeyer.

Schrenck-Notzing, Albert von. 1888. *Ein Beitrag zur therapeutischen Verwendung des Hypnotismus*. Leipzig: Vogel.

———. 1892. *Die Suggestions-Therapie bei krankhaften Erscheinungen des Geschlechtssinnes: Mit besonderer Berücksichtigung der conträren Sexualempfindung*. Stuttgart: Enke.

———. 1895. *Der Prozess Czynski: Thatbestand desselben und Gutachten über Willensbeschränkung durch hypnotisch-suggestiven Einfluss, abgegeben vor dem oberbayerischen Schwurgericht zu München von Prof. Dr. Grashey in München, Prof. Dr. Hirt in Breslau, Dr. Freiherr von Schrenck-Notzing in München, Prof. Dr. Preyer in Wiesbaden*. Stuttgart: Enke.

———. 1900. "Die gerichtlich-medizinische Bedeutung der Suggestion." *Archiv für Kriminalanthropologie und Kriminalistik* 5:1–36.

———. 1904. *Die Traumtänzerin Magdeleine G. Eine psychologische Studie über Hypnose und dramatische Kunst*. Stuttgart: Enke.

———. 1914. *Materialisationsphaenomene: Ein Beitrag zur Erforschung der mediumistischen Teleplastie*. Munich: Ernst Reinhardt.

———. 1920. *Phenomena of Materialization: A Contribution to the Investigation of Mediumistic Teleplastics*. Translated by E. E. Fournier d'Albe. New York: E. P. Dutton.

Schuller, Marianne. 1989. "Hysterie als Artefaktum: Zum literarischen und visuellen Archiv der Hysterie um 1900." In *Literatur in einer industriellen Kultur*, ed. Götz Großklaus and Eberhard Lämmert, 445–67. Stuttgart: Cotta.

Sconce, Jeffrey. 2000. *Haunted Media: Electronic Presence from Telegraphy to Television*. Durham, NC: Duke University Press.

Scott, Walter D. [1908] 1917. *The Psychology of Advertising*. Boston: Small, Maynard & Co.

Sedgwick, Eve Kosofsky. 1985. *Between Men: English Literature and Male Homosocial Desire*. New York: Columbia University Press.

Seeling, Otto. 1922. *Hypnose, Suggestion und Erziehung: Eine Handreichung für jeden Gebildeten, insbesondere für Eltern und Erzieher, Juristen und Polizeibeamte*. Leipzig: Gehlen.

———. 1928. "Hypnotische Verbrechen." *Schweizerische Zeitschrift für angewandte Psychologie* 4:337–40.

Sellmann, Adolf. 1912. *Der Kinematograph als Volkserzieher*. Pädagogisches Magazin 470. Langensalza: Beyer.

Seltzer, Mark. 1992. *Bodies and Machines*. New York: Routledge.

Showalter, Elaine. 1997. *Hystories: Hysterical Epidemics and Modern Media*. New York: Columbia University Press.

Siegert, Bernhard. [1993] 1999. *Relays: Literature as an Epoch of the Postal System*. Translated by Kevin Repp. Stanford, CA: Stanford University Press.

Sighele, Scipio. 1891. *La folla delinquente: Studio di psicologia collective*. Turin: Bocca.

———. 1901. "Le crime collectif." In *Compte rendu du 5ième congrès international d'anthropologie criminelle*, 68–78. Amsterdam: Imprimerie J. H. de Bussy.

Simmel, Ernst. 1918. *Kriegsneurosen und "psychisches Trauma."* Munich: O. Nemnich.

Simmel, Georg. [1890] 1992. "Die Selbsterhaltung der socialen Gruppe: Sociologische Studie." In *Aufsätze und Abhandlungen 1894 bis 1900*. Vol. 4 of *Gesamtausgabe*,. ed. Heinz-Jürgen Dahme und David P. Frisby, 311–72. Frankfurt am Main: Suhrkamp. Originally published in *Jahrbuch für Gesetzgebung, Verwaltung und Rechtspflege des Deutschen Reiches*, n.s. 22:589–640.

———. [1908] 1992. *Soziologie: Untersuchungen über die Formen der Vergesellschaftung*. Vol. 11 of *Gesamtausgabe*, ed. Otthein Rammstedt. Frankfurt am Main: Suhrkamp.

Smith, Adam. [1758] 1967. "The Principles Which Lead and Direct Philosophical Enquiries: Illustrated by the History of Astronomy." In *The Early Writings of Adam Smith*, ed. J. R. Lindgren, 30–109. London: Kelley.

———. [1776] 1976. *An Inquiry into the Nature and Causes of the Wealth of Nations*. Edited by E. Cannan. 2 vols. in one. Chicago: University of Chicago Press.

Smith, John H. 1989. "Abulia: Sexuality and Diseases of the Will in the Late Nineteenth Century." *Genders* 6:102–24.

Sollier, Paul. 1903. *Les phénomènes d'autoscopie*. Paris: F. Alcan.

Solomons, Leon M., and Gertrude Stein. 1896. "Normal Motor Automatism." *Psychological Review* 3:492–512.

Somló, Felix. 1917. *Juristische Grundlehre*. Leipzig: Meiner.

Soyka, Otto. 1921a. *Die Traumpeitsche*. Vienna: Rikola.

———. 1921b. *Der Seelenschmied*. Berlin: Keils.

Spunda, Franz. 1921. *Devachan: Magischer Roman*. Vienna: Strache.

Stein, Gertude. 1898. "Cultivated Motor Automatism: A Study of Character and Its Relation to Attention." *Psychological Review* 5:295–306.

Steinecke, Hartmut. 1972. "Das Schlafwandeln: Zur Deutung des Motivs in Hermann Brochs Trilogie." In *Hermann Broch: Perspektiven der Forschung*, ed. Manfred Durzak, 69–88. Munich: Fink.

Stoker, Bram. [1897] 1979. *Dracula*. London and New York: Penguin.

Stoll, Otto. 1894. *Suggestion und Hypnotismus in der Völkerpsychologie*. Leipzig: Koehler.

Stratz, Rudolph. 1926. *Filmgewitter: Roman*. Berlin: August Scherl.

Strobl, Karl Hans. 1920. *Umsturz im Jenseits*. Munich: Rösl.

Sword, Helen. 2001. *Ghostwriting Modernism*. Ithaca, NY: Cornell University Press.

Tannenbaum, Eugen. [1922] 1994. "Dr. Mabuse, der Spieler: Der neue Uco-Film im Ufa-Palast am Zoo." In Norbert Jacques, *Dr. Mabuse, der Spieler*. Edited by Michael Farin and Günter Scholdt, 291–94. Hamburg: Rogner & Bernhard. Originally published in *Berliner Zeitung am Mittag*, April 28.

Tarde, Gabriel. [1890] 1903. *The Laws of Imitation*. Translated by Elsie Crews Parsons. New York: Henry Holt & Co. Original edition: *Le lois de l'imitation: Étude sociologique* (Paris: F. Alcan).

———. 1893. "Les crimes des foules." In *Actes du troisième congrès international d'anthropologie criminelle*, 73–90. Brüssel: Hayez.

Tatar, Maria M. 1978. *Spellbound: Studies on Mesmerism and Literature*. Princeton, NJ: Princeton University Press.

Thomé, Horst. 1991. "Vorwort: Arthur Schnitzlers Anfänge und die Grundlagenkrise der Medizin." In *Medizinische Schriften* by Arthur Schnitzler, 11–59. Frankfurt am Main: Fischer.

———. 1993. *Autonomes Ich und "Inneres Ausland": Studien über Realismus, Tiefenpsychologie und Psychiatrie in deutschen Erzähltexten (1848–1914)*. Tübingen: Niemeyer.

Többen. 1921–22. "Über verbrecherische Ausnutzung suggestiver Fähigkeiten." *Monatsschrift für Kriminalpsychologie und Strafrechtsreform* 12:331–41.

Todorov, Tzetvan. 1975. *The Fantastic: A Structural Approach to a Literary Genre*. Translated by Richard Howard. Ithaca, NY: Cornell University Press.

Tsivian, Yuri. 1994. *Early Cinema in Russia and Its Cultural Reception*. Translated by Alan Bodger. London and New York: Routledge.

Tuke, Hack. [1872] 1884. *Influence of the Mind upon the Body in Health and Disease,*

Designed to Elucidate the Action of the Imagination. 2d ed. London: J. and A. Churchill.

———. 1884. *Sleep-Walking and Hypnotism.* London: J. and A. Churchill.

Twain, Mark. [1894] 1984. *"Pudd'nhead Wilson" and "Those Extraordinary Twins."* Edited with an introduction by Malcolm Bradbury. London and New York: Penguin.

Unger, Josef. 1859. "Zur Lehre von den juristischen Personen." In *Kritische Ueberschau der deutschen Gesetzgebung und Rechtswissenschaft*, ed. Ludwig Arndts, Johann Caspar Bluntschli, and Joseph Pözl, 6:145–88. Munich: Verlag der litterarisch-artistischen Anstalt.

Valdès, André. 1891. *La prise du regard: Roman d'hypnotisme.* Paris: Flammarion.

Vareilles-Sommières, Gabriel de. 1902. *Les personnes morales.* Paris: Pichon.

Vestenhof, A. Hoffmann von. 1913. *Der Mann mit den drei Augen: Eine sonderbare Geschichte.* Munich: Langen.

Vorberg, Gaston. 1908. *Guy de Maupassants Krankheit.* Grenzfragen des Nerven- und Seelenlebens 60. Wiesbaden: Bergmann.

Waffelaert, Jean. 1888. "Les démoniaques de la Salpêtrière et les vrais possédés du démon." *La Science Catholique: Revue des Questions Religieuses* 2:273–87, 352–69, 571–93.

Wager, Walter Herman. 1975. *Telefon.* New York: Macmillan.

Wagner, Benno. 2002. "Poseidons Gehilfe. Kafka und die Statistik." *Marbacher Magazin: Sonderheft zu Kafkas Fabriken* 100:109–38.

———. 2004. "Überlieferung und Kommentar." In Franz Kafka, *Amtliche Schriften: Kritische Ausgabe*, ed. Klaus Hermsdorf and Benno Wagner, 814–979. Frankfurt am Main: S. Fischer.

———. 2005. "Verklärte Normalität. Gustav Freytags Soll und Haben und der Ursprung des 'Deutschen Sonderwegs.'" *Internationales Archiv für Sozialgeschichte der deutschen Literatur* 30:14–37.

———. 2006. "Insuring Nietzsche: Kafka's Files." In *New German Critique* 99 (Fall): 83–119.

Wagner-Jauregg, Julius. 1919. *Telepathie und Hypnose im Verbrechen.* Vienna: Verlegt von der Vereinigung der Gerichtssaalreferenten der Wiener Tagespresse.

Walloth, Wilhelm. 1897. *Im Banne der Hypnose: Ein psychologischer Roman*, Jena: H. Costenoble.

Walpole, Horace. [1764] 1993. *The Castle of Otranto: A Gothic Tale.* Edited by R. L. Mack. London: Everyman.

Warstat, Willi, and Franz Bergmann. 1913. *Kino und Gemeinde.* Lichtbühnen-Bibliothek 3. Mönchengladbach: Volksvereins-Verlag.

Weber, Alfred. [1910] 1927. "Der Beamte.' In *Ideen zur Staats- und Kultursoziolo-*

gie, 81–101. Karlsruhe: Braun. Originally published in *Die Neue Rundschau*, vol. 21, no. 4.

Weber, Max. [1910–20] 1985. *Wirtschaft und Gesellschaft: Grundriß der verstehenden Soziologie*. Edited by Johannes Winckelmann. Tübingen: Mohr.

———. [1917–19] 1992. *Wissenschaft als Beruf (1917–19): Politik als Beruf (1919)*. Edited by W. J. Mommsen and W. Schluchter. Vol. 17 of *Gesamtausgabe*. Tübingen: J. C. B. Mohr (Siebeck).

Wells, H. G. [1896] 1989. "The Red Room." In *The Oxford Book of English Ghost Stories*, ed. Michael Cox and R. A. Gilbert, 172–79. Oxford and New York: Oxford University Press.

———. [1897] 1983. *The Invisible Man*. New York and London: Bantam.

Wiene, Robert. 1919. *Z*. Reproduction of the original intertitles; Schriftgutarchiv der Stiftung Deutsche Kinemathek Berlin.

Wolf, Burkhardt. 2006. "Die Nacht des Bürokraten: Franz Kafkas statistische Schreibweise." *Deutsche Vierteljahrsschrift für Literaturwissenschaft und Geistesgeschichte* 80:97–127.

Worbs, Michael. 1983. *Nervenkunst: Literatur und Psychoanalyse im Wien der Jahrhundertwende*. Frankfurt am Main: Europäische Verlagsanstalt.

Ziolkowski, Theodore. 1985. "In Search of the Absolute Novel." *New York Times Book Review*, March 11.

Zitelmann, Ernst. 1873. *Begriff und Wesen der sogenannten juristischen Personen*. Leipzig: Duncker & Humblot.

Zola Émile. [1885] 1967. *Germinal*. Vol. 5 of *Œuvres completes*, ed. Henri Mitterand. Paris: Fasquelle.

———. [1891] 1967. *L'argent*. Paris: Fasquelle.

INDEX